The Sea-gunner's Vade-mecum

THE

SEA-GUNNER's VADE-MECUM;

BEING

A NEW INTRODUCTION TO

PRACTICAL GUNNERY,

EXPRESSLY ACCOMMODATED TO THE USE OF

THE ROYAL NAVY, &c.

AND INCLUDING

THE RULES OF DECIMAL ARITHMETIC;

SO MUCH OF

Practical Geometry

AS MAY BE REQUIRED IN THE ART;

AN EXPLANATION OF THE

DUTY OF A MASTER-GUNNER;

WITH THE FORMS OF ACCOUNTS, PAPERS, &c.;

THE COMPOSITION OF USEFUL

ARTIFICIAL FIRE-WORKS;

AND

A VARIETY OF INFORMATION WITH INSTRUCTIONS USEFUL TO GUNNERS, BOTH AT SEA AND ON-SHORE.

By *ROBERT SIMMONS*,

ONE OF THE SENIOR GUNNERS OF THE NAVY,

ASSISTED BY

SEVERAL EXPERIENCED OFFICERS OF THE FLEET.

" England expects every Man to do his Duty !"
Lord Nelson, off Trafalgar.

LONDON:

PRINTED FOR STEEL AND CO.

CHART-SELLERS TO THE HONORABLE BOARD OF ADMIRALTY,

AT THEIR NAVIGATION-WAREHOUSE,

70, CORNHILL, NEAR THE ROYAL EXCHANGE.

1812.

PRICE 9s.

F 1

ENTERED AT STATIONERS' HALL.

Hildyard, Printer,
Fetter Lane, Holborn, London.

John Lords
16. S. Navy

TO

THOMAS WOLLEY, *Esquire,*

LATE CAPTAIN OF HIS MAJESTY's SHIP

SALVADOR DEL MUNDO,

THIS INTRODUCTION TO NAVAL GUNNERY

IS RESPECTFULLY DEDICATED,

BY HIS MOST OBEDIENT

AND VERY HUMBLE SERVANT,

ROBERT SIMMONS.

24th April, 1812:

PREFACE.

THIS Volume is constituted on the principle of a little publication, composed by the Author some time since, and intituled " *The Sea-Gunner's Pocket Companion :*" that work having been favorably received, and very frequently demanded since out of print.

The original intention of the Author was, merely to instruct those persons, in subordinate situations, who aspired to the rank of Gunner in the Royal Navy; and the book was therefore limited to a small collection of useful information, formed almost solely for the purpose of aiding those who have not been blessed with a more liberal education than himself. But, imperfect as that collection was, its utility to the service has been acknowledged; and this acknowledgement has occasioned a more extended view of the subject. The result is, a much larger collection of information, more conveniently arranged. The additions, which are considerably more than equal to the whole of the former book, will, it is presumed, render it a very useful companion to every officer and seaman of the British Fleet.

THE WORK IS ARRANGED AS FOLLOWS:

1st. The Rules of Decimal Arithmetic, with ex-
    amples.

2nd. Definitions in Geometry, with problems, and
    the methods of ascertaining distances, &c.

3rd. The Duty of a Gunner in the Royal Navy; with
    forms of accounts, letters, certificates, &c.

4th. General Principles of Gunnery, including defi-
    nitions, &c.

5th. Miscellaneous Information and instructions, al-
    phabetically arranged: under which head will
    be found many interesting particulars not gene-
    rally known in the service; including, also,
    the composition of useful artificial fire-works;
    the exercise of the great guns and small-arms;
    regulations of quarters; preparation and rules
    for conducting engagements, &c. with various
    useful tables.

CONTENTS.

CONTENTS.

ERRATUM.

Page 30, line 1, for A *insert* C.

THE
SEA-GUNNER's VADE-MECUM,
&c.

SECTION I.

OF DECIMAL ARITHMETIC.

THE first rudiments of Gunnery, as well as of Ship-building, have their foundation in Arithmetic and Practical Geometry.— With the first rules of the former we presume that our readers are already acquainted; if they be not, it is requisite that they become so, before proceeding to the perusal of this work. We commence, however, with the arithmetic of decimals, the rules of which are here briefly stated, not merely for the purpose of imparting this essential information, in the first instance, to those who are entirely ignorant of the subject, but, more particularly, for the purpose of a ready reference to those who may have been already initiated, but whose memory may happen to fail them, on certain occasions, when practice may be required, and such reference cannot be made to any other work.

EXPLANATION OF SIGNS AND CONTRACTIONS, &c.

$=$ .... Signifies......	is equal to.
$\times$	multiply or multiplied by.
$\div$	divided by.
$-$	*minus*, or subtract.
$+$	*plus*, or add.
4^2	square of 4.
4^3	cube, or third power of 4.
$\sqrt{4}$...................	square root of 4.
$\sqrt[3]{4}$...................	cube root of 4.

DEFINITIONS.

A FRACTION is a broken number, or part of unity, or of an integer or 1; being represented by two separate terms. Thus

B

$\frac{3}{4}$ represents three fourths or quarters of any thing forming a whole.

If equal to or exceeding an integer, the fraction is *improper;* as $\frac{5}{5}$ five fifths, or $\frac{10}{7}$ ten sevenths. When less, they are *proper,* although there is seldom any occasion for employing this distinction.

A MIXED NUMBER is a whole number and a fraction joined, as $3\frac{3}{8}$, $4\frac{4}{7}$, &c.

The upper term of a fraction is called the *Numerator,* and the lower term the *Denominator.* The latter denotes the number of parts into which the integer is divided, and the former signifies the number of parts of the denominator contained in the fraction.

The value of any fraction is equal to its numerator divided by the denominator, as $3 \div 4$; and, consequently, the greater the denominator is, the less is the fraction; and *vice versa.*

A DECIMAL FRACTION is one whose denominator is 10, 100, 1000, &c. as $\frac{3}{10}$, $\frac{3}{100}$, $\frac{3}{1000}$, &c. and is expressed thus, .3, .03, .003. The decimals being placed to the right hand of the integers, and separated from them by a dot. Any number of cyphers, being placed to the right hand of a decimal, does not alter its value; but every other figure placed to the right, is worth only one tenth of what it would be, were it one place farther to the left.

Thus,   .1 signifies one tenth.

.11 .... eleven hundredths.

.112 .... one hundred and eleven thousandths.

The denominator being always of that class of numbers produced by the multiplication of the numerator by 10. Thus, as 1 multiplied by 10 gives 10; 112 being multiplied by 10 gives 1120, *i. e.* thousandths, consequently the denominator is 1000, &c. &c.

A MIXED DECIMAL is an integer and a decimal united; as, 4.2563.

A CIRCULATING DECIMAL is one whose value cannot be accurately expressed by any vulgar fraction. Thus, 3333, &c. is less than one third by an infinitely small fraction. The reason is obvious; for, 10 divided by 3 quotes 3 and a remainder of 1. If cyphers be added to infinity, nothing will result but a continual series of 333, &c. the remainders being perpetually less. Fractions with the denominators 7 and 9 are in this predicament; and many others, with larger denominators.

A REPEATING DECIMAL has one figure or several figures continually repeated. As 20.2433, &c. which is a single or simple repetend: and 20.2424, &c. which are equivalent to circulating decimals.

ADDITION OF DECIMALS.

RULE. Place tens under tens, hundreds under hundreds, &c. Then sum up as in whole numbers, and separate the integers from the decimals by a dot.

EXAMPLE.—Add together 10.257, 5.393, 4.937, 3.873, 2.92.

$$
\begin{array}{r}
10.257 \\
5.393 \\
4.937 \\
3.873 \\
2.92 \\
\hline
\text{Sum......27.380}
\end{array}
$$

SUBTRACTION OF DECIMALS.

RULE. Proceed as in the preceding rule, then subtract, as in whole numbers.

EXAMPLE.—Subtract 10.5798635 from 21.8768.

$$
\begin{array}{l}
21.8768000....\text{(Add cyphers.)} \\
10.5798635 \\
\hline
\text{Answer....11.2969365}
\end{array}
$$

MULTIPLICATION OF DECIMALS.

RULE. Multiply as in whole numbers, and cut off as many figures from the product, proceeding from right to left, for decimals, as there are decimal figures in the multiplier and multiplicand.

B 2

EXAMPLE.—Multiply 13.59876 by 15.58797.

$$13.59876$$
$$15.58797$$

$$9519132$$
$$12238884$$
$$9519132$$
$$10879008$$
$$6799380$$
$$6799380$$
$$1359876$$

Answer....211.9770629172

As there are 5 places of decimals in the dividend, and 5 in the division, cut off 10 figures from the product, as above.

DIVISION OF DECIMALS.

RULE. Divide as in whole numbers; then cut off, as above, as many places from the quotient, as the decimal places in the dividend exceed those in the divisor. If there is a deficiency of figures in the dividend, add cyphers.

EXAMPLE.—Divide 161.57 by 21.573.

$$21.573)161.57000000(7.48945$$
$$151011$$

$$105590$$
$$86292$$

$$192980$$
$$172584$$

$$203960$$
$$194157$$

$$098030$$
$$86292$$

$$117380$$
$$107865$$

$$9515$$

The decimal places in the dividend are 8, in the divisor 3; therefore mark off 5 figures from the quotient—Answer, 7.48945.

REDUCTION OF DECIMALS.

CASE 1. To reduce a vulgar fraction to a decimal fraction of nearly equal value.

RULE.—Add cyphers to the numerator; and divide by the denominator. The quotient is the decimal required. If cyphers may be added, *ad infinitum,* without producing an exact quotient, the decimal is a circulating one.

EXAMPLE 1.—Reduce $\frac{11}{12}$ to a decimal.

12)1100000000000

9166666666, &c. Answer.

The above is a circulating decimal.

EXAMPLE 2.—Reduce $\frac{15}{16}$ to a decimal.

16)150000

.9375 Answer.

EXAMPLE 3.—Reduce $\frac{31}{32}$ to a decimal.

32)3100000

96875 Answer.

CASE 2. To find the value of a decimal fraction of a pound, or any other denomination.

RULE. Multiply the decimal successively by the different component parts from the highest to the lowest.

EXAMPLE 1.—What is the value of .76 of a pound sterling?

.76
20 Shillings.

15.20
12 Pence.

2.40
4 Farthings.

1.60 ....Answer, 15s. $2\frac{1}{4}d.$

EXAMPLE 2. What is the value of .96 of a lb. avoirdupois ?

$$.96$$
16 Ounces.
———
15.36
16 drams.
———
5.76 ....Answer, 15 oz. 5.76 drams.

EXAMPLE 3.—How many feet in length is the decimal .553 of a pole.

A pole $= 16\frac{1}{4}$ feet.
$$.553$$
$16\frac{1}{4}$ .. feet.
———
$9.324\frac{1}{4}$
12 .. inches.
———
3.894
3 .. barley corns.
———
2.682 ....Answer, 9 ft. 3 in. $\frac{3}{4}$.

CASE 3. To reduce the known parts of an integer to a decimal.

RULE. Form a vulgar fraction, the denominator of which shall be the number of times that the lowest denomination in the known parts to be reduced, is contained in the integer: the numerator will be the *number* of the lowest denomination contained in the known parts to be reduced.

EXAMPLE 1. What part of a pound sterling is 1s. $5\frac{3}{4}d.$?

In a pound are 960 farthings ; and in 1s. $5\frac{3}{4}d.$ are contained 71 farthings ; consequently the vulgar fraction is $\frac{71}{960}$.

960)71000000000

Decimal .739583333, &c. Answer.

EXAMPLE 2. What part of a furlong are 101 yards, 2 feet, 9½ inches?

Yds. ft. in.	A furlong=220 yards.
101 2 9½	220 yards.
3	3 feet.
305 feet.	660
12	12 inches.
3669 inches.	7920 inches.
2	2
7339 half inches.	15840 half inches.

Fraction $\frac{7339}{15840}$) 7339000000

.46332007, &c. Answer.

DUODECIMALS; OR, CROSS MULTIPLICATION.

DUODECIMAL ARITHMETIC is the art of multiplying feet, inches, &c. into each other, by a process different from that of common or decimal arithmetic.

In duodecimals the calculation decreases by twelves, from the place of feet, towards the right hand. Inches in this rule are commonly denominated *primes*, and are marked thus '; the next division after inches are called *parts* or *seconds*, and marked thus, "; the next are *thirds*, marked thus, '''; &c.

RULE. Under the multiplicand write the corresponding denominations of the multiplier, i. e. feet under feet, inches under inches, &c.

2. Multiply each term in the multiplicand, beginning at the lowest, by the feet in the multiplier, and set each result under its respective term; observing to carry an unit for every 12, from each lower denomination to its next superior.

3. Multiply every term in the multiplicand by the inches in the multiplier, and set the result of each term one place removed to the right of those in the multiplicand.

4. Proceed in the same manner with the seconds, and all the other denominations, setting the product of each line one place

farther to the right than the preceding one. The sum of all these lines will be the product required.

Feet ......by......feet......give.... feet.
Feet ......by......primes........... primes.
Feet ......by......seconds......... seconds.
Primes ....by......primes........... seconds.
Primes ....by......seconds......... thirds.
Primes ....by......thirds........... fourths, &c.
Seconds...by......seconds......... fourths.
Seconds...by......thirds........... fifths.
Seconds...by......fourths......... sixths, &c.
Thirds ....by......thirds........... sixths.
Thirds ....by......fourths......... sevenths.
Thirds ....by......fifths............ eighths, &c.

EXAMPLE 1. Multiply 7 feet 6 inches by 5 feet 4 inches.

```
ft.  in.
 7   6
 5   4
 ─────
35
     2   6
     2   4
         2   0
 ─────────────
```

Product.... 40 0' 0" Square feet.

Here, in the first instance, 5 feet multiplied by 7 feet, give 35 feet; then 6 inches by 5 feet produce 30 inches, or 2 feet 6 inches.—Next, 7 feet, multiplied by 4 inches, give 28 inches, or 2 feet 4 inches; and 6 inches by 4 inches, give 24 seconds, or 2 inches.—The sum of all the products is 40 square feet, as shown in the operation.

EXAMPLE 2. Multiply 54 feet 6 inches and a quarter by 23 feet nine inches and a half.

54 feet 6¼ inches, is.......54° 6' 3"
22 feet 9½ inches, is......22 9 6
                           ─────────────
                           108 0 0
                           108 0 0
                            11 0 0
                           ── 5 6
                            40 6 0
                           ── 4 6
                           ── 0 2 3'''
                             2 3 0
                           ──── 3 1 6''''

Product.... 1242 7 5 4 6

NOTE. The contents of the area of a superficies, or the cubical contents of a solid, may be very readily found by the fractional parts of the foot being given in common decimals, as shown under the word FOOT, in the last division of this work, which is alphabetically arranged.

INVOLUTION.

INVOLUTION is the multiplication of any number by itself, a given number of times; the product is called a *power*.

Every number is the first power of itself; consequently, when multiplied by itself, it is called the 2nd power or square; when multiplied once more by itself, the 3d power or cube; if again, the 4th power, &c.; so that the number or *index*, called also *exponent*, of the power exceeds the number of multiplications by 1.

It is therefore evident that, to ascertain the value of any power, nothing more is requisite than to multiply the original number, or *root*, into itself, a number of times less by one, than the index of the power required.

c

EXAMPLES.—To find the square of 23.

$$23$$
$$23$$
$$\overline{}$$
$$69$$
$$46$$
$$\overline{}$$
$$529 \text{ The answer.}$$

Required the cube of 42.

$$42$$
$$42$$
$$\overline{}$$
$$84$$
$$168$$
$$\overline{}$$
$$1764$$
$$42$$
$$\overline{}$$
$$3528$$
$$42$$
$$\overline{}$$
$$3528$$
$$7056$$
$$\overline{}$$
$$74088 \text{ The answer.}$$

If the number of figures should be odd, dot the first figure, and afterwards every second figure towards the right. The operation may be considerably shortened by the following observations.

The product of two powers multiplied into each other, is that power whose index is the sum of the indexes of the two factors; thus the cube × the square = the 5th power; for $3+2=5$. The index of the cube being 3, and of the square, 2.

Also, when a power is multiplied by itself, the product is a power whose index is double that of the multiplier. Thus the square × the square = 4th power. The cube × the cube = 6th power, &c.

INVOLUTION BY DECIMALS

Is very nearly the same as in whole numbers.

RULE. Multiply as usual, and cut off as many figures from the quotient for decimals, as there are decimal figures in the dividend and divisor.

EXAMPLE. Find the square of 4.5

$$4.5$$

$$\begin{array}{r} 225 \\ 180 \\ \hline 20.25 \end{array}$$ Answer.

Find the cube of 5.5

$$5.5$$

$$\begin{array}{r} 275 \\ 275 \\ \hline 30.25 \\ 3.5 \\ \hline 15125 \\ 15125 \\ \hline 166.375 \end{array}$$ Answer.

The method of shortening the operation by the addition, &c. of the indices has been fully explained in the article Involution.

EVOLUTION.

EVOLUTION is the extraction of roots; a root of any power is the number that, being multiplied into itself a number of times, less by one, than the index of the power, will produce the power. The root takes its denomination from the number of multiplications $+1$; so that is called the 2d, 3d, or 4th root, as it is multiplied 1, 2, or 3 times, in order to produce the power. Roots, besides the mark $\sqrt{}$, are sometimes designated by a fraction; as $\frac{1}{2}$, $\frac{1}{3}$, $\frac{1}{4}$, for the 2d, 3d, or 4th root.

TO EXTRACT THE SQUARE ROOT.

BEGIN from the left hand; and on every second figure towards the right, place a dot. Find the next less root to the first period, and place it to the right hand of the given number, as in division. Subtract the square of this root from the first

c 2

period; and to the remainder, annex the next period, for a dividend.

Double the root already found, and place it to the left hand of the dividend.

Consider what figure can be annexed to this divisor; by which, if the sum represented by the union of the two figures be multiplied, it shall be equal to, or next less than, the dividend.

Having found this figure and its product, subtract the latter from the dividend; to the remainder annex the next period for a new dividend; then, double the figures already found for a divisor, and proceed as before, till the operation be complete.

EXAMPLE. Find the square root of

$$17.305\overset{\smile}{6} \quad (4.16 \text{ Answer.}$$
$$16$$

$$81) \quad 1.30$$
$$81 \times 1 = .81$$

$$826) \quad .4956$$
$$826 \times 6 = 4956$$

What is the square root of 256 ?—Answer 16.

Do............. 3......1.732050.
Do............. 5......2.236068.
Do............. 10......3.162278.
Do.............3025......55.
Do.............4896......6.99714.
Do.............2495......4.99499.

In order to extract the roots of vulgar fractions, reduce them to decimals, or find the root of the denominator; and place the root of the numerator above it.

EXTRACTION OF THE CUBE ROOT.

RULE 1. Divide the given number into periods of 3 figures each; find the next less cube of the first period; set the root in the quotient; deduct the said cube from the 1st period; and, to the remainder, annex the following period for a *resolvend*.

2. Find the triple square of the root already found; and place three times the root under it; but one figure more to the right. Add them together. The sum is a divisor.

3. Cut off the last figure of the resolvend; and divide the remaining figures by the divisor; annex this to the figure in the quotient already found.

4. Cut off from the quotient the figure last found; multiply the square of the figures preceding it by 3; then, multiply three times the said figures by the square of the figure cut off: and, lastly, find the cube of the figure cut off; add them all together in the above order, placing the 2d product one figure more to the right hand than the 1st, and the 3d one more than the second.

5. The sum is called the *subtrahend*; which must be as nearly equal to the *resolvend* as possible, but not exceed it: if it does, repeat the operation for finding it, till it is either less than, or exactly equal to, the subtrahend.

6. Deduct the subtrahend from the resolvend; to the difference annex the next period of the given number; then proceed as before to find a divisor, &c.

Required the cube root of

$$1^2 \times 3 = 3 \qquad (2350976359(1[3[2[9[6 \text{ Quotient}$$
$$1 \times 3 \quad 3 \qquad\qquad 1$$

Divisor 33   135[0   Resolvend.

$$1^2 \times 3 \times 3 = 9$$
$$1 \times 3 \times 3^2 = 27$$
$$3^3 \ldots\ldots \quad 27$$

Subtrahend 1197

Resolvend   1350
Subtrahend 1197

153.97[6 new Resolvend.

$$13.^2 \times 3 = 507$$
$$13 \times 3 = 39$$

Divisor   5109

$$13^2 \times 3 \times 2 = 1014$$
$$13 \times 3 \times 2^2 = 156$$
$$2^3 = 8$$
$$102968$$

Resolvend   153976
Subtrahend 102968

New Resolvend   51008.35[9

$$132^2 \times 3 = 52272$$
$$132 \times 3 = 396$$

Divisor 523116

$$3 \text{ times } 132^2 \times 9 = 470448$$
$$3 \text{ times } 132 \times 9^2 = 32076$$
$$9^3 = 729$$

Subtrahend   47366289

Resolvend   51008359
Subtrahend 47366289

.3642070000[0 new Resolvend.

$$3 \text{ times } 1329^2 = 5298723$$
$$3 \text{ times } 1329 = 3987$$

Divisor   52991217

$$3 \text{ times } 1329^2 \times 6 = 31792338$$
$$3 \text{ times } 1329 \times 6^2 = 143532$$
$$6^3 = 216$$

Subtrahend   3180669336

Resolvend   3642070000
Subtrahend 3180669336

Difference   461400664

Answer, 13296 nearly.

And so proceed.

Examples.   What is the cube of 1000 ? Answer 10.

Do.............. 3375....15 Answer.

Do.............. 17 ....2.571282.

Do.............. 25 ....2.924018.

Do.............. 42 ....3.476027.

A SIMPLER METHOD OF EXTRACTING THE CUBE ROOT.

Rule 1. By trial, find the nearest cube to the given number, and call it the assumed cube.

2. Then, as the sum of the given number, and double the assumed cube, is to the sum of the assumed cube, and double the given number, so is the root of the assumed cube to the root required, nearly.

3. Assume the cube of the root last found as a new *assumed cube*, and proceed as before, by which a root will be found approximating still more nearly to the real root. This is a sufficiently exact method for all general purposes. The oftener the operation is repeated, the more exact will be the result.

EXAMPLE Required the cube root of 128000.

It lies between 50 and 51.

Assumed cube 125000. Root 50.

As 128000+twice 125000 or : 125000+twice 128000 or 378000 : 381000 : : 50—so 50 to 50.4 nearly. Cube of 50.4=128024, and 064=exceeding 128000 by 24.064 only.

LOGARITHMS.

LOGARITHMS are a series of numbers, or rather roots of numbers, calculated in order to facilitate those operations, which cannot be performed, without extreme labour and delay, by common arithmetic.

By means of a table of logarithms, multiplication is performed by addition, and division by subtraction.

The integer prefixed to a logarithm is called its index; thus 2 is the index of the logarithm 2.2081725.

The Index of the logarithm of 10 is 1; of 100 is 2; of 1000, 3; of 10000, 4,&c. When the number for which a logarithm is wanted lies between 1 and 10; 10 and 100; 100 and 1000; &c. a reference must be made to a table of logarithms.

The index of the logarithm of an integer or mixed number is always 1 less than the number of integer places in the natural number. Thus, between 100 and 1000, it is 2; 1000 and 10000, 3, &c.

The index is generally omitted in tables for the sake of brevity.

To find the Logarithm of any mixed Decimal Number.

RULE. Find the logarithm as if it were a whole number, and prefix the index of the integer part.

The logarithm of 259.7, is 41447 ; to which, if the index be prefixed, the logarithm is 2.41447.

TO FIND THE LOGARITHM OF A VULGAR FRACTION.

SUBTRACT the logarithm of the denominator from the logarithm of the numerator, borrowing 10 in the index, when the denominator is the greatest, the remainder is the logarithm required.

What is the logarithm of ⅝ ?

$$\text{Logarithm of } 5 = 69897$$
$$9 = 95424$$

$$9.74473 \text{ Answer.}$$

MULTIPLICATION BY LOGARITHMS.

ADD the logarithms together of the multiplier and multiplicand, the sum is the logarithm of the answer required.

Multiply 9 by 253.

$$\text{Logarithm of } 9 = .95424$$
$$253 \quad 40312$$

$$1.35736$$

35736 is the logarithm of 2277, the Answer.

DIVISION BY LOGARITHMS.

SUBTRACT the logarithm of the divisor from the logarithm of the dividend ; the difference is the logarithm of the quotient.

Divide 477 by 3.

$$\text{Logarithm of } 477 \quad .67852$$
$$3 \quad 47712$$

$$20140$$

2014 = logarithm 159, the Answer.

INVOLUTION BY LOGARITHMS.

MULTIPLY the logarithm of the root by the index of the power to which it is to be raised; the product is the logarithm of the answer.

Required the 5th power of 11.

$$\begin{array}{r} \text{Logarithm of } 11 = 1.4139 \\ \times \quad\quad 5 \\ \hline 5.20695 \end{array}$$

20695 is the logarithm of 161051, the Answer.

EVOLUTION BY LOGARITHMS.

DIVIDE the logarithm of the given number by the index of the power; the quotient is the logarithm of the root.

EXAMPLE. What is the cube root of 15625?

Logarithm of 15625 = 4.19382. 4.19382 ÷ 3 = 1.397606. 1.397606 = logarithm of 25, the Answer.

· RULE OF THREE BY LOGARITHMS.

RULE. Add together the logarithms of the 2d and 3d numbers, and from their sum, deduct the logarithm of the 1st. The difference will be the logarithm of the answer.

EXAMPLE. If 110 give 19, what will 94 give?

110 : 94 : : 19 :

$$\begin{array}{r} \text{Logarithms } 2.04139. \quad 1.97313 : : 1.27875 \\ 1.97313 \\ \hline 3.25188 \\ \text{Deduct} \quad 2.04139 \\ \hline \text{Difference} \quad 1.21049 \end{array}$$

.21049 logarithm of 16.22, the Answer.

SECTION II.

DEFINITIONS IN GEOMETRY,

WITH PROBLEMS,

AND THE

METHODS OF ASCERTAINING DISTANCES, &c.

DEFINITIONS.

THE first definition in Geometry is a POINT or dot, which is abstractedly considered as having no parts or magnitude; neither length, breadth, or depth.

A LINE is considered as length without-breadth.

A SUPERFICIES, or surface, is an extension, having only length and breadth.

A BODY or SOLID, is a figure of three dimensions; namely, length, breadth, and thickness.

Hence surfaces are the extremities of solids; lines the extremities of surfaces; and points the extremities of lines.

Lines are either right, or curved, or mixed of these two.

A *right* or *straight line* is one which lies evenly between its extreme points, and is the shortest distance between those points.

A *curve* continually changes its direction between its extreme points.

Parallel lines are those which have no inclination towards each other; or which, being every where equi-distant, would never meet, although ever so far produced.

AN ANGLE is the inclination or opening between two lines, having different directions, and meeting in a point; hence a *Plane Angle* is a space or corner formed by two straight lines meeting each other.

When a straight line AD standing upon another CB, makes angles ADC, ADB, on each side, equal to one another; each of these angles is called a *Right Angle*; and the line AD is said to be *Perpendicular* to the line CB.

An angle is usually expressed by three letters ; that placed at the angular point being always in the middle : as D, in the preceding figure, is the angle of ABC.

An *Obtuse Angle* is that which is greater than a right angle, as ABC.

An *Acute Angle* is that which is less than a right angle, as DBC.

By an ANGLE of ELEVATION is meant the angle contained between a line of direction, and any plane on which the projection is supposed to be made ; as the angle formed by the direction of the bowsprit with the plane of the horizon.

SUPERFICIES are either plane or curved.

A PLANE, or Plane superficies, is that with which a right line may every way coincide ; but, if not, it is curved.

Plane figures are bounded either by right lines or curves. Those that are bounded by right lines have names according to the number of their sides, or of their angles ; for they have as many sides as angles ; the least number being three.

A figure of three sides and angles is called a TRIANGLE. And it receives particular denominations from the relations of its sides and angles. Hence, a *Plane Triangle* is a figure bounded by three right lines.

An *Equilateral Triangle* is that which has three equal sides.

An *Isosceles Triangle* is that which has only two equal sides.

A *Scalene Triangle* is that which has all its sides unequal.

A *Right-angled Triangle* is that which has one right angle.

In a right-angled triangle, the side opposite to the right angle is called the *hypothenuse,* and the other two sides the *legs,* or sometimes, the *base* and *perpendicular.*

An *Oblique-angled Triangle* is that which has no right angle.

An *Obtuse-angled Triangle* has one obtuse angle.

D 2

An *Acute-angled Triangle* has all its three angles acute.

In the same triangle, opposite to the greater side, is the **greater** angle; and opposite to the greater angle is the greater side.

All plane figures, bounded by four right lines, are called QUADRANGLES, or *quadrilaterals.*

A *Square* is a quadrangle, whose sides are all equal, and its angles all right angles.

A *Rhombus* is a quadrangle, whose sides are all equal, but its angles not right angles.

A *Parallelogram* is a quadrangle, whose opposite sides are parallel.

A *Rectangle* is a parallelogram whose angles are all right angles.

A *Rhomboid* is a parallelogram whose angles are not right angles.

All other four-sided figures, besides the above, are called either *Trapeziums,* or *Trapezoids.* The latter having only one pair of opposite sides parallel.

A right line joining any two opposite angles of a four-sided figure, is called the *diagonal.*

All plane figures contained under more than four sides are called *Polygons.*

Polygons having five sides are called *Pentagons;* those having six sides, *Hexagons;* with seven sides, *Heptagons;* with eight sides, *Octagons;* with nine sides, *Nonagons,* &c.

A *Regular Polygon* is that whose angles and sides are all equal.

The *Base* of any figure is that side on which it is supposed to stand, and the *Altitude* is the perpendicular falling thereon from the opposite angle. The height, or altitude, is, therefore, a perpendicular let fall from an angle, or its vertex, to the opposite side, called the base.

If a triangle and parallelogram have equal bases and equal altitudes, the triangle is half the parallelogram

A CIRCLE is a plane figure, bounded by a curve line, called the *Circumference,* every part whereof is equally distant from a point within the same figure, called the *Centre.*

Any part of the circumference of a circle is called an *Arch.*

Any right line drawn from the centre to the circumference of a circle, is called a *Radius*.

All the radii of the same circle are equal.

The circumference of every circle, great or small, is supposed to be divided into 360 parts, called *degrees ;* each degree into 60 equal parts, called *minutes ;* and each minute into 60 equal parts, called *seconds*.

A *Quadrant* of a circle will therefore contain 90 degrees, being a fourth part of 360.

Equal angles at the centres of all circles will intercept equal numbers of degrees, minutes, &c. in their circumferences.

The *measure* of every plane angle is an arch of a circle, whose centre is an angular point, and is said to be of so many degrees, minutes, &c. as are contained in its measuring arch.

All right angles, therefore, are of 90 degrees, or contain 90 degrees, because their measure is a quadrant. Acute angles contain less than 90 degrees, and obtuse angles more than 90 degrees.

The three angles of every plane triangle, taken together, contain 180 degrees, being equal to two right angles, as demonstrated hereafter.

In a right-angled plane triangle, the sum of its two acute angles is 90 degrees.

The *Complement* of an arch, or of an angle, is its difference from a quadrant or right angle.

The *Supplement* of an arch, or of an angle, is its difference from a semi-circle, or two right angles.

The quantities or magnitudes of arches and angles are determined by certain straight lines, appertaining to a circle, called chords, sines, tangents, &c.

The *Chord* of an arch is a straight line, joining its extreme points, as FRO.

A *Diameter* is a chord passing through the centre, and dividing the circle into two equal and similar parts, as DCV, the half of which, as DC, is a *Radius*.

A *Segment* is any part of a circle, bounded by an arch and its chord, as D *n*, B *m*.

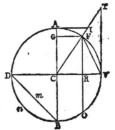

A *Semi-circle* is half the circle, or a segment cut off by a diameter, and contains, therefore, 180 degrees.

A *Sector* is any part of a circle bounded by an arch, and two radii, drawn to its extremities.

The *Sine* of an arch is a line drawn from one end of the arch, perpendicular to the other side or radius, as F R, in the preceding figure; and it is half the chord of twice the arch.

The *Versed Sine* of an arch, is that part of the diameter intercepted between the sine and the end of the arch, as R V.

The *Tangent* of an arch is a line, V T, proceeding from either end, perpendicular to the radius joining it; its length is limited by a line drawn from the centre through the other end.

Hence one line is a tangential, or a tangent, to another, when both are produced, and it touches it without cutting.

The *Secant* of an arch is the line proceeding from the centre, and limiting the tangent of the same arch, as C T.

The *Co-sine* and *Co-tangent*, &c. of any arch is the sine and tangent, &c. of its complement, or what it wants of ninety degrees.

Therefore, in the foregoing figure, FO is the chord of the arch FVO, and FR is the sine of the arches FV, FAD; RV, RD, are the versed sines of the arches FV, FAD.

VT is the tangent of the arch FV, and of its supplement.

CT is the secant of the arch FV.

AI is the co-tangent, and CI the co-secant of the arch FV.

The chord of 60°, the sine of 90°, the versed sine of 90°, the tangent of 45°, and the secant of 0, are all equal to the radius.

In making use of these lines, it is obvious that we must always make use of the same radius, otherwise there would be no settled proportion between them.

The whole mensuration of figures may be reduced to the measure of triangles, which are always the half of a rectangle of the same base and altitude; and, therefore, their area is obtained by taking the half of the product of the base multiplied by the altitude or height. Consequently, the mensuration of distances may be reduced to the doctrine of triangles, or TRIGONOMETRY.

CONIC SECTIONS are figures which are formed by the intersection of a cone with a plane, either perpendicularly, horizontally, or obliquely; for, according to the different positions of the cutting plane, five different figures or sections are produced; namely, a triangle, a circle, an ellipse, a parabola, and an hyperbola. The three latter are, however, the only figures to which the term Conic Sections is properly applied.

If the cutting plane pass through the vertex of the cone, and any part of the base, the section will be a *triangle* as V H G.

If the plane cut the cone parallel to the base, or make no angle with it, the section will be a circle, as *h g*.

If the cone be cut obliquely through both sides, or if the plane be inclined to the base in a less angle than the side of the cone, the section is an *ellipse*, as T S *c n*.

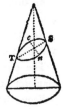

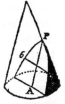

If the plane cuts the cone parallel to one side, or if the cutting plane and the side of the cone make equal angles with the base, the section is a *parabola*, as P A *b b*.

If the cutting plane makes a greater angle with the base than the side of the cone makes, the section is called an *hyperbola*, as A C D: and, if the plane be continued so as to cut an opposite cone, the latter is called the opposite hyperbola to the former, as B E.

The *vertices* of a conic section are the points where the cutting plane meets the opposite sides of the cone, or the sides of the vertical triangular section, as A and B. The ellipse and the opposite hyperbolas, therefore, have each two vertices; but the parabola only one; unless the other be considered as at an infinite distance.

The *axis* or *transverse diameter* is the line or distance A B between the vertices, and the middle point of the transverse is the centre of the conic section.

A *Diameter* is any right line drawn through
the centre, and terminated on each side by
the curve : and the extremities of the diameter, or its intersections with the curve,
are its vertices, as C D.

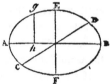

The *transverse diameter* of an *hyperbola* is
that part of the axis intercepted between the vertices of the opposite sections.

The *conjugate axis* is a line, E F, drawn through the centre of
the section and perpendicular to the transverse.

An ordinate is a line perpendicular to the transverse axis, as
g *h*.

An abscissa is that part of the axis A *h*, between the ordinate
and the vertex.

The *parameter* of any diameter is a third proportional to that
diameter and its conjugate.

From these definitions it will appear, that the conic sections
are in themselves a system of regular curves naturally allied to
each other, and that one is changed into another by increase or
diminution. Thus the curvature of a circle being ever so little
increased or diminished passes into an ellipse. Also, the centre
of the ellipse going off infinitely, and the curvature being thereby
diminished, it is changed into the parabola : and again, the curvature of the parabola, being ever so little changed, produces the
first of the hyperbolas; the innumerable species of which will all
arise in gradation by a diminution of the curvature, until at
length, the last hyperbola will end in a right line. Whence it is
manifest, that every regular curvature, like that of the circle,
from the circle itself to a right line, is a conical curvature, and
distinguished with its peculiar name, according to the degree of
curvature.

In short, a circle may change into an ellipsis, the ellipsis into
a parabola, the parabola into an hyperbola, and the hyperbola
into a plane isosceles triangle; and the centre of the circle, which
is its focus, divides itself into two foci, so soon as the circle
begins to degenerate into an ellipsis : but, when the ellipsis
changes into a parabola, one end of it flies open, one of its foci
vanishes, and the remaining focus goes along with the parabola

until the latter degenerates into an hyperbola : and, when the hyperbola degenerates into a plane isosceles triangle, this focus becomes the vertical point of the triangle, namely, the vertex of the cone ; so that the centre of the base of the cone may be said to pass gradually through all the sections, until it arrive at the vertex.

THEOREMS.

THEOREM I. When a right line, as AB, stands upon another right line, as CD, they form two angles, DAB and BAC, which, together, are equal to two right angles.

DEMONSTRATION, &c.

If AB were perpendicular to CD, each of the angles would be a right angle ; but, as EAB is the excess of BAC above a right angle, and DAB is less than a right angle by the same quantity, the angles DAB and BAC must be equal to two right angles.

Hence, if ever so many right lines stand thus on one point A, on the same side of a right line CD, the sum of all the angles are equal to two right angles, or 180 degrees ; and, all the angles formed about the same point, by any number of lines, are altogether equal to four right angles.

THEOREM II. If two right lines intersect each other, the opposite angles are equal.

DEMONSTRATION, &c.

By theorem the first, the angles BED, DEA, are equal to two right angles ; for the same reason, the angles AEC, CEB, are also equal to two right angles ; and, by subtracting a common angle on each side, the remaining angles will be equal. Consequently, the angle DEB is equal to the angle AEC, and the angle AED to BEC.

THEOREM III. If a straight line AB, intersect two parallel straight lines, CD, EF, the alternate or opposite angles will be equal, and the outward angle a will be equal to the inward and opposite angle e.

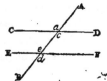

E

DEMONSTRATION.

If we suppose the space between C D and E F to be a line, the outer opposite angles are equal by the last theorem. By the same reason the angle *a* is equal to the angle *e*, and the angle *c* to the angle *d*. Consequently, the alternate angles are equal, &c.

THEOREM IV. In any right-lined triangle the sum of the three angles is equal to 180 degrees, or two right angles; and, if one side of the triangle, as B C, be continued or produced, the outward angle, A C D will be equal to the sum of the two inward and opposite angles A and B.

DEMONSTRATION.

Through the point A draw a right line EF, parallel to B D; then, by Theorem III the angle E A B is equal to the angle A B C, and F A C to A C B : hence the three angles included in the semicircle are equal to the three angles of the triangle. Again, the three angles in the semi-circle are equal to two right angles, or 180 degrees; and the three angles of the triangle are also equal to two right angles.

The two angles D C A, A C B, are, likewise, equal to two right angles, as before shown; and are, of course, equal to the three angles of the triangle. Subtracting, therefore, the common angle A C B, the angle A C D must be equal to the opposite angles C A B, A B C.

HENCE ; 1. The sum of any two angles of a triangle subtracted from 180 degrees, gives the third angle.

2. If the sum of any two angles of a triangle be equal to the sum of any two angles of another, the remaining angle of the first triangle must be equal to the remaining angle of the other triangle.

3. The sum of the two acute angles of a right-angled triangle, is equal to a right angle ; and, therefore, if one be given, the other is found by subtracting it from 90 degrees.

4. The four angles of every quadrilateral figure are altogether equal to four right angles.

THEOREM V. Parallelograms, standing on the same base, or equal bases, and between the same parallels, are equal.

DEMONSTRATION, &c.

As A B is equal to C D, so must A a be equal to B b; B a being common to both: and, because A C equals B D, as the angle A equals the angle C, the triangle AC a is equal to the triangle BD b; and if, from both these triangles, the common triangle B e a be taken, there will remain the trapezium A B e C equal to the trapezium a b D e. Now the trapezium A B e C, added to the triangle C e D, is equal to the parallelogram A B c D; and the trapezium a b D e, added to the triangle C e D, is equal to the parallelogram a b C D; consequently, the parallelogram A B C D is equal to the parallelogram a b C D.

Hence, all triangles standing upon the same base, or upon equal bases, and between the same parallels, are equal; for all triangles are the halves of their circumscribing parallelograms; and, if the whole be equal, their halves must also be equal.

THEOREM VI. In any right-angled triangle, the square of the hypothenuse, or side opposite to the right angle, is equal to both the squares of the sides containing it.

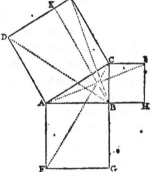

DEMONSTRATION, &c.

Let the triangle A B C have a right angle at B; then will the square of A C be equal to the sum of the squares of A B, B C.

For, upon A B, B C, C A, describe the squares A E, B F, B I; draw likewise B K parallel to E C, and join B D, B E, A I, and C F.

Now the angle D A C is equal to the angle F A B, each being a right angle, and, by adding the angle B A C, common to both, the angle B A D is equal to the angle F A C. Also, because A B is equal to AF, and A D equal to A C, by construction; the triangle B A D is equal to the triangle F A C.

E 2

The parallelogram A K is equal to twice the triangle B A D, and the square A G is equal to twice the triangle A F C; consequently, the parallelogram A K is equal to the square A G.

In like manner it may be shown that the parallelogram C K is equal to the square C H; therefore the square A E is equal to the sum of the parallelogram A K, C K, and the sum of the squares A G, C H.

Hence, from two sides of a right-angled triangle given, the third may be easily found; for, if the two sides containing the right angle are given, the hypothenuse may be found by adding the squares of the two given sides together, and extracting the square root of the sum. Or, if the hypothenuse and one of the legs be given, the square of the given leg subtracted from the square root of the hypothenuse will leave a remainder, the square root of which will be the side required.

———

GEOMETRICAL PROBLEMS.

The case of drawing instruments used for Geometrical Purposes, generally consists of a pair of compasses, with a shifting leg, to admit a steel pen or a pencil holder; a pair of compasses, with a spring joint, for taking or marking distances with the greatest accuracy; a pair of bows for sweeping small circles; a steel drawing pen; a drawing pen and pencil holder for the compasses; a pen-knife and pencil; a parallel rule for drawing lines parallel to each other; and, a plane scale, generally of ivory, having upon it the following graduated lines, viz.: upon one side, a protractor and a line of chords for measuring and laying off angles, with a decimal diagonal scale of equal parts, divided into half and quarter inches, and subdivided into hundredth parts of an inch. The other side of the scale is occupied with lines, graduated into equal parts, as one inch $\frac{7}{8}$, $\frac{3}{4}$, $\frac{5}{8}$, $\frac{1}{2}$, $\frac{3}{8}$, $\frac{1}{4}$, and $\frac{1}{8}$, of an inch. The latter are, generally, used in the construction of plans, as so many parts of one inch to a foot, and one division at the end of each, is subdivided into twelve parts, for inches, accordingly.

With these instruments the following and other problems may be correctly performed.

1. *To divide a given right line into two equal parts.*

From the points A and B, with any distance greater than the half of A B, describe with compasses, arcs cutting each other in *e* and *d*. Draw the line *e* C *d*, and it will divide the given line into two equal parts.

2. *From a given point, in or near the middle of a given line, to draw a perpendicular to the given line.*

On each side of the point *d* take any two equal distances *d* A, *d* B; and, from the points A B, with any radius greater than *d* A, *d* B, describe two arcs intersecting in C. The line *d* C, drawn through the intersection, will be the perpendicular required.

3. *From a given point, near the end of a given line, to draw a perpendicular to the given line.*

From the point B, with any radius, describe the arch *c e i;* and, from *c* with the same radius, turn the compasses twice over on the arc, as at *e* and *i*. Then, from *e* and *i*, describe the arcs intersecting in O. Now draw B O, and it will be the perpendicular required.

Another method.

From any point C, as a centre, with the radius C B, describe an arc cutting the given line in A and B. Through A and C draw a straight line to intersect the arc at O. Draw B O, and it will be the perpendicular required.

4. *From a given point, as* C, *to let fall a perpendicular to a given line* A B, *when the point is nearly over the middle of the line.*

From the point C, with any radius, describe an arc cutting A B in *e* and *i* From the points *e* and *i* describe arcs intersecting as at *o*. Then draw C *o*, the perpendicular required:

5. *From a given point, as* A, *nearly over the end of a right line, to let fall a perpendicular.*

From C draw a straight line, at pleasure, to meet A B at any point, as *e*. Bisect C*e* at *m*; and, from the point *m*, and distance C*m* or A*m*, describe the arch cutting A B in *n*. Now draw C*n* and it will be the perpendicular required.

* In practice, perpendiculars may be more readily raised and let fall, by means of a square, or the protractor on the plane scale before mentioned.

6. *To divide a given angle into two equal parts.*

Let B A C be the given angle. From A as a centre describe the arc B C; and, from B and C, with the same radius, describe the arcs intersecting in O. Draw A O and it will divide the angle as required.

7. *To divide a right angle into three equal parts.*

From A, with any radius, describe the arc B C; and, from B with the same radius, cross the arc in *d*, likewise from C in *e*. Through the points *d e* draw A*d*, A*e*, and they will trisect the angle as required.

8. *To draw a line, as* D E, *parallel to a given right line,* A B.

From the given points A and B, with the requisite distance, describe the arches D and E; then lay a ruler to touch the back of the arches, and by it draw the line D E, which will be parallel to the given line as required.

9. *To draw a line, parallel to a given line* A B, *which shall pass through an assigned point, as* C.

From any point *u*, in the line A B, with the distance C*u*, describe the arc C*o*. From C, with the same radius, describe the arc *i u*. Take the arc C*o* in the compasses, and apply it from *u* to *i*. Through C and *i* draw the line D E, which will be the parallel required.

10. *To divide a given line into a proposed number of equal parts.*

Let it be required to divide the line A B
into six equal parts. From the point A draw
any line A D, making an angle with the line
A B ; then through the point B, draw a line
B C, parallel to A D; and, from A, with any small opening in
the compasses, set off a number of equal parts on the line A D,
less by one than the proposed number (which, in this example, is
5) ; then, from B, set off the same number of the same parts
on the line B C   Join 5 and 1, 4 and 2, &c. and these lines will
cut the given line as required.

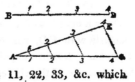

11. *To divide a given line in the same Proportion as a given divided*
line.

Let A C be the line to be divided, and
B D the graduated line. From A draw a
line A E, equal to B D, and upon it
transfer the divisions of that line. Join
E C, and, parallel to it, draw the lines 11, 22, 33, &c. which
will divide the line A C as required.

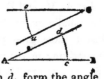

12. *At a given point, as A, in a given line A B, to make an angle*
equal to a given angle.

From the point C, with any radius, describe an arc *o u.* From A, with the same
radius, describe the arc *d c.* Take the distance *o u* in the compasses, and apply it from
c to *d;* then will the line A *d,* drawn through *d,* form the angle
as required.

13. *At a given point, on a right line, to make an angle of any*
proposed number of degrees.

From the point A, with the radius equal to 60
degrees, taken from the scale of chords, describe
the arc *c e.* Then take, in the compasses, from
the same scale of chords, the proposed number
of degrees, and apply them from *e* to *c.* A line A *c,* drawn through
the point *c,* will then form the required angle.

Angles exceeding 90 degrees are set off at twice. But these, or any other angles, may be more readily laid off with the protractor, by laying the centre to the point A, and the base along A B; a dot at the proposed number of degrees will then mark the angle.

14. *To measure a given angle, as* A, *above.*

. With the chord of 60 degrees describe the arc *c e;* then take the arc in the compasses, and the extent, applied to the scale of chords will shew the number of degrees in the angle.

If the arc exceeds 90 degrees, it may be taken off at twice, as above.

The angle may, however, be more readily measured by applying the protractor, as described in the preceding problem.

15. *To find the centre of a circle.*

Draw a chord, as A B, and bisect it perpendicularly with C D, which will be a diameter. Then bisect C D in the point O, and that will be the centre of the circle.

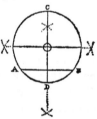

16. *To describe a circle through any three given points not situated in a right line.*

Let A, B, and D, be the given points. From the middle point B draw the lines B A, B D. Bisect these lines perpendicularly by the lines intersecting in the point C. Upon C, as a centre, with the radius C A, then describe the circle required.

₊ In the same manner may the centre of an arc be found.

17. *To make an equilateral triangle on a given line.*

From the points A and B, with the distance A B, describe arcs intersecting in C. Draw A C, B C, and it is done.

An isosceles triangle may be made in the same manner, taking for the distance the given length of one of the longer sides.

18. *To make a triangle with three given lines.*

Let the lines be A B, A C, and B C. From the
point B and distance B C describe an arc. From
the point B, with the distance A C, describe
another, intersecting the former. The intersection gives the point which will form the triangle required.

19. *To make a square on a given line.*

Draw B D equal and perpendicular to C D. From
B and C, with the distance C D, describe arcs intersecting in A. Then draw C A and A B, which will
form the square required.

20. *To describe a parallelogram or rectangle.*

Let the length of the proposed rectangle be
A B, and its breadth A C. Draw A C perpendicular to A B; and, from the point A, with
the given breadth, describe an arc. From the
points B and C, describe other arcs intersecting in D, which give
the point forming the parallelogram.

In the same manner may an oblique parallelogram be described,
by drawing A C with the given angle instead of perpendicular.

21. *To construct Plane Scales, &c.*

1. The decimal diagonal scale.

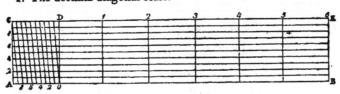

Draw the line A B, and divide it into any number of equal parts
for the primary divisions. Next erect the perpendiculars A C,
&c. equal in height to the given breadth of the scale. Divide
each of the perpendiculars A C and B E into ten equal parts, and
through the divisions draw parallel lines of the whole length of
the scale. Then divide the length of the first division C D into
ten equal parts, both on C E and A B, and connecting the points

F

by diagonal lines, the scale will be finished, and may be numbered at pleasure.

Scales of this description are made use of for taking off dimensions or numbers of two or more figures. For instance, if the largest divisions be taken as units, the smaller divisions between A and o will be tenth parts, and the divisions in the height will be hundredth parts. If the larger divisions be taken as tens, the next smaller will be hundredths, and the smallest thousands, &c. Each set of divisions being tenth parts of the former ones.

EXAMPLES. To take the distance representing one and three tenths (1.3) from the scale, set one foot of the compasses on the base line, to the larger division 1, and open the other leg to 3 in the smaller divisions between A and 0. The extent will be the distance required.

To take a distance equal to 25, set, in like manner, one foot of the compasses on the larger division 2, and extend the other to the smaller division 5 on the base, which will be the distance.

For 346, the larger divisions being in this case taken as hundredths, set one leg in three, upon the line marked 6 at the end, and extend the other to the diagonal 4, which will be the extent required.

And, conversely, may the length of any line, be measured relatively to another of a determinate length.

2. *A diagonal Scale, for Feet, Inches, and Eighths of an Inch.*

This is constructed upon the same principle as the former. The larger divisions representing feet, the subdivisions, A to 0 inches, and the graduations in the height, eighths of an inch. Hence, to take off an extent equal to four feet six inches and three-eighths of an inch, place the compasses upon the parallel marked 3 at the end of the distance from the primary division 4 to the diagonal line 6, and that will be the extent required.

Plate I

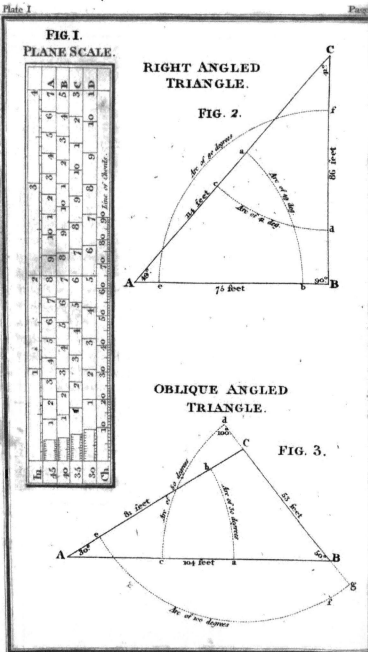

FIG. I.
PLANE SCALE.

RIGHT ANGLED
TRIANGLE.

FIG. 2.

OBLIQUE ANGLED
TRIANGLE.

FIG. 3.

Publish'd Apr. 20 1812 by Steel & C? Chart-sellers to the Honf. Board of Admiralty, at their Navigation Warehouse, N. 70 Co.

TRIGONOMETRY, BY SCALE AND COMPASSES.

*** *In all the following seven cases, we shall make use of, and refer to, the scale* C, Fig. 1, Plate 1, *for measuring the sides of a triangle; and by the line of chords (marked* Ch.), *given on the same figure, for measuring the angles. The triangle, Fig. 2, Plate 1, serves for all the cases.*

CASE I.

The two acute angles at A and C, and the base A B, being given, to find the perpendicular B C.

In the triangle A B C the given angle at A is 49 degrees, and the given angle at C is 41 degrees, and the base A B is 75 feet. *Required* the number of feet in the perpendicular B C?

Make A B equal to 75 parts of the scale C, (fig. 1, plate 1.) and make B C perpendicular to A B by problem 3, page 29. Then, setting one foot of the compasses in the beginning of the line of chords (*Scale, fig.* 1.) extend the other foot to 60 degrees, (which is called the *radius,* or *chord* of 60) and, with that extent, setting one foot in A (fig. 2.) sweep the arc *a b* with the other foot ; and, taking 49 degrees from the line of chords in your compasses, set that extent from *b* to *a;* and, through the point *a,* from A, draw the line A *a* C, meeting the perpendicular at C. Then, taking the line B C between the points of your compasses, apply that extent of the compasses to the scale, (C, fig. 1.) and you will find it to be 86 parts or divisions of that scale : and, as the base A B is reckoned in feet, so must the perpendicular B C be. Hence the perpendicular required is 86 feet.

CASE II.

The two acute angles at A and C, and the base A B, being given, (as in case I.) *Required* the hypothenuse A C?

Project the triangle A B C, as shewn in case I. Then take the hypothenuse A C in your compasses, and applying that extent to the scale C (fig. 1.) you will find it to be 114 parts ; which are feet, if the base A B be taken in feet ; yards, if taken in yards ; or, fathoms, if taken in fathoms.

CASE III.

The two acute angles A and B being given, viz. A 49 degrees and C 41 ; and, also, the hypothenuse A C 114 feet. *Required* the number of feet in the base A B ?

The triangle A B C being projected, (as shewn in case I.) take the base A B in your compasses ; and, by measuring it on the same scale (C, fig. 1.) as above, it will be found to contain 75 feet.

CASE IV.

The base A B being given, viz. 75 feet, and the perpendicular B C 86 feet. *Required* the number of feet in the hypothenuse A C ?

Make A B equal to 75 parts of the above scale, and draw B C perpendicular to A B, by problem 3, page 29, making B C equal to 86 parts of the scale. Then draw the hypothenuse A C, and measure its length by your compasses on the same scale, which length will be found to be 114 parts ; which are feet, because A B is reckoned in feet.

CASE V.

·The base A B, and perpendicular B C, being given (as above), *Required* the two acute angles at A and C ?

Construct the triangle as directed in case IV. Then, with the chord of 60 degrees, taken in the compasses, (see case I.) set one foot in the angular point A, and, with the other foot, describe the arc *a b* ; then, without altering the compasses, set one-foot in the angular point C, and, with the other foot, describe the arc *c d*. Lastly, take these arcs at their extremities in your compasses, and, by measuring them on the line of chords, (See problem 14, page 32,) you will find *a b* (the measure of the angle A) to be 49 degrees ; and *c d* (the measure of the angle C) to be 41 degrees. Or, having found either of these angles, subtract it from 90 degrees, and the remainder will be the measure of the other.

CASE VI.

The base A B, and the hypothenuse A C, being given, the former being 75 feet, and the latter 114. *Required* the acute angles A and C ?

Make A B equal to 75 parts of the scale before referred to ; and, from the end B, draw B C indefinitely, but of sufficient length, and perpendicular to A B. Then, taking 114 parts of the same scale in your compasses, set one foot in the end A of the base A B, and, with the other foot, cross the perpendicular B C in C, and draw A C. Then measure the angles at A and C, as directed in case V, and you will find that the former contains 49 degrees, and the latter 41.

CASE VII.

The base A B, and the hypothenuse A C, being given, according to the preceding measures : *Required* the acute angles A and C, and the perpendicular B C ?

Project the triangle A B C as directed in case VI. ; then measure the angles A and C, as in that case, and the former will be found to be 49 degrees, and the latter 41. And, by taking the length of the perpendicular B C in your compasses, and applying that extent to the scale C (fig. 1.), it will be found to be 86 parts, which are feet, as the base is taken in feet.

THE FOREGOING ARE ALL THE CASES OF RIGHT-ANGLED PLANE TRIANGLES ; AND THE FOLLOWING ARE THE SEVERAL CASES OF OBLIQUE-ANGLED PLANE TRIANGLES.

⁎ *In all these cases we shall use the same scales of equal parts and chords as were used in the former. The triangle* (fig. 3, pl. I.) *serves for all the cases.*

In every oblique-angled plane triangle, as A B C, fig. 3, plate I. the sum of all the angles is equal to 180 degrees, which is equal to two right angles, or twice 90 degrees.

CASE I.

Two sides, and an angle opposite to one of them, being given : *Required* the angle opposite to the other side ?

In the triangle A B C there are given the side A B, 104 feet ; the side B C, 53 feet ; and the angle at A, 30 degrees : and the question is, to find the number of degrees in the angle at C.

Take 60 degrees from the line of chords, (as before shewn,) and, with that extent, setting one foot of the compasses in the angular point C, with the other foot describe the arc *e f g*; then, setting one foot at the extremity *e* of the arc, extend the other foot to the other extremity *g*, and apply that extent to the line of chords. But, as it happens, in the present case, that this extent is greater than 90 degrees, which is the whole length of the chord line, and, consequently, the angle at C is greater than a right angle; therefore, taking the whole length of the line of chords in your compasses, set that extent from *e* to *f* on the arc *e f g*; and, then, taking the remaining part *f g* of the arc in your compasses, measure it backwards on the line of chords from the point of 90 degrees, and it will be found to be ten degrees; which, added to the former 90, makes 100. So that the angle C contains 100 degrees: which was required.

CASE II.

The three angles, and one of the sides, being given; to find either of the other sides.

In the triangle A B C there are given the angle at A, 30 degrees; the angle at B, 50; the angle at C, 100 degrees; and, the side A C, 81 feet (by the scale C, fig. 1.) *Required* the number of feet contained in the side A B?

Construct the triangle; then take the line A B in your compasses, and measure its length on the scale; when it will be found to contain 104 of the equal parts of that scale, which are to be considered so many feet, because the given side A C is in feet.

CASE III.

Two sides, and an angle opposite to one of them, being given: *Required* the other side.

In the triangle A B C there are given; the side A B, 104 feet; the side A C, 81 feet; and, the angle at A, 30 degrees. What is the length of the side B C?

Construct the triangle; then take B C in your compasses, and measure its length on the scale, and you will find it to be 53 parts or feet: which was required.

CASE IV.

Two sides, and an angle being included between them, being given; to find the other angles.

In the triangle A B C there are given ; the side A C, 81 feet ; the side B C, 53 feet ; and, the included angle at C, 100 degrees. *Required* the angles at A and B ?

Construct the triangle ; then measure these angles as before shewn, and you will find the angle A to be 30 degrees, and the angle B 50 : which was to be done.

CASE V.

Two sides, and their included angle being given, to find the third side.

In the triangle A B C the same particulars are given as in case IV. ; and it is required to find the third side B C.

Construct the triangle ; then take B C in your compasses, and measure it on the same scale as you have hitherto used for this triangle, and you will find it to be 53 feet.

CASE VI.

The three sides being given, to find the three angles.

In the triangle A B C are given, the side A B, 104 feet ; the side A C, 81 feet ; and, the side B C, 53. *Required* the number of degrees in each of the angles A, B, and C ?

Construct the triangle, as shewn in problem 18, page 33, then measure the angles as before shewn, and you will find the angle at A to be 30 degrees ; the angle at B, 50 ; and, the angle at C, 100.; which was required.

We now proceed to the practical application of Trigonometry, in finding heights and distances, &c.

TO FIND THE HEIGHTS AND DISTANCES OF OBJECTS AT SEA.

CASE I. If the object be perpendicular, and the distance to it can be measured, find the angle of altitude with a quadrant, and measure the distance to it as exactly as possible ; and thus you will have the angles and base given * to find the perpendicular ;

---

* The best instrument for taking altitudes, or angular heights, is the well-known Hadley's quadrant ; a description of which, with its uses, is contained in every modern Treatise on Navigation.

or, if you go backward and forward until the angle be 45° the distance between you and the object will be the perpendicular height.

EXAMPLE. Suppose that the altitude of a castle, or topmast-head, be 27° 20′, when the given distance from it is 100 fathoms, by admeasurement; what is its perpendicular height?

This is similar to case I. in the resolution of right-angled triangles. For, draw the base A B, which make equal to 100 fathoms; upon B erect the perpendicular B C; at A, with the

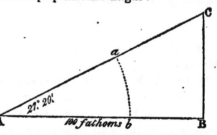

chord of 60°, make an arch, *a b*, upon which lay off the given angle 27° 20′; from A draw a line through *a*, the termination of the arch, until it cut the perpendicular in C; then will B C be the height of the tower above the eye of the spectator, equal to 51.7 fathoms.

CASE II. If the altitude of a mountain, observed at sea, be 30° 10′; and then, after sailing from it, in a direct line for three miles, the altitude be again observed, and found to be 18° 47′, what is its perpendicular height?

Draw the ho-zontal line D C on any point, as suppose A; make

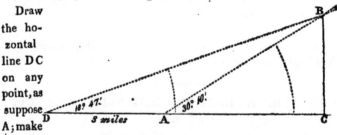

the angle B A C equal to 30° 10′; from A set off three miles towards D; on D make the angle B D C equal 18° 47′, and, from where the line B D cuts the line A B, as at B, let fall the perpendicular BC on the base D C; then will B C represent the perpendicular height of the mountain; or, two miles and four tenths of a mile.

CASE III. To ascertain the distance of any object of which the height is known.

Suppose the point C to be a topmast-head at 86 feet above the surface of the water, and its observed altitude to be 49 degrees : what is the horizontal distance from the mast to the observer ?

Draw the line A B indefinitely, as a base ; and, on its extremity B, erect the perpendicular B C, equal to 86. Then subtract the observed angle 49° A

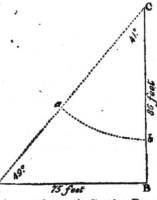

from 90°, or a right angle, which leaves the angle C 41°. Draw the arc *a b*, which make equal to 41°. Then, through the points C*a*, draw the line C A ; and the distance from A to B, measured on the scale of equal parts, will be the distance required, viz. 75 feet.

The triangle in this case is similar to that on plate 1.

The distance of remote objects, whose heights are known, may be ascertained from the curvature of the earth, by means of tables included in the Treatises on Navigation ; but this particular does not appear to be of so much practical utility as to require notice in this work.

CASE IV. If, in coasting along shore, a cape or headland be seen, bearing N. E. by N., and the ship then sails 20 miles on a N. N. W. course, until the cape bears E. N. E, what is its distance from the last station.

Draw the compass N. E. S. W.—
Let A represent the place of the
ship at her first station; lay off
two points, or $22\frac{1}{2}$ degrees from
N. towards W. *, and draw the N.
N. W. line A C, equal to 20 miles;
from C draw the line C B, parallel
to the E. N. E. line, until it meet
the N. E. by N. line A B; then
will B represent the cape of land,
and C B the distance of the ship at
her last station; which is 29.93
miles.

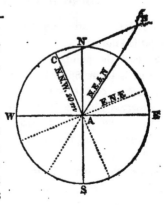

CASE V. If, in coasting along shore, two head-lands be seen,
the one bearing N. N. E. 12 miles, the other S. E. by S. 19 miles,
what are the bearing and distance of one from the other?

Draw a compass, as in the preceding case, and let A represent
the ship's place at the time of
taking the bearing of the two head-
lands; lay off two points from N.
towards E., through which draw
the line A B, which make equal to
12 miles; then lay off three points,
or 33° 45', from S. towards E,
through which draw the line A C,
made equal to 19 miles, and join
the lines B and C; then will B C
represent the distance of the two

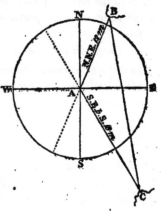

head-lands, viz. 27.54 miles. The angle B will be equal to 35°,
and the angle C to 21° 14'.

Then, from the angle B 35°   0'
     Deduct the angle C 21   14

         Difference....13   46 or N. 13° 46' W., the bearing
                                    of C from B.

* The points of the compass are reckoned from North and South to East
and West, 1, 2, 3, &c.; and the angle from any one point to the next is equal
to 11° 15'; consequently two points are 22° 30'; 3 points 33° 45', &c.

Case VI. On sailing along, two head-lands are seen, the one bearing North, and the second W. N. W., or N. $67\frac{1}{2}°$ W. The ship then sails N. E. (N. 45° E.) 18 miles, until the first bears W. by N. (N. $78\frac{3}{4}°$ W.), and the second W. S. W. (S. $67\frac{1}{4}°$ W.). Required the bearing and distance of the two head-lands from the last station ?

Draw the compass as in the preceding page. Let A represent the ship at her first station; produce (or continue) A N to D, the bearing of the first cape being North; lay off six points from the N. towards W., and draw the W. N. W. line A C for the bearing of the second cape. Draw the N. E. line A B, equal to 18 miles; then will B represent the ship's place at her second

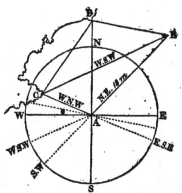

station; from B draw B D, parallel to the W. S. W line, meeting the two first lines in the points D and C; then will D represent the first, and C the second, head-land; of which the bearings may be found by reference to the compass, and the distances by scale as before shewn.

In the same manner may the bearing and distance of three or more objects be readily found; namely, by simply taking the bearing of each from two given stations, and constructing a figure as above.

In the estimation of distances, in the order of sailing in squadrons, the subjoined table will be found very useful. In thus sailing there are two modes; the one called Close Order, and the other Open Order. By the first is meant at the distance of from one and a half to two cables length, or about one quarter of a mile; and, by the latter, or open order, is understood an interval of from three to four cables length, or about half a mile. But the distances are varied occasionally, according to circumstances, and may be ascertained, as shewn in the following page.

· The following table for finding the distance between ships of the line was most obligingly communicated by the Honorable

Admiral Waldegrave, now Lord Radstock, for *Steel's Treatise on Naval Tactics*, from which it is here reprinted, with additions.

A TABLE for finding the distance of Ships in the line.

Guns.	100	90	80	80	74 L.	74 S.	64	60	50
Distance in Fathoms.	Angle.	Angle.	3 decks Angle.	2 decks Angle.	Angle.	Angle.	Angle.	Angle.	Angle.
50	31° 50½′	30° 45′	29° 57′	35° 43′	31° 13′	30° 16′	27° 50′	26° 45½′	25° 34½
100	16 21½	15 43½	15 23½	16 49	16 7½	15 34½	14 4½	13 28½	12 5½
150	11 3½	10 37	10 18½	11 25	10 48½	10 26	9 30	9 5½	8 39
200	8 18½	7 59	7 44½	8 29½	8 7½	7 50	7 8	6 49½	6 29
250	6 39	6 23½	6 12	6 50	6 30	6 16½	5 42	5 27	5 11½
300	5 32½	5 18½	5 9½	5 39¾	5 24½	5 13½	4 44½	4 32½	4 19½
400	4 9	3 59½	3 52½	4 15	4 3½	3 55	3 34	3 24	3 14
500	3 19½	3 11½	3 5½	3 24	3 15	3 8	2 51	2 44	2 36
600	2 46	2 39	2 35	2 50	2 42½	2 36½	2 22¼	2 17	2 10
700	2 22¼	2 17	2 12½	2 25½	2 19	2 14	2 2	1 57	1 51
800	2 5	1 59	1 56	2 8	2 2	1 58½	1 46¼	1 42½	1 37½
900	1 51	1 46½	1 43½	1 53½	1 48	1 44½	1 35	1 31	1 27
1 mile	1 38	1 34	1 31½	1 40½	1 36	1 32½	1 24	1 20½	1 17
2 miles	0 49	0 47½	0 45¾	0 50½	0 48	0 46½	0 42	0 40	0 38
3 miles	0 33	0 31½	0 30½	0 33½	0 32	0 31	0 28	0 27	0 25½
4 miles	0 24½	0 23½	0 23	0 25½	0 24	0 23¼	0 21	0 20¼	0 19¼

Explanation.

Observe, with a Hadley's quadrant, well adjusted, the angle made from the observer's eye to the maintop-gallant-mast hounds or rigging, of the next ship, by bringing the hounds or rigging down to the surface of the sea: then refer to the table, and, under the rate of the ship observed in the upper column, take the angle which is nearest to that on the quadrant; and, on the same parallel in the left-hand column, will be found the distance of that ship's main-mast from the observer, in fathoms or miles.

When the angle observed does not agree with any in the table, and the corresponding distance is required accurately, proceed thus:

Suppose the observed angle of the rigging of the **Princess Royal** of 90 guns to be 8° 40′ ; required her distance ?

The nearest greater angle in the table is $10:37'$ answering to 150 fathoms distance
The nearest lesser angle is . . . . 7:59 ——————— 200 ————————

Their difference is. . . . . 2:38 answering to 50 fath. difference.

Then, from. . . . . $8:40'$ the observed angle.
Subtract. . . . . 7:59 the nearest lesser angle.

Leaving. . . . . 0:41 difference.

Then proceed thus :

fath.
If $2:38'$ is equal to 50 what is $0:41'$ equal to ?

60   50
———   ——— Answer,
158′   158′(2050′(13 fathoms.
                        158
                        ———
                        470
                        474

Therefore, deducting 13 fathoms from 200 fathoms, will give the distance required, 187 fathoms.

REMARKS.

The ship's are supposed to have six months stores on-board, and the nautical mile to contain 1015 fathoms, 60 of which make one degree of the meridian. In computing the table, the observer's eye hath been supposed to be elevated 30 feet above the surface of the sea, which answers to the gangways of three-decked ships, or to the poop of a ship of 74 guns.

When the line of battle a-head is formed in close order, it must not be forgotten, that, the distance between the observer and the observed ship's main-mast, found by the table, may by very different from that which is between the taffarel of the one and the jib-boom-end of the other ; it is also evident, that, when the observer is on the gangway, the distance found will be nearly equal to that which is between main-mast and main-mast ; but, should he be on the poop, it will be almost half the length of the ship less. When the distance of the ship observed is considerable, and the main-top-gallant-sail is hoisted, the yard may be very safely used, in observing the angle, instead of the rigging; and it is for this reason, as well as for the arbitrary lengths of the main-top-gallant-mast-heads, that the hounds have been used. It may be proper to observe, that the ships' having been supposed to have six months stores continually on-board, will, in some measure, compensate for the inclination of the mast, when they may be of a lighter draught of water.

A TABLE *exhibiting the distances of Ships of the Second and Third Rate from each other, according to the subtending angle.*

To bring the vane of a second or third-rate ship of war to her water-line, you will have on your quadrant as expressed in the table, according to the corresponding distances in cables' length.

Height of the eye.	Height of the object.	Distance of a second rate in cables.	Angle on the quadrant.			Height of the object.	Distance of a third rate in cables.	Angle on the quadrant.		
The eye 26 feet above the surface.	Prince George's vane 184 feet above the surface.	1	14°	27'	06"	A seventy-four's vane 170 feet above the surface.	1	13°	27'	05"
		2	7	17	49		2	6	44	40
		3	4	52	27		3	4	30	10
		4	3	39	26		4	3	22	43
		5	2	55	33		5	2	42	11
		6	2	26	15		6	2	15	20
		7	2	05	25		7	1	55	50
		8	1	49	45		8	1	41	25
		9	1	38	13		9	1	30	09
		10	1	27	50		10	1	21	08
		11	1	19	45		11	1	13	46
		12	1	13	23		12	1	07	35
		13	1	07	32		13	1	02	25
		14	1	02	40		14	0	57	00
		2 miles.	0	49	45		2 miles.	0	55	19
		2½ ditto.	0	47	50		2½ ditto.	0	44	15
		3 ditto.	0	39	45		3 ditto.	0	37	00

N. B. The Prince George's gangway is 29 feet above the surface. The difference of ten feet in the height of the eye, makes very little difference in the angle.

DISTANCES WHEN CHASING.

In order to ascertain, when chasing, whether shot from the bow-chase guns will reach a ship, which may be chased, take a quadrant, properly adjusted, and look through the sight-vane and horizon-glass; moving the index until the ship be seen; then bring the head of the topgallant sails or topsails even with the water's edge; and, if the top of the sails appear to rise, on repeating the observation, she, of course, will be nearer; or, if lower, farther off. When the index cuts about 20 degrees, on elevating the gun, by taking the quoin nearly out, a nine-pounder may, probably, reach; paying particular attention to the rise and fall of the ship at the moment the gun is fired.

TO ASCERTAIN A DISTANCE BY THE FLASH AND REPORT OF A GUN.

The sound, or report, of a gun, is found to fly at the rate of 1142 feet in one second of time : by this rule may, therefore, be estimated the distance of the gun from the spectator. For example; if, between seeing the flash of a gun and hearing the report I count nine seconds, then is the place whence the gun was fired 10,278 feet distant. For,

    1142 feet
       9 seconds

6)10278 (1713 fathoms, or one nautic mile and 698 fathoms;
          allowing the mile to be 1015 fathoms.

SECTION III.

THE DUTY OF A GUNNER IN THE ROYAL-NAVY;

WITH

FORMS OF ACCOUNTS, LETTERS, CERTIFICATES, &c.

THE Duty of a Gunner, in the Royal Navy, is to take charge of the artillery and ammunition on-board; to examine and observe that the former are always kept in order, and fitted with tackles and other furniture; and to teach the sailors the exercise of the cannon.

The office of a Master-Gunner is, therefore, important and respectable; as, in the person who fills it, and performs its various duties, there should exist no inconsiderable portion of the energies contributive to ultimate success in conflict; to which his preparation and disposal of the materials for serving the guns, in time of action, and his skill and attention during the same, especially in making a well-directed fire, are essential. Added to all this, by his prudence, forethought, and good management, the lives of many brave men may be preserved.

Probity, courage, and skill, should, therefore, always mark the character of him who holds this situation, that its respectability may be properly maintained.

Although mathematical knowledge will, unquestionably, operate very advantageously in the recommendation of a candidate for this office, yet, experience has shown, that an extensive knowledge of these sciences is not essential to practice at sea. The subjoined form of the Gunner's passing certificate, will show precisely what is required in order to a qualification.

It cannot be expected, that every young sea-gunner, or those on board a ship who have a prospect of stepping forward into this line of the service, have been favored with opportunities for scien-

tific study; especially when it is considered that the persons
selected to fill the office, are, by the regulations of the naval service, to be promoted from the rank of petty-officers; and who,
of course, must have passed some years in the service previous to
their obtaining such appointment, and have been unavoidably
precluded from those opportunities of application to study which
persons in other spheres of life enjoy.

It is certain, that, to be perfect master of gunnery, a man
should have first obtained a competent, if not a thorough, knowledge of the mathematics; as judgement is thereby readily assisted
and practice accounted for. Yet thus much may be said in favor
of those who have not the advantage of scholastic education, that
a sober, honest, and aspiring, man, who is an able sailor, may
acquire, by solitary application and little difficulty, sufficient information to enable him to discharge the duty of master-gunner
with credit to himself, as a good officer, and with advantage to
the service.

According to the regulations of the navy, as shown hereafter,
no person is to be examined for a gunner unless he shall produce
certificates of his good conduct from the respective captains he
has served with, and also a certificate from the navy-office to ascertain the time he has been in his Majesty's navy, one year of
which he must have served as a rated petty-officer, and in actual
service at sea; certificates of which he must produce. He must,
also, produce a specimen of his hand-writing; in order that his
ability for keeping the requisite books and accounts may be ascertained; and must, likewise, prove to the captain and officers appointed to examine him, that he is perfectly acquainted with the
business of a seaman.

FORM OF A GUNNER'S PASSING CERTIFICATE.

These are to certify, the right honorable the lords commissioners
for executing the office of lord high admiral of Great Britain and
Ireland, that, in pursuance of directions from   , commis-
sioner of the navy, residing at   , we have examined Mr.
in all the articles ordered by their lordships for the examination of gunners for his Majesty's sea-service, and do humbly report as follows:

1st. That he is skilled in vulgar and decimal arithmetic, in the

H

extraction of the square and cube roots, and in practical problems in geometry and plain trigonometry.

2d. He is capable of knowing when a cannon is truly bored, and not honey-combed.

3d. He knows how to dispart a cannon, so as to direct it justly to the place aimed at.

4th. He knows how to tertiate, or round the thickness of the metal of a cannon at the touch-hole, trunnions, and muzzle.

5th. He knows how to adjust a shot to a cannon, and a due proportion of powder.

6th. He is capable of taking and judging of heights and distances, and more especially at sea.

7th. He is able to find the weight of a cannon, and doth know the names and denominations thereof, and the names of the particular parts of them, the dimensions of their bores and shot for them, and the weight of the shot..

8th. He knows the length and fortification of a cannon of each sort and size, and how many persons will be necessary to attend each piece in time of service.

9th. He knows when the trunnions of a gun are placed justly in the carriage ; whether the carriage itself be fit, and of a due length for the gun ; and whether the trucks are equally high, and revert and return equally quick.

10th. He knows how to charge and discharge a piece of ordnance, readily, and artist like, and how to spunge the same ; and to muzzle and secure the same in bad weather.

He has produced to us certificates from captains   and under whom he has served, of his diligence and sobriety ; and, also, a certificate from the principal officers and commissioners of his Majesty's navy, shewing that he served   in his Majesty's service at sea. and we do humbly certify our opinion, that he is a person. fitly qualified to be master-gunner on-board any of his Majesty's ships of war of the third rate.

Given, under our hands, the . day of   , 1812.

Master-gunner ⎰ Glory,
     of his   ⎱ Anson,
Majesty's ship   Blake.

ABSTRACT FROM THE GENERAL REGULATIONS RELATING TO HIS MAJESTY'S NAVAL SERVICE ; PARTICULARLY THOSE AFFECTING THE GUNNER.

THE commissioned officers of his Majesty's navy are divided into the following ranks and denominations, viz.

Flag-officers. — Captains, who command post-ships. — Commanders, who command sloops.—Lieutenants.—Sub-lieutenants.

The order in which officers shall take precedence and command in the ship to which they belong, is as follows :—Captain or commander.—Lieutenant.—Sub-lieutenants.—Master.—Second Master.—Gunner. —Boatswain. — Carpenter.—Master's mate. —Midshipmen.

Every officer is to repair to the ship to which he shall be appointed, without delay, after receiving information of his being appointed or ordered.

Every officer, from the time of his joining the ship to which he shall be appointed, to that of his being discharged from it, is to be constant in his attendance on-board, never going out of the ship, except on the public service, without having obtained permission from the commanding-officer on-board ; nor shall he remain out of the ship during the night, nor after the setting of the watch, without having express permission to do so ; nor be absent from the ship for more than twenty-four hours at one time, without the permission of the commander-in-chief, or the senior officer present.

Every officer in the fleet, from the time of his joining the squadron or ship to which he shall be appointed, to that of his being removed from it, shall wear the uniform established for officers of his rank or station ; except when he shall have leave from the lords commissioners of the admiralty, or the commander-in-chief, to be absent from his duty ; or, when he shall have express permission from his commanding-officer to appear without it, which is never to be granted unless he may have leave to go to some considerable distance from the port where the ship, to which he belongs, shall be anchored.

Every officer, in his station, is to conduct himself, in the discharge of his duty, with the most perfect respect to his superiors, and the most implicit obedience to their orders ; and every officer is, on all occasions, to shew to all other officers every degree of respect and attention, which their respective situations may entitle them to expect.

Every officer in the fleet is to obey every order of his superiors, and to discharge every part of his duty with the utmost zeal and alacrity; and he is not only to discharge the duties particularly attached to his own station, but he is also, as far as circumstances will admit, to assist all other officers in whatever duties they may have to perform. He is, on all accasions, to promote the good of the public service, in all its branches ; and so to conduct him-self, in every situation, as to be an example of morality, regu-larity, and good order, to all who may be subject to his command.

Every officer is to observe attentively the conduct of all the officers unders his command, and of the ship's company in general ; urging them, individually and collectively, to a zealous and per-fect performance of their duty; commending all those whose good conduct shall merit commendation; and censuring, punishing, or reporting to his superior, as circumstances may require, those whose misconduct shall deserve it.

If an officer shall observe any misconduct in his superior, or shall suffer any personal oppression, injustice, or other ill-treat-ment, he is not, on that account, to fail, in any degree, in the respect due to such superior officer ; but he is to represent such misconduct or ill-treatment to the captain of the ship to which he belongs, or to the flag-officer commanding the squadron in which he serves, or to the commander-in-chief, as circumstances may require.

Every officer is strictly enjoined to refrain from making any re-marks or observations on the conduct or orders of any of his superior officers, which may tend to bring them into contempt; and most carefully to avoid the saying or doing of any thing, which, if seen or heard by, or reported to, the ship's company, may discourage them, or render them dissatisfied with their con-dition, or with the service on which they shall then be employed, or with any service on which they may be ordered. And, if any officer shall so far forget so essential a part of his duty, as, either by his conduct or observations, to endeavour to lessen the respect due to his superior or his orders, or to dishearten the ship's com-pany, or any part of them, or to render them dissatisfied, every officer, and every other person, who shall observe such conduct, or shall hear such observations, is strictly charged to report it immediately to the captain of the ship, or to the commander-in-chief, as circumstances may require; and, if any officer, or other person, shall observe such conduct, or hear such observations, and 'shall not report them as herein directed, he shall be considered as accessary to the offence, and shall be punished accordingly. But this injunction is not intended to prevent an officer, who receives an order, from making to the officer from whom he receives it, a proper and respectful representation of any bad effects which he shall think may result to his Majesty's service from its being obeyed; nor to prevent any person from representing, either to the officer by whom the order was issued, or to his superior, any injury, injustice, or oppression, he may suffer, or may have reason to apprehend he shall suffer, by such order being carried into execution: nor is it intended to prevent an officer, or any person whatever, from taking such measures as the custom of the service allows, to obtain redress for any injustice or injury done to him (as directed in the preceding article of these instructions)' or protection from tyranny or any oppression he may suffer by the conduct or orders of his superiors.

If an officer, or other person, shall have occasion to represent the misconduct of any officer, or shall have cause of complaint, he is to represent it to the captain of the ship to which he belongs; but, if the captain shall not attend to his representation, or if the captain be the officer whose misconduct he shall think it necessary to represent, or of whose ill-treatment he shall have cause to complain, he is to make his representation to the commander-in-chief, to the senior officer present, or to the secretary of the admiralty, as circumstances may require.

Every officer is strictly enjoined to avoid all unnecessary public expense; and, as far as may depend upon him, to prevent it in others; to be himself, and to oblige all officers under his command to be, as economical as possible in the expenditure of stores, and not to admit of their being converted to any other than their proper use; except in such manner, and into such articles, as are allowed on the establishment of the navy; and, if an officer shall discover any wasteful expense of timber, or other materials, appropriated to the repairing of the ship, or any negligence or idledleness in the artificers employed on such repairs, he is immediately to report it to the captain, or the commanding-officer onboard, that such steps may be taken as the degree of neglect or of wasteful expense may require.

Every officer is most strictly enjoined to be particularly correct in all the accounts which he may have to render, of the purchase, receipt, expenditure, or return, of stores or provisions; always representing them as being expended, or otherwise disposed of, precisely in the manner in which they were disposed of, and in no other.

Every officer is strictly enjoined to report to the captain of the ship to which he belongs, or to the commander-in-chief, or to the secretary of the admiralty, as circumstances may require, any neglect, collusion, or fraud, which he may discover in any contractors, agents, or other persons, concerned in supplying his Majesty's ships with stores or provisions; or in executing any works in the naval department, either on-board or on-shore: whether such stores or provisions be under his charge, or such works under his inspection, or under that of any other officer.

Every officer is strictly forbidden to have any concern or interest in the purchasing of, or in contracts made for the supplying of, provisions or stores of any kind for the use of his Majesty's ships; or in contracts made for the executing of any works in the naval department; or to receive any emolument, fee, or gratuity, whatever, either directly or indirectly, on account of such contracts or purchases, from those who have an interest in such contracts or purchases.

Every flag-officer, before he strikes his flag, and every captain, commander, and other officer, before he leaves the ship to which he belongs, is to sign all books, accounts, and certificates, which may be necessary to enable the officers of the ship to pass their respective accounts, or to receive their pay, provided he be satisfied that such books, accounts, or certificates, ought to be signed; but, every officer is strictly enjoined to examine very carefully all muster-books, accounts of the receipt, expenditure, or other disposal, of stores or provisions, and all other books, accounts, or papers, before he signs them; and to sign such only as he shall believe to be correct. And every officer is also enjoined not to sign any certificate for any specific service, without ascertaining that such service has been actually performed; nor any certificate of general conduct and character, but such as the general conduct. of the person to whom it is given shall really deserve.

If an officer shall, at any time, receive from his superior an order which may be contrary in any respect to any article in these general instructions, or to any particular order he may have received from the lords commissioners of the admiralty, or from any superior officer, he is to represent in writing such contrariety to the officer from whom he shall have received the order; but if, after such representation, that officer shall direct him to obey the order he has given him, he is to obey it, and report the circumstances to his commander-in-chief, or to the secretary of the admiralty, as may be necessary.

If stores or provisions of any description be lost, embezzled, or spoiled, or if any extraordinary public expense be incurred, by the misconduct or negligence of any officer, the pay of that officer shall be made answerable for the amount of such provisions, stores, or extraordinary expense; and, if the pay due to him shall not be equal to the amount thereof, his future pay, or half-pay, shall be stopped until the public shall be perfectly reimbursed for every expense whish his misconduct or negligence may have occasioned.

Every officer is to be particularly careful, when he signs any letters, books, certificates, &c. or when he draws bills on his Majesty's service, to insert, after his name, the rank which he holds in the service.

By the regulations respecting the appointment of officers, it is ordained, that—1. No person shall be appointed to any station in which he is to have the charge of stores, unless he can read and write, and is sufficiently skilled in arithmetic to keep an account of them correctly.

2. No person shall be appointed gunner of any of his Majesty's ships, who shall not have served on-board one or more of his Majesty's ships one year as a petty-officer, and shall produce certificates of his good conduct, and undergo such examinations as may from time to time be directed.

3. Whenever there shall be a necessity for appointing an officer to act in any station during the absence of another, an officer of

the same rank as, or of the rank immediately below that of, the absent officer is to be appointed, if there be one on the station.

4. None of the standing warrant-officers of a ship are to be removed by any flag-officer, without their consent.

5. If an officer, whose situation requires that he should undergo an examination before he can be promoted, shall have left England without having passed such examination, the commander-in-chief may give orders for his being examined by officers properly qualified to examine him. A candidate for a lieutenant or sub-lieutenant's commission, is to be examined by three of the senior captains of the squadron. A candidate for the appointment of master, or second master, by one of the senior captains, and three of the best qualified masters. A candidate for a gunner's warrant, by one master and three gunners, in the presence of a captain, &c.

6. If a commission or warrant officer of any ship shall die, and the service should require that another should be immediately appointed, the senior captain present is to appoint a proper person to act until the pleasure of the admiralty or of his commander-in-chief shall be known; but no other than the commander-in-chief shall appoint to any vacancy occasioned by any other cause than death; unless, from some extraordinary circumstances, the number of officers in a ship be so reduced as to make it absolutely necessary to appoint others.

7. If the captain and all the lieutenants, and all those who may be doing duty as lieutenants, shall be killed in battle, or taken prisoners, or die, and there be no other ship present, the master is to succeed to the command, and is to appoint a sufficient number of master's mates and midshipmen to act as lieutenants, if any properly qualified remain on-board; but, if none such remain, he is to give the command of a watch to any other persons whom he may find qualified for such a trust. If the master be also killed, or taken prisoner, or die, the command shall devolve on the second master, after him on the gunner, after him on the boatswain, and after him on the carpenter. Any captain or commander may supercede all these appointments, and make such others as he shall think proper.

8. If a lieutenant, or master, succeed to the command of a ship, of whatever rate it may be, he shall receive the pay and al-

lowances of a commander only; unless, on account of his zeal
and good conduct, the admiralty shall direct that he be paid according to the rate of the ship he may command. But, if a
second-master, gunner, boatswain, or carpenter, succeed to the
command, he shall not be entitled to the pay and allowance of a
commander, but shall have such allowances as, on consideration
of his conduct, the admiralty shall think he deserves.

General Instructions for Warrant-officers.

1. The warrant-officers of his Majesty's ships, when in ordi-
nary, are to examine frequently the condition of the store-rooms
appointed to receive their respective stores, and are to inform the
master-shipwright of the dock-yard of any defects in them which
may require to be repaired, that they may be fit to receive the
stores whenever the ship shall be put into commission; and when
any ship is commissioned, the warrant-officers are to use their
utmost endeavours to get their stores on-board as expeditiously as
the other duties, necessary to the equipment of the ship, will
admit.

2. When they receive stores on-board; whether at the fitting
out of the ship, or in any subsequent supply, they are to be very
particular in ascertaining that they are good in quality, and that
they receive the full quantity specified in the note sent with them;
and they are immediately to report to the captain any defect or
deficiency which they may discover in them.

3. They are to indent for all the stores they receive from his
Majesty's dock-yards, as well as from his Majesty's ordnance-
magazines, before the ship proceeds to sea; and they are to be
very careful in observing that they do really receive all those for
which they indent, as they will always be considered as having
received them.

4. They are to keep an account, according to the forms delivered
to them, of the receipt, expenditure, (expressed in words, and
not in figures), condemnation by survey, or supplying of stores;
always specifying the place where, and the person from whom,
the stores are received, or the person to whom they are supplied.

5. There shall not be any interlineations in the accounts of
stores expended; but, if an officer shall discover that he had for-

gotten tò insert, in its proper place, the expenditure of any article which had really been expended, he is to represent the circumstance to the master, who, being satisfied of the truth of such representation, is to allow it to be inserted in the account of expenses for the next month, and to note his having done so in the ship's log-book, specifying in both the reason for its being so inserted.

6. No waste of stores not perishable will ever be allowed, except from unavoidable accidents, which are to be particularly mentioned in the log-book, where the quantity of every article is to be specified. Two of the principal officers present at such accident are to certify that it happened; and, if the quantity of the stores lost be considerable, the quantity remaining is to be ascertained by survey.

7. If stores of any description be lost or damaged through the neglect, or by the misconduct, of any officer or other person, the officer having charge of such stores is to report such misconduct or neglect to the captain, that the value of the stores may be charged against the wages of the person guilty of it.

8. Every officer shall be responsible for the conduct of his yeoman, to whom he is not to entrust the keeping of his accounts, but is to keep them with great accuracy himself. He is most carefully to avoid the stating of any stores as being expended which have not been used, or the stating of them as having been expended for any other purposes than those to which they were actually applied.

9. Every officer shall be responsible for any errors he makes in his accounts; and he shall pay out of his wages the full value of all stores not properly accounted for, or improperly expended, unless he shall produce an order from his captain to expend them in a manner contrary to the regulations contained in these instructions, and the allowed practice of the service.

10. Officers are not to suffer the yeomen to take stores from the store-rooms without their express order. They are frequently to examine the quantity remaining, and, if they have doubts of its being as great as it ought be, they are to apply for its being surveyed.

11. When they are supplied with stores by other officers, whether of the same ship, or of any other, they are to charge them-

themselves with those stores, and are to mention their having done so in the receipt they give for them.

12. One officer shall not supply another with stores, nor lend any, without an order in writing from the captain; and, when he does supply or lend them, he is to demand a receipt, in which the quantity of every article is to be written in words at length, and in which it is to be mentioned by whose order they were supplied; and he is also to give, under his hand, to the officer supplied, a voucher of delivery, specifying the stores with the same particularity as the receipt.

13. Officers, when appropriating rope, canvas, or any other article, to use, are to be very attentive to conform to the established length, and other dimensions, of whatever it may be intended to make.

14. When they convert stores to any other use than that for which they were originally intended, they are to expend them, in their accounts, as having been so converted, and are to charge themselves with whatever they convert them into.

15. When masts, sails, colours, or other stores, are blown away or lost, they are to be very particular in the quantity they expend in that manner; as they will probably be required to make oath to the truth of that part of their accounts.

16. When stores are damaged or worn out, the officer who has charge of them is to apply to the captain for their being surveyed; and, after their being surveyed, he is to be careful to apply them to whatever use the surveying-officers shall appoint, charging himself with those articles into which he may be directed to convert them.

17. They are to visit their store-rooms very frequently, to see that they are kept clean, that they are well aired, and that the stores are so arranged as to admit of any part of them being easily got at when wanted.

18. They are never to carry, nor to suffer others to carry, lights into their store-rooms, except in good lanterns; the doors of which are never to be opened in the store-rooms.

19. They are strictly charged not to put into the magazine, the wings, or any of the store-rooms, any wine or spirituous liquors; nor to keep any quantity in their cabins, except such as the captain shall expressly permit them to keep there.

20. When the ship is to be dismantled, either for the purpose of being refitted, or being paid off, they are to be particularly careful in preventing their stores, rigging, &c. from being cut, or in any way damaged; they are to see that all the stores they send from the ship are tallied, and very carefully put into the boats or vessels which are to carry them; and to take every possible precaution to prevent their receiving damage in their way to the store-houses.

21. When a warrant-officer is about to be removed from a ship, or when he wishes to pass his accounts, which he will be allowed to do at the end of every twelve calendar months, he is to apply to the captain for a survey on his stores, who will obtain from his commanding-officer an order for that purpose, if his ship be not alone, and under such command; otherwise the captain is himself to order the survey, that the quantity of stores remaining onboard may be correctly ascertained.

22. When a warrant-officer dies, the captain is immediately to apply to the commanding-officer present, to order, or if the ship be alone, he is himself to order, a survey on the stores remaining on-board; one copy of the report of such survey is to be sealed up with the papers of the officer who died, and another copy is to be delivered to his successor, to be considered as his first charge.

23. As all warrant-officers may, at times, be called to survey stores, they are strictly charged to perform that duty with the utmost attention, and to make all their reports with the strictest truth and impartiality; so that, when called on, they may be able, conscientiously, to make oath to the correctness of the report they have made.

24. When ordered to survey stores represented as being unfit for service, they are to examine every part of them very carefully; and, if they find them unfit for the service for which they were originally intended, they are to point out, in their report, any other service to which they may be appropriated.

25. When ordered to survey stores for the purpose of ascertaining their quantity, whether to enable the officer in whose charge they are placed, to pass his accounts, or to transfer them from one officer to another, they are not to take any account of any part of them from the officer who has charge of them, but, as far as it shall be possible for them to do so, they are themselves to ascertain their real quantity.

Particular Instructions to the Gunner.

1. So soon as one of his Majesty's ships is ordered to be commissioned, the gunner is to apply to the store-keeper of the ordnance at the port, for the established number of guns, with the proper quantity of ammunition and stores, which he is carefully to examine before they are put in the hoys; and he is to report to the store-keeper any imperfection or deficiency he may discover in them.

2. The gunner, having received directions for that purpose from the captain, is to inform the store-keeper when the ship will be ready to receive the guns; he is to attend to receive them on-board, and is to see that every gun is put into its proper carriage, and placed in its proper port; No. 1 being the formost gun on the larboard side, and No. 2 the foremost on the starboard side, on each deck.

3. He is, whenever other duties will admit of it, to employ his mates and the men of his crew in fitting the breechings and tackles, that they may be ready for the guns when they are carried on-board.

4. He is to examine very carefully into the state of the magazine, that he may be certain of its being properly fitted and perfectly dry before the powder is carried on-board; but, if he should find any appearance of dampness, he is to report it to the captain, that it may be properly dried.

5. He is to inform the captain when the powder will be ready to be sent on-board, that the fire in the galley may be put out before the vessel which carries it is suffered to go alongside. While the powder is taking into the ship, no candles are to be kept lighted, except those in the light-room; nor is any man to be allowed to smoke tobacco. So soon as the whole is stowed in the magazine, the gunner is to see the doors, the light-room, and the scuttle, carefully secured, and is to deliver the keys to the captain, or to such other officer as he shall appoint to take charge of them.

6. The powder is to be taken on-board at the following places only, unless ordered otherwise on particular occasions, viz. Plymouth Sound or Cawsand Bay, Spithead, Blackstakes, Longreach:

and ships being ordered into any port are to take out their powder before they pass either of those places.

7. He is never to go into the magazine without being ordered to go there; he is never to allow the doors of the magazine to be opened but by himself; he is not to open them until the proper officer is in the light-room; and he is to be very careful in observing that the men who go into the magazine have not about them any thing which can strike fire; and he must take care that no person enter the magazine without wearing the leather slippers supplied by the ordnance.

8. He is never to keep any quantity of powder in any other part of the ship than the magazine, except that which the captain shall order to be kept in the powder-boxes, or powder-horns, on deck; and, when he delivers cartridges from the magazine, he is to be very particular in observing that they are in cases properly shut; and whenever it may be necessary to remove powder from the ship, he is to use the utmost caution that all the passages to the magazine may be wetted, so that accidents may be prevented.

9. He is not to stave, nor to convert to any other use, the empty powder-barrels, but is to keep them; and, when the ship comes into port, to return them to the store-keeper of the ordnance, who is directed to pay him one shilling for every empty barrel he shall return in good condition. He is to mark with white paint, in legible characters, those barrels into which powder has been returned from cartridges,

10. He is to turn the barrels of powder once at least in every three months, to prevent the separation of the nitre from the other ingredients of the powder; he is also to examine frequently the barrels, and, if he find any of them defective, he is to remove the powder into some of the barrels which have been emptied. He is frequently to examine the cartridges which are filled, that he may remove the powder from any of them that he finds defective.

11. When powder of various qualities shall be sent on-board, he is to be very attentive in using them in the order which the board of ordnance shall prescribe.

12. When any extra quantity of stores or ammunition is supplied for foreign service, he is to be attentive to use those first which have been the longest time on-board, unless he shall receive particular directions to the contrary.

13. He is frequently to examine the state of 'the guns, their locks, and carriages, that they may be immediately repaired or exchanged if they be defective; and he is frequently to examine the musquetry, and all other small arms, to see that they are kept clean and in every respect perfectly fit for service.

14. He is to be attentive in keeping the shot-racks full of shot, the powder-horns and boxes of priming-tubs full, and a sufficient quantity of match primed and ready for being lighted at the shortest notice.

15. Guns received from the ordnance stores shall be scaled before they are loaded for service, and, if it shall be necessary to scale them at any other time, the gunner shall represent it to the captain, who is to give him an order for that purpose, in which the cause of its being done is to be particularly specified.

16. In filling cartridges, whether for service, or for scaling, he is never to exceed the quantity specified in the table*, but he is to fill a sufficient number to be ready for quick firing, with such reduced quantities as the captain shall direct.

17. When a ship is preparing for battle, he is to be particularly attentive to see that all the quarters are supplied with every thing necessary for the service of the guns, the boarders, firemen, &c.; he is to see all the screens thoroughly wetted, and hung round the hatchways, and from them to the magazine, before he opens the magazine doors,

18. He is, during an action, to take all opportunities of filling powder, that there may be no cessation of firing from want of ammunition; and he is to be attentive to send out cartridges with the quantity of powder reduced or increased, as the captain shall, from time to time, send him directions.

19. After an engagement, he is to apply to the captain for a survey on the powder, shot, and other stores, remaining under his charge, that the quantity expended in the engagement may be ascertained.

20. When he is exercising the men at the guns, he is to see that they perform every part of their exercise with the utmost correctness, particularly explaining to them, and strongly enforcing, the necessity of their pointing the guns carefully before

* See the article POWDER, in the last division of this work.

they fire them, and of spunging them well, with the touch-hole closely stopped, immediately after they have been fired.

21. He it to supply, at such times as the captain shall direct, ammunition for the guns and musquetry, not exceeding in each month, for six months after the guns are first received on-board, one charge of powder and one round of shot for one-third of the number of the upper deck guns, in ships of two or three decks ; or one-fourth for ships of one deck; and twelve charges of musquet-cartridges with ball, and twenty-four without ball, for each man of one-third part of the seamen of the ships company, and for all the marines ; not exceeding, after the first six months, one half of that quantity for the guns or musquets.

22. He is to be careful in keeping the boxes of hand-grenades and grape-shot in dry places ; and to expose frequently the grape-shot to the sun and wind, to prevent the bags from being mildewed. He is never to start the hand-grenades, but is to return those which are not used in the boxes in which he received them.

23. He is never to allow any match to be burnt in the day, nor more than two lengths, at the same time, in the night, without being ordered so to do by the captain. When match is burning, it is always to hang over water in tubs; and the gunner's mate of the watch is to attend to it.

24. If a detachment of seamen or marines shall; at any time, be sent from the ship, the gunner is to make out an inventory of the arms, ammunition, and stores, which are sent with it ; which is to be signed by the officer appointed to command the detachment, and to be witnessed by the captain's clerk, who is to examine the quantity supplied ; and, on the return of the detachment, the gunner, in presence of the officer who commanded it, and the captain's clerk, is to examine the arms, &c., which are brought back, and to report the deficiency, if any, in each article, to the captain ; who, from the manner in which the officer shall account for such deficiency, will determine whether it be proper to allow the articles to be expended by the gunner in his accounts, or charged against the pay of the officer, or any person under him, by whose carelessness or misconduct the whole, or any part of them, was lost or destroyed.

25. When a salute is to be fired, the gunner is to be very atten-

tentive to take such precautions in drawing the guns as may insure there not being a shot in any of them; and, if vessels of any description be so near as to risk the being damaged by the wads, he is to draw them also; and he is to lay up and point the guns so as to prevent their doing mischief, although a wad or shot, notwithstanding the precautions he has taken, may have been left in one of them.

26. He is to take every possible precaution to prevent any ball-cartridge being given to the men among the blank-cartridges issued to exercise.

27. Whenever he shall be directed to strike any guns into the hold, he is to pay them all over with a thick coat of warm tar and tallow mixed together; and, after having washed the bore of the gun with fresh water, and very carefully spunged and dried the inside, he is to put a good full wad, dipped in the same mixture, about a foot within the muzzle, and to see that the tompion is well driven in and surrounded with putty; and he is to drive a cork tight into the touch-hole, and to secure it there.

28. He is to be extremely attentive in examining all the guns, in seeing them carefully drawn and thoroughly spunged, before they are returned into store, He is also to examine very carefully the magazine, to see that no loose powder remains in any part of it after the powder has been returned into store; and he is to be very careful that there are not any cartridges left in the cartouch-boxes when they are sent on-shore.

29. He is to be very careful of the tools he receives from the store-keeper of the ordnance for the use of the armourer *, whom he is to furnish with such only as he may want for immediate use; and he is to require him to account particularly for all those with which he shall be furnished.

30. He is to be very attentive to the conduct of the armourer and his mates, to see that they discharge their duty properly; that they keep the musquets, and other small arms, clean and in good order; always repairing them when they are defective, and not suffering them, through neglect, to become too bad to be repaired. At the end of the voyage, or at any other time that the ship's company is paid, he is to give the armourer and his mates

---

* The Armourer is appointed by warrant from the board of ordnance.

K

certificates of their good conduct, if they shall have so performed their duty as to deserve them, but not otherwise.

31. If, from any extraordinary circumstances, when a ship is on a foreign station, the small arms should be so damaged that they cannot be cleaned or repaired by the armourer, the gunner is to represent their condition to the captain, who is to direct a lieutenant and the master to survey them; and, if their report shall confirm the representation of the gunner, he is to apply to the commander-in-chief to give orders for their being repaired; but, if the commander-in-chief be not present, the captain is himself to get them repaired by workmen on-shore, being very careful not to pay more for their repairs than the established price of the country; the gunner is to attend frequently, and the armourer constantly, to see that the work is properly done; but, if there be an officer of the ordnance at the place, the captain is to direct him to get them repaired.

32. As the brass-sheaves and iron-pins of blocks for gun-tackles, from being much exposed to salt water, are frequently set fast with rust, he is to be particularly attentive, when this is the case, to cause the iron-pins to be knocked out, and to be oiled or greased.

33. He is to be very careful not to suffer the bare gun-metal adzes, which are supplied by the ordnance for the use of the magazine, to be struck against the copper hoops of the powder-barrels; but always to have the wooden-setters applied to them, to convey the stroke from the adze, there being several instances of strong sparks of fire having been produced from the collision of a metal-adze against a metal-setter, or a copper-hoop.

INSTRUCTIONS ON TAKING SURVEYS OF STORES.

. ALL applications for surveys shall be made in writing to the captain by the officer who has charge of the provisions or stores to be surveyed, and shall be transmitted by the captain to the flag-officer commanding the division of the fleet to which he belongs, who is to order the surveys applied for to be taken, except in cases which the commander-in-chief shall reserve for his particular directions. But captains not serving in a fleet, or, if serving in a fleet, not being at the time in company with the flag-officer commanding the squadron, or division, to which they belong, are to transmit such applications to the senior officer present.

2. Surveys are to be taken on the following occasions, viz. on masts, yards, sails, and stores, of every description, when they appear to be worn out, and to be rendered unserviceable by use.

On masts, yards, sails, stores, and provisions, when they appear to be rendered unserviceable by accidents, by leaks, by vermin, or by any other cause, independent of their being worn out by use.

On stores and provisions, which, when received on-board, appear to be deficient in quantity, or defective in quality.

On stores and provisions remaining on-board, when the officer who has charge of them wishes to pass his accounts; or, when he or any other officer has reason to suspect that the quantity of any species remaining is less, from the quantity expended, than it ought to be; or when, by the death or absence of an officer who has charge of any stores or provisions, or by his being removed from the ship, the charge of them is to be transferred to some other person.

3. The officers employed on surveys are to be one master, and two officers of the class of him whose stores are to be surveyed; they are all, if possible, to belong to other ships than that to which the stores to be surveyed belong; but the master of that ship, and the officer who has charge of those stores, are to be present, to give what information may be required, and to prevent partiality or injustice, or to represent it to the captain, if they perceive without being able to prevent it. But if there be a necessity for an immediate survey, when there are not a sufficient number of ships present to furnish, or when the sickness of their officers prevent other ships from furnishing the number of officers required, the master of the ship may be ordered to assist at such survey; but, if the ship be alone, such survey is to be taken by one of the lieutenants, the master, and one of the master's mates; but, in this case, a survey shall be taken again, if other ships shall join company before the surveyed stores, &c. have been disposed of.

4. The report made by officers appointed to survey stores, &c. is to specify by whose order it is taken, and for what purpose;

what are the articles ordered to be surveyed.; the quantity and quality of those articles remaining on-board, or the actual state of any which shall be particularly represented as deficient or defective; the number or quantity is always to be written in words at length; and, if any stores complained of be found to be no longer fit for their proper use, the report is to specify whether they be fit for any other, and for what, or whether they be no longer fit for any purpose whatever.

5. If any appearance of neglect shall be discovered by the surveying-officers, it is to be particularly noticed in their report, whether it be the officer who has charge of the stores, or any other person who may have been guilty of it; but, if an appearance of fraud be discovered, the surveying-officers are not only to notice it in their report, but they are also to deliver to the captain a separate report, informing him of their suspicions of such fraud having been committed, and of their reasons for suspecting it.

6. There are to be three copies of all reports of stores, provisions, &c. which are to be surveyed, each signed by all the surveying officers; one of which reports, written on the back of the order for the survey, is to be delivered to the officer who has charge of the stores, &c. which are surveyed; one copy to the captain of the ship to which the stores belong; and one, by the captain, to the officer by whose order the survey was taken; but when the stores &c. surveyed, are to be transferred to the charge of another officer, a fourth copy, signed in the same manner, is to be delivered to the officer to whose charge the stores, &c. are to be transferred.

7. The copy of the report, delivered to the officer who had charge of the stores or provisions surveyed, is to be transmitted by him to the proper office, with his other books and papers, when he passes his accounts.

The copy delivered to an officer to whom the charge of stores or provisions is transferred, is to be considered as his first charge of stores or provisions, and is to be sent, with his books and papers, when he passes his accounts. The copy delivered to the officer, by whose order the survey is taken, is to be by him transmitted to the proper board, by the first safe opportunity; and the copy delivered to the captain of the ship is to be sent, with his books and papers, when he passes his accounts.

8. The surveying-officers are not to direct any stores or provisions to be thrown over-board, except such as, by their putrescent state, may be prejudicial to the health of the ship's company; whatever they find in such state, they are themselves to see thrown into the sea before they leave the ship, and they are to mention their having done so in their report. All other stores not convertible to any use, they are to direct the officer having charge of them to return into store, whenever a ship shall go to a port where there is a store-keeper, or other officer authorised so receive them.

9. If any officer shall wilfully sign any false report of the quantity or condition of the stores or provisions he is ordered to survey, or shall discover any fraudulent practices in the management of such stores or provisions, without making proper mention of them in his report, or if any persons shall give any false account of stores or provisions, by which any surveying-officers may be deceived, and be led to make out an improper report, he is to be immediately suspended, and his misconduct reported to the commander-in-chief, or to the secretary of the admiralty, that he may tried by a court-martial.

10. When any officer, employed on a foreign station, shall be represented to the commander-in-chief as being in such a state of health as to render it necessary for him to go to another climate, the commander-in-chief is to order three captains, assisted by the physician of the fleet, and the surgeons of the ships they command, to survey him; and, if they shall be satisfied that to continue in the service in which he is employed would be attended with danger to his life, and that a change of climate is necessary to his recovery, they are to report accordingly, particularly specifying the disease or hurt which makes such change of climate necessary; but, if they shall discover any misrepresentation in such officer's case, or any disposition in him to withdraw himself unnecessarily from the service on which he is employed, they are to report their opinion to the commander-in-chief, that all who have concurred in such misrepresentation may be dealt with as circumstances may require.

FORMS

OF

ACCOUNTS OF SUPPLIES,

EXPENSE, RETURNS, AND REMAINS;

WITH THOSE OF

ORDERS, LETTERS, CERTIFICATES, &c.

ADMONITORY NOTES.

WHEN the Gunner receives his first appointment, he will, upon application, receive Instructions from the Commissioners, relative to his accounts, &c.—Yet, here it may be proper to observe—

1. It will be requisite to have a ROUGH EXPENSE BOOK, taking care to keep it in the same manner as your complete book, and to be signed by your captain monthly, when approved of by him, before entered into the complete book; particularly when from England, as an accident may happen in sending it home to the Tower, and then the rough book will appear to pass your accounts.

The first charge, supplies, and returns, are to be entered in the Supply and Return Book, being a true copy of original indents. Every twelve months accounts in the said book are to be signed by the captain, and the indentures and returns only sent to the ordnance-office; as, if accidentally lost, the book will be a voucher.

2. *If a gunner fits out a ship and then leaves her,* which has frequently been the case, before he has indented for, or taken charge of, the stores, his pay-ticket and certificates are not alone sufficient for him to obtain his pay; he must, also, have a certi-

ficate from the ordnance-office, to certify that he has no stores on charge, his successor being the person who takes charge of them.

ORDER FOR PAINTING GUN-CARRIAGES.

(Dated Ordnance-Office, 29th April, 1807.)

THE established colours are red, white, chocolate, and yellow. You are hereby required and directed to take particular care that the guns and carriages belonging to the ship or vessel you are gunner of be painted in the established colours above-mentioned, and no other ; and that the paint delivered from the ordnance be not applied to any other purpose than that for which it was intended.

BLANK FORM OF GUNNER's SUPPLIES.

An Account of Gunner's Stores supplied to his Majesty's ship   , captain   , commander, between the   day of   , and the   , day of   ,

Time when.	Place where.	By whom.	Quality.	Quantity.

BLANK FORM OF GUNNER's EXPENSE.

An Account of the expense of Gunner's Stores on-board his Majesty's ship   , captain   , commander, between the   day of   , and the   day of

Time when.	Place where.	For what use expended.	Quality.	Quantity.

BLANK FORM OF GUNNER's RETURNS.

An Account of Gunner's Stores returned from his Majesty's ship   , captain   , commander, between the   day of   , and the   day of   ,

Time when.	Place where.	To whom.	Quality.	Quantity.

EXAMPLE OF THE FORM OF MONTHLY EXPENSE.

An Account of the expense of Gunner's Stores on-board his Majesty's ship _____, J.B., Esq. commander, between the 1st and 31st day of January, 18

Place where.	Month. Days.	In what service expended.	N° Guns.	Quality.	Quantity.
Plymouth-Sound	2	Fired to salute vice-admiral A.B............	Fifteen	} Powder total	Thirty pounds.
		Ditto to make the signal for all master merchantmen	One		
	3	Ditto to unmoor.....................	Two	{ Flannel cartridges, 18 pounders	} Twenty in No.
At sea.........		Ditto to weigh...................	One	} Round shot, 18	} One in No.
	4	Ditto to bring a ship-to............	One	} pounders	} One in No.
		Used in priming the above guns........		Quill tubs	Twenty in No.
		SMALL STORES EXPENDED.			
		Made into musquet cartridges		Fine paper.	One quire
		Fired away in wads, and converted into spun-yarn.		Junk	One cwt. one quarter
		Split in pieces not returnable.........		Tompions, 18 pounders.	Two in No.
		Converted into three breechings and four tackle-falls, the old returned into store		Rope of { 5 inch...... { 2 ditto.....	Two in No. fathoms. ditto.
				Sweet oil	Two quarts.
				Emery { Course ..... { Fine	One ounce. Ditto.
		For cleaning and new flinting the small arms......		Flints { Musquet ...... { Pistol	Fifty in No. Twenty-five in No.
		Captain		Gunner	

L 2

A Working Abstract of the Supplies, Returns, Expense, and Remains, on-board H. M. ship   , J. B., Esq. captain, between the 1st of January and the 30th of June, 18   , with the Remains on the said 30th of June.

Articles.	First charge.	January.		February.				March.				April.				May.		June.			
		E	Rs	S	Rd	E	Rs	S	Rd	E	Rs	S	Rd	E	Rs	E	Rs	S	Rd	E	Rs
Ordnance, pounders Ships' carriages Round { Shot —18 &c.	1090	1	1089		60	.....	1029														
Carronades { pounders — 18	14	.....	14																		
Flannel cartridges { 18	1010	20	990		50	.....	940														

N. B. First charge is taken by survey, or supplied from the ordnance-office.—E for Expense.—Rs. for Remains.—S. for Supplies.—Rd. for Returned into Store. If there are no supplies or returns there is no necessity for a supply or returned column.—See the Form of Supply, Expense, and Remains, in January, above ; as, also, the Returns in February.

FORM OF RECEIPT FOR GUNNER'S STORES RETURNED.

Officer of ordnance, } *March* , 18 .
Priddy's Hard Magazine,

Received into store at this place, from on-board his Majesty's ship , whereof Mr. is master-gunner, the copper-hoops under-mentioned, on the said ship's refitting at this port for foreign service.

By order of the board, the day of , viz.

Copper-hoops for half barrels, twenty No. serviceable.

FORM OF A DEMAND FOR STORES.

A demand for the supply of gunner's stores, for the use of his Majesty's ship , H. N., captain, in Hamoaze, this day of 18 .

     Viz.

(Here state the articles required.)

COPY OF AN AFFIDAVIT, IF ANY STORES ARE LOST OVERBOARD.

This deponent, Mr. , gunner of his Majesty's ship , H. N., esq. captain, maketh oath, that like articles inserted in the Expense-book are actually lost; and that his expenses are just and true, to the best of his knowledge.

                                      , gunner.

Sworn before me this day of

FORM OF A LETTER TO THE CAPTAIN, FOR AN ORDER TO SURVEY.

SIR, H. M. ship , 18 .

The time having elapsed for passing my annual accounts as gunner of his Majesty's ship under your command, I have to request that you will please to apply to the commander-in-chief for order to survey the stores that now remain in my charge.

       I am, Sir, your most obedient,

To , esq.
   captain of H. M. ship

ORDER FOR THE SURVEY ON GUNNER'S STORES.

By Hawser Trunnion, esq. rear-admiral of the White, and commander-in-chief of his Majesty's ships and vessels at Spithead, and in Portsmouth harbour.

Whereas the honorable Seymour Finch, captain of his Majesty's fire-ship the Salamander, has, in consequence of an application from the gunner of that ship, requested me to order a survey on the gunner's stores remaining in her, to enable him to pass his annual accounts:

You are, therefore, hereby required and directed forthwith to repair on-board the said fire-ship, and take a strict and careful survey on the gunner's stores, remaining in her, accordingly, reporting to me, from under your hands, your proceedings therein.

Given, under my hand, on-board his Majesty's ship Nelson, at Spithead, this 14th day of February, 181 .

H. TRUNNION.

To

The gunners of his Majesty's ships

Blake,

Valiant,

Cressy,

Centaur,

Rodney,

Laurel,

Camel, or any three of them.

By the command of the admiral.

REPORT OF SURVEY AND PERAMBULE.

Pursuant to an order from rear-admiral Trunnion, commander-in-chief, of this day's date, unto us directed,

We, whose names are hereunto subscribed, have been on-board H. M. ship   , and have taken a strict and careful survey of the stores remaining in the charge of Mr.   , gunner of the said ship, and find as follows, viz.

(Particulars.)

All which stores we find to be as above-mentioned, and have left the same in the charge of the said Mr.   , gunner. And we hereby declare that we have taken the survey with such care and equity, that we are willing, if required, to make oath to the impartiality of our proceedings.

Given, under our hands, on-board H. M. ship, at

FORM OF AN ORDER TO KEEP POWDER FILLED.

By   , esq., commander of his
Majesty's sloop

You are hereby required and directed, constantly to keep the following proportion of powder filled complete for service; and when any part thereof shall be expended, you are to report to me the same, in order that a sufficient quantity may be filled to keep such proportion complete, viz.

Six-pounders at whole allowance, ten rounds, or one hundred and eight cartridges.
At two-thirds allowance, eight rounds.
At half-allowance, ten rounds.
Swivels at whole allowance, fourteen rounds.
Musquet-cartridges balled, nine hundred.
Pistol cartridges balled, three hundred.

Given, under my hand, on-board his
Majesty's said sloop   , this
day of   , 181 .

To   T. R.
Mr.   , master-gunner of his
Majesty's sloop   .

CERTIFICATE RELATIVE TO POWDER BARRELS.

These are to certify, that there remains on-board his Majesty's ship   a sufficient quantity of empty powder barrels to contain the powder now on-board.

Given, under my hand, on-board, his
his Majesty's ship

, captain.

To the officers of ordnance, at

(The above certificate is to ascertain that a sufficient number of empty barrels be left on-board to contain the powder then in cartridges.

CERTIFICATE RELATIVE TO ORDNANCE STORES, IN CASE OF BEING
SUPERCEDED.

These are to certify, the right honourable the Principal Officers
of his Majesty's ordnance, that, having had a survey on the
day of 　　　 , 181 , for passing my annual accounts, as gunner
of his Majesty's ship 　　　 , H. N., esq., commander, and there
being no expense of ordnance stores from the day of the survey to
the present day ; and, being appointed to his Majesty's ship 　　 ,
and Mr. 　　　 being appointed to supercede me, he has taken
charge of all the ordnance stores from that survey.

　　　　　　　　Given, under our hands, on-board H. M.
　　　　　　　　　ship 　　 , this 　　 day of 　 , 1812.
　　Witness 　　　　　　　　　　　　　　　 , gunner.
　　　　　　　 , captain.
　　　　　　　 , master.
　　　　　　　 , succeeding gunner.

FORM OF CERTIFICATE FOR DRYING POWDER.

　These are to certify, the right honorable the principal officers
of his Majesty's ordnance, that Mr. 　　　 , gunner of his Majesty's
ship 　　　 , was actually employed on-shore, at the place appointed, in airing, drying, and sifting, 　　 barrels of gunpowder,
which he has returned in good order.

　　　　　　　　Given, under my hand, on-board
　　　　　　　　H. M. ship

　　　　　　　　　　　　　　　 , captain.

A LIST AND CERTIFICATE FOR PAINTING GUNS AND CARRIAGES.

　A list of men employed painting the guns and carriages belonging to his Majesty's ship 　　　 , 　　　 , esq., commander,
between the 　　 day of 　 , and the 　　 day of 　 , 181 ,
Sundays excepted.

Men's Names.	Number of Days.	Rate per Day.	Currency.	By whom received.

These are to certify, the right honorable the principal officers of his Majesty's ordnance, that the men named in the list were actually employed the number of days as above-mentioned.

Given, under my hand, on-board his Majesty's ship

, captain.

CERTIFICATE TO SHOW THAT THE GUNS AND CARRIAGES HAVE NOT BEEN PAINTED WITHIN THE LAST TWELVE MONTHS.

These are to certify, the principal officers of his Majesty's ordnance, that the guns and gun-carriages on-board his Majesty's ship , under my command, have not been painted between the of , 181 , and the date hereof.

Given, under my hand, on-board his Majesty's ship , this day of , 181 .

, captain.

FORM OF CERTIFICATE OF AFFIDAVIT FOR LOSS OF PAPERS AND DUE EXPENSE OF STORES; THE SHIP BEING LOST.

These are to certify, that , late gunner of his Majesty's ship the , hath voluntarily made oath, that he never sold or embezzled any part of the King's stores committed to his charge, during the time he was gunner of the said ship, between the , and the ; and that the books and papers necessary for passing his accounts for the above time were lost with the said ship , on the day of , when she struck and foundered near

(In case of capture a similar affidavit is required, varied according to circumstances.)

M

FORM OF CAPTAIN'S CERTIFICATE TO A GUNNER.

These are to certify, the principal officers and commissioners of his Majesty's navy, that Mr.   served as master-gunner of his Majesty's ship   , under my command, from the day of   to the   day of   , during which time he discharged his trust faithfully, as a sober and diligent officer.

Given, &c.

, captain.

FORM OF THE ORDNANCE INDENTURE.

This indenture, made the   day of   , in the   year of the reign of our sovereign lord George the Third, by the grace of God of the United Kingdom of Great Britain and Ireland King, defender of the faith, &c. between   , master-general of the ordnance, and the principal officers of the same, on behalf of the King's most excellent Majesty, on the one part, and   , master-gunner of his Majesty's ship   , on the other part, witnesseth, that the said master-gunner hath received into his custody, out of his Majesty's stores within the office of ordnance, the ordnance, ordnance stores, and habiliments of war, hereafter-mentioned, well fixed and serviceable in every respect for fitting out the said ship in his Majesty's service. By order of the board, dated the   . And the said master-gunner doth covenant with the said officers, that, at the end of the service, he shall or will deliver or cause to be delivered back into his Majesty's magazines, every part or parcel of the said stores which shall not be truly expended in the said service, with a true and perfect account of the expenditure of the residue.

	Pounders ..
	....
Ordnance......:..................................	....
	....
	....
	Pounders..
Ship-carriages, with one bed and one coin to	....
each	....
	....

Carronades .... { Pounders..
....
....

———— carriages .... { Pounders..
....
....

Axletrees .... { Pounders..
.. F. H. ...
....

Trucks, pairs .... { Pounders..
....
.. F. H. ...
....

Beds and coins, spare........................ { Pounders..
....
.. B. C. ...
....

Coins for coining guns, new pattern ....

Round shot .... { Pounders..
....
....
....

Grape shot, complete........................ { Pounders..
....
....
....

Boxes for grape-shot ....

Double-headed hammered-shot................. { Pounders..
....
....

Paper-cartridges .... { Pounders..
....
....
....

Copper powder-measures .... { Pounders..
....
....
....

M 2

Cases of wood .... {
Pounders...
....
....
....

Ladles and spunges, complete with staves........ {
Pounders...
....
..La.Sp...

Rope spunges, with rammer heads............. {
Pounders...
....
....
....

Wadhooks, with rammer heads and staves complete .... {
Pounders...
....
....
....

Staves, spare, for ladles, &c...............................

Heads and rammers, spare. .... {
Pounders...
....
.. H. R. ...
....

Sheep-skins to coat spunges, dozens, odd ....
Spunge-tacks for ditto. ....

Tompions for guns. .... {
Pounders...
....
....
....

Corned-powder, in copper hooped.. { Whole barrels...........
Half barrels ....

Copper hoops for .... { Whole barrels ....
Half barrels ....

Hazle hoops, spare...... Pieces. ....
Budge-barrels ....
Copper hoops on ditto. ....
Copper adzes. ....
Copper drivers...................................
Copper vises . ...
Match...................... Cwt. qrs. lbs.................
Tanned hides.................................

Lanterns. . . . . $\begin{cases} \text{Muscovy.} \ldots \ldots \ldots \ldots \ldots \\ \text{Ordinary, or tin.} \ldots \ldots \ldots \\ \text{Dark.} \ldots \ldots \ldots \ldots \ldots \ldots \end{cases}$

Powder-horns . . . .

Priming irons . . . .

Aprons of lead. . . . . $\begin{cases} \text{Large .} \ldots \\ \text{Small.} \ldots \ldots \end{cases}$

Hand-screws. . . . . $\begin{cases} \text{Large .} \ldots \\ \text{Small .} \ldots \ldots \end{cases}$

Hand-crow-levers . . . . $\begin{cases} 6 \text{ feet.} \ldots \\ 5 \text{ feet.} \ldots \end{cases}$

Crows of iron. . . . . $\begin{cases} 5\frac{1}{2} \text{ feet.} \ldots \\ 1\frac{1}{2} \text{ feet.} \ldots \end{cases}$

Ladle-hooks. . . . . Pairs . . . . . .

Linch-pins. . . . . Pairs . . . . . .

Forelock-keys. . . . . Pairs . . . . . .

Pen-mauls . . . .

Spikes. . . . . $\begin{cases} 10\frac{1}{2} \text{ inches .} \\ 9 \text{ inches .} \end{cases}$

Nails. . . . . $\begin{cases} 40 \text{ penny. .} \\ 30 \text{ penny. .} \\ 20 \text{ penny. .} \\ 10 \text{ penny. .} \\ 6 \text{ penny. .} \end{cases}$

Baskets. . . . .

Breechings. . . . . $\begin{cases} 7 \text{ inches. .} \\ 6\frac{1}{2} \ldots \ldots \\ 5\frac{1}{2} \ldots \ldots \\ 4\frac{1}{2} \ldots \ldots \\ 3\frac{1}{2} \ldots \ldots \end{cases}$

Tackles, complete with blocks and hooks. . . . . . . $\begin{cases} 3 \text{ inches. .} \\ 2\frac{1}{2} \ldots \ldots \\ 2 \ldots \ldots \\ 1\frac{1}{2} \ldots \ldots \end{cases}$

Port-ropes. . . . . $\begin{cases} 3 \text{ inches. .} \\ 2\frac{1}{2} \ldots \ldots \\ 2 \ldots \ldots \\ 1\frac{1}{2} \ldots \ldots \end{cases}$

Port-tackles. . . . . $\begin{cases} 2 \text{ inches...} \\ 1\frac{1}{3} \text{ . . . .} \end{cases}$

Runners for ditto . . . . $\begin{cases} 2\frac{1}{4} \text{ inches. . .} \\ 2 \text{ . . . . . .} \end{cases}$

Muzzle-lashings. . . . . $\begin{cases} 2 \text{ inches...} \\ 1\frac{1}{2} \text{ . . . .} \end{cases}$

Thimble-straps. . . . . $\begin{cases} 2 \text{ inches...} \\ 1\frac{1}{2} \text{ . . . .} \end{cases}$

Double-thimbles for the breechings to pass through $\begin{cases} 12 \text{ pounders} \\ 32 \text{ . . . .} \\ 24 \text{ . . . .} \\ 18 \text{ and } 12 \text{ . .} \\ 9 \text{ and } 6 \text{ . . . .} \\ 4 \text{ and } 3 \text{ . . . .} \end{cases}$

Tarred rope, spare. . . . . $\begin{cases} 7 \text{ inches...} \\ 6\frac{1}{2} \text{ . . . .} \\ 5\frac{1}{2} \text{ . . . .} \\ 4\frac{1}{2} \text{ coils fath.} \\ 3 \text{ . . . .} \\ 2\frac{1}{2} \text{ . . . .} \\ 2 \text{ . . . .} \end{cases}$

Blocks, spare, pairs. . . . . $\begin{cases} 10 \text{ inch } \begin{cases} \text{Double. . . . . . .} \\ \text{Single. . . . .} \end{cases} \\ 8 \text{ inch } \begin{cases} \text{Double . . . . . .} \\ \text{Single. . . . .} \end{cases} \\ 6\frac{1}{4} \text{ inch . . Single. . . . .} \\ 5 \text{ inch . . Single. . . . . . .} \end{cases}$

Tackle-hooks, spare . . . . $\left.\begin{cases} \text{Large. . . . . .} \\ \text{Small. . . . . .} \end{cases}\right\}$ Pairs . . . . .

Tallow. . . . . Cwts. qrs. lbs. . . . .

Marline. . . . . Skains . . . .

Junk. . . . . Tons, Cwts. qrs. . . . .

Hand-grenades, fixed. . . . .

Fixed fuzes, spare for ditto. . . . .

Boxes for hand-grenades. . . . .

Melting-ladles . . . .

Musquets. . . . . $\begin{cases} \text{Marine. . . . .} \\ \text{Ship's company} \end{cases} \begin{cases} \text{Bright. .} \\ \text{Black . .} \end{cases}$

Bayonets. . . . .

Scabbards for bayonets...

Slings for musquets...

Musquetoons..

Pistols with ribs, pairs ....

Cartouche-boxes ....

Belts for ditto..

Frogs for bayonets ....

Boxes for cartridges .... { Musquet....
 { Pistol......

Musquet-rods ....

Flints .... { Musquet...
 { Pistol......

Shot......Cwts. qrs. lbs... .... { Musquet...
 { Pistol......

Fine paper, reams, quires..

Funnels of plate ....

Sweet-oil, gallons, quarts ....

Pole-axes ....

Swords ....

Scabbards for ditto...

Belts..

Strong pikes...

Halberts...

Drums, complete...

ARMOURER'S TOOLS.

Vises....................................... { Standing...
 { Hand......

Wrenches..

Stakes..Poiz 4 lb....

Hammers .... { Hand......
 { Small......

Punches and cold-chizzels...

Iron braces ....

Square bits, of sorts..

Screw-plates, with 7 taps ....

Drills, of sorts...

Drill-bows...

Drill-boxes..

Drill-strings, knots ....

Breast-pieces. ....

Rubbers, poiz 3 lbs.. ....

Files .... {
     Hand ....
     Large bastard......
     8 penny bastard ....
     Large flat smooth...
     12d smooth........
     9 penny smooth...
     6 ——— ....
     3 ——— ....
     6 ——— rough. ....
     2 ——— ....
     Slitting. ....
}

File-handles...

Emery...................................... {
     Coarse, lbs. ....
     Fine, lbs............
}

Burnishers. ....

Lock-nails. ....

Side-nails...

Breech-nails ....

Spring-hooks...

Forge tongs, small, pairs ....

Wiping-rods. .... {
     Musquet...........
     Pistol.............
}

Chests for the tools, with padlocks and keys ....

       Signed, sealed, and delivered, for the use of his
       Majesty, in the presence of

*** *The half-yearly return to the ordnance-office, directed to the
right honorable the Master-general, &c. for which forms are
supplied by the office, correspond with the preceding list.*

SECTION IV.

GENERAL PRINCIPLES OF GUNNERY,

INCLUDING

DEFINITIONS, &c.

THE science of Gunnery, besides the management and care of artillery, includes the mathematical doctrine of PROJECTILES; and, in the application of that doctrine to practical use, it embraces a wide range of calculation, of which the general principles are considerably modified by the result of experimental philosophy. To express the laws which regulate this science in their full extent, and with any near approach to precision, would require the aid of complex algebraical analysis; but it is merely our avowed purpose, in this work, to give such a general view of approved deductions as to prepare the practical gunner for the comprehension of more elaborate statements, whenever his pursuits may demand it.

A PROJECTILE or PROJECT, according to the definition of Dr. Hutton, is any body which, being put into a violent motion, by an external force impressed upon it, is dismissed from the agent, and left to pursue its course. Such as a stone thrown out of the hand or a sling, an arrow from a bow, a ball from a gun, &c.

And, by PROJECTILES is meant the science of the motion, velocity, flight, range, &c. of a projectile, put into violent motion by some external cause, as the force of gunpowder, &c. This is the foundation of gunnery.

The AMPLITUDE or RANDOM is the range of the shot, or the

N

horizontal right line which measures the extent over which it has passed.

The IMPETUS is the force with which it is projected from the mouth of the piece, and the height to which it would ascend according to the laws of gravity.

The ELEVATION is the angle which the line of direction makes with the horizon, or plane in which the gun is placed. The greatest range is at an elevation of 45 degrees ; or, when the angle bisects the space between zenith, (or the point directly over head,) and the horizon or plane.

All bodies, being indifferent as to motion or rest, will necessarily continue in the state they are put into, except so far as they are hindered, and forced to change it, by some new cause. Hence, a projectile, put in motion, must continue eternally to move on in the same right line, and with the same uniform or constant velocity, were it to meet with no resistance from the medium, nor had any force of gravity to encounter.

In the first case, the theory of projectiles would be very simple indeed ; for there would be nothing more to do, than to compute the space passed over in a given time by a given constant velocity ; or either of these from the other two being given.

But, by the constant action of *gravity* *, the projectile is continually deflected more and more from its right-lined course, and that with an accelerated velocity ; which, being combined with its projectile impulse, causes the body to move in a curvilineal path, with a variable motion, which path is the curve of a *parabola* ; and the determination of the range, time of flight, angle of projection, and variable velocity, constitutes what is usually meant by the doctrine of projectiles, in the common acceptation of the word.

The preceding explanation is, however, to be understood of projectiles moving in a non-resisting medium ; for, when the resistance of the air is also considered, which is enormously great, and which very much impedes the first projectile velocity, the path deviates greatly from the parabola, and the determination of

---

* For an explanation of *Gravity*, and of the other terms which occur in this section, see the following section of the present work.

the circumstances of its motion becomes one of the most complex and difficult problems in nature.

Hence it will appear that the flight of shot is retarded by the resistance of the atmosphere, operating in conjunction with the laws of gravity and motion. By the former, all objects suspended in the air are drawn towards the centre of the earth, with a velocity whose ratio increases in proportion to the square of the time; falling through 16 feet in one second, 64 in 2, and so forth. Hence will appear the necessity of pointing guns with at least a small elevation of angle, as otherwise the action of gravity would draw the shot to the ground before they had finished their course, or that the projecting velocity was exhausted.

In the theory of gunnery it was long supposed, that, from the combined effect of the velocity of the ball and its motion towards the earth, it described a parabola in its course, as above described; the resistance of the air being thought too inconsiderable for notice: but experience has proved this hypothesis to be erroneous, and that the impediment which the shot encounters during its flight is the principal object of regard when artillery are to be fitted for actual service. . . . . . .

The parabolic hypothesis is, in fact, only of utility to show the difference between theory and practice, when inferences are required to be deduced from experiments made under varying circumstances.

According to a calculation of Mr. D. Bernoulli, a ball which ascends only 7819 feet in the air, would have ascended 58750 in vacuo; and Mr. Robins calculates that the range of a 24lb. ball at 45 degrees is not one fifth of what it would be, were the resistance of the air prevented.

The proportion of the velocity with which a bomb or shell falls on an object to that with which it issued from the mouth of the piece is increased by the quantum of what it acquires by its fall, according to the laws of gravity.

The velocity communicated to balls of different weight, by the same quantity of powder, is as the square root of their weights.— The resistance to balls of unequal diameter, but the same velocity, is as their surfaces, or the square of their diameters.

There is little difference in the velocity of shot fired from guns of the same length and unequal weight; the variations of experiments, even under the same circumstances, being more than equal to the apparent difference.

The velocity given by guns of 22 calibers in length was ascertained by experiments at Woolwich in 1788, 89, 90, to be equal to that given by long guns of 15½ calibers, after passing through the following spaces :

With half the shot's weight. .... 285 feet.
        one third................................. 200
        one fourth............................... 150
        one sixth................................ 115

Hence it appears that the velocity given by a charge of half the shot's weight is reduced to an equality with that given by one third, after passing through 200 feet.

The RESISTANCE increases in a greater proportion than the square of the velocity, according to the following table, extracted from the writings of Dr. Hutton, and the result of experiments made by that eminent mathematician, with a globe of 1.965 inch diameter.

Velocity in feet per second.	Resistance by experiment. Ounces.	Resistance by theory. Ounces.	Ratio of experiment to theory.
5	0.006	0.005	1.20
10	0.024½	0.020	1.23
15	0.055	0.044	1.25
20	0.100	0.079	1.27
25	0.157	0.123	1.28
30	0.23	0.177	1.30
40	0.42	0.314	1.33
50	0.67	0.491	1.36
100	2.72	1.964	1.38
200	11.	7.9	1.40
300	25.	18.7	1.41
400	45.	31.4	1.43
500	72.	49.	1.47
600	107.	71.	1.51
700	151.	96.	1.57
800	205.	126.	1.63
900	271.	159.	1.70
1000	350.	196.	1.78
1100	442.	238.	1.86
1200	546.	283.	1.90
1300	661.	332.	1.99
1400	785.	385.	2.04
1500	916.	442.	2·07
1600	1051.	503.	2.09
1700	1186.	568.	2.08
1800	1319.	636.	2.07
1900	1447.	709.	2.04
2000	1659.	786.	2.0

From this table it appears that, at 1300 feet, the resistance by experiment is double that by theory ; at 1600 or 1700 feet the excess is the greatest, and gradually decreases till 2000 feet, when the former once more doubles the latter.

The RANGES with a medium one pounder gun, at different angles of elevation, were as follow:

Powder.	Elev. of gun.	Veloc. of ball.	Range.	Time of flight.
2 oz.	15°	860 feet	4100	9 seconds
4	15	1230	5100	12
8	15	1640	6000	14½
12	15	1680	6700	15¼
2	45	860	5100	21

With a velocity of 1650 feet, and two thirds of the weight of the ball in powder, a 24 lb. ball may be thrown between 2 and 3 miles; generally about two miles and three quarters.

By the above statement may be observed the range at 15 degrees and 45 degrees, with the same powder and velocity, 860; and that 4 ounces of powder, notwithstanding the increased velocity, gave the same range as 2 ounces at 45°, the latter angle being so much more advantageous than 15 degrees.

The Ranges of different balls, according to experiments made by lieut.-general Du Metz, stand thus:

Ball 24 lb.	Powder 12 lb.	Miles 2.5
16	10½	2.3
12	8	2.12
8	5½	1.9
4	2¾	1.73

The greatest distance to which a BOMB or SHELL of 5 or 600 weight, will range, is between 2 and 3 miles.

VELOCITY.—The velocity of a light six-pounder, length 4 feet 8 inches, charge one third the weight of the shot, 1558 feet per second. Of a six-pounder, heavy, 6 feet 8 inches long, charge one third; 1671 feet per second. Of a light three-pounder, length 3 feet 4 inches, charge one third; 1371 feet per second. Of a heavy three pounder, length 5 feet 9½ inches, charge one third; 1514 feet per second.

If a globe, or spherical ball, move in a resisting medium, with a velocity much exceeding that with which the particles of the medium would rush into a void space, so that a *vacuum* be left behind the globe in its motion, the resistance of this medium will be much greater than what would take place in a slower motion. But the greater part of military projectiles, at the time of their discharge, acquire a whirling motion round their axis, which will cause them to strike the air very differently from what they would do with no other than a progressive motion.—Thus, the resistance will not be directly opposed to their flight, but will act in a line oblique to their course, and thereby cause them to deviate very considerably from the regular track that they would otherwise have followed.—If, from the construction of the barrel, as in rifle-pieces, the ball should acquire a regular motion around its axis, co-*incident* with the line of its flight, it will reach the mark with more certainty, owing to the equal distribution of the impulse of the medium upon its surface.

The RESISTANCE OF THE AIR, with the usual allotment of powder, is much less to large shot than to the smaller. For, though a 24-pound ball has four times the surface, and, consequently, four times the resistance, of a three-pounder, yet, as it has eight times the solidity, the proportion of the resistance to the *momentum* will be but half as much in the 24 lb. ball as in the other. Consequently, in musket-balls, the effect of the resisting medium will be yet of greater importance.

The depth to which a bullet penetrates in a solid substance is a better criterion of its velocity than the distance to which it ranges; for the *initial velocity*, with which it is projected from the piece, decreases the farther it proceeds in its flight. But the proper charge of any piece of artillery is not that allotment of powder which will communicate the greatest velocity to the bullet, nor is it to be determined by an invariable proportion to the weight of the ball; but it is that quantity which will produce the least velocity necessary for the purpose required, and ought to vary accordingly. Large charges are chiefly useful for ruining parapets or battering in breach, when the object is near to the piece.—But, if the parapet be so thin, as to be pierced through with a small charge, more powder or a greater velocity would diminish the effect, in lieu of increasing it. The bullet, for instance, which has just force sufficient to go through the side, generally breaks and splinters the last surface, causing by far more ravage than when it retains a considerable force after passing through; for the penetration will be, in general, no more than an orifice, which is, in a great degree, closed up by the springiness of the wood.

In making a breach, it is more effectual to fire from two batteries, or more, at the object, than from one battery only, with the same number of guns.

If bombs are thrown with an intention of setting fire to buildings, the more powder they are charged with, the greater will be
the effect; but, if the purpose be only to injure the enemy, the
smallest quantity of powder which will cause the shell to burst is
quite sufficient to disable human beings.

It will be obvious too, as we proceed, that large charges are
not attended with any other advantage, proportionate to the expense of powder.

GUNPOWDER, in its explosion, generates a fluid, which possesses an elasticity about 1600 times greater than that of common
air.—Its heat is supposed to be equal to that of red-hot iron; for,
although the force increases in a greater proportion than the
quantity, so as to produce, perhaps, in the explosion of a magazine, a degree of heat even sufficient for the vitrification of metals,
yet the quantity required to excite this heat is infinitely greater
than what can be employed for military purposes. If a bullet be
fired with two thirds of its own weight in powder, and afterwards
with one third, the difference of the ranges will be scarcely greater
than the irregularities which happen in repetitions of the same
trial with the same piece, charge, and elevation; for the resistance of the air accumulates in a degree far exceeding the excess
of velocity from the greater charge. The quantity of powder calculated to produce the greatest velocity in a gun is such as would
nearly fill up three eighths of the piece, and therefore by far too
great for practice, even had it not been ascertained that the
greatest velocity does not produce an adequate effect in service.

The weight and length of artillery, with the nature of the *bore*
and *windage*, are also to be considered in the art of gunnery; for
a longer piece communicates a greater velocity than a small one,
although the difference is not great, unless the length be extremely disproportioned. If a musket-barrel, of common length
and bore, be fired with a leaden bullet, and half its weight in
powder, and if the same barrel be afterwards shortened by one
half, and again fired with the same charge; the velocity in the
shortened barrel will be about one sixth part less than it was when
the barrel was entire; and if, instead of shortening the barrel, it
be increased to twice its customary length (nearly eight feet) the
velocity will not be increased more than an eighth part. Moreover, by diminishing a twenty-four pounder one foot in length,

with its customary charge of powder, no greater change is occasioned than about one fortieth part of its velocity; which is a variation too minute to be ascertained with certainty by any mode of trial hitherto discovered.

By the WINDAGE of one twentieth, nearly one third or one fourth part of the powder is lost in explosion. The whole of the powder is fired before the bullet is moved from its place, and the pressure on the bullet grows weaker as the bullet is farther impelled. If a charge of powder takes up one foot of the cylinder, whose whole length is nine feet, then, at the mouth of the piece, the powder exerts but one ninth of pressure that it does near the charge. The velocity with which the bullet moves from the mouth of the piece is the effect of the pressures united through each different space; but its acceleration decreases as it approaches the extremity of the barrel; for, besides the decrease of pressure already noticed, the efficacy even of this *quantum* of it is less while the bullet is in motion than when at rest. If the bullet be placed home upon the powder, so that with a smaller charge it is nearer the breech than with a larger, the collective pressure of the smaller charge will be somewhat more than in proportion to its quantity; but the disproportion must not be very great, for, we have before observed that the action of large quantities of powder is greater than in proportion to the quantity; as if the charge of a musket be compared with the explosion of a few grains, or the effects of a magazine blowing up, with the force of a cannon's charge.

The velocity of powder, without a ball before it, Mr. Robins states at about 7000 feet per second; but the celebrated Euler is inclined to think that it may be considerably more. Even the state of the atmosphere will affect the powder by rendering it moist in a greater or less degree; but, with the same proportion of moisture, small quantities of powder are diminished in force more than larger. Mr. Robins makes an ingenious conjecture, that, in the explosion of large quantities of powder, moisture may possibly add to its force, when converted into vapour, which produces such effects in the steam engine. To this remark, however, he does not attach any importance; but rather glances at it, as a hint, than delivers it as a principle.

It seems, too, that there is a degree of heat which, though not sufficient to fire the powder, will melt the brimstone and destroy the texture of the grains. Thus, if separate grains of powder be dropped upon red-hot iron, they will burn with a small blue flame for some time without exploding. Mr. Robins, by this expedient, has been able to cover two or three inches with a blue lambent flame, without explosion, or observing, upon subsequent examination, that the grains had lost their colour or their shape. Care must be taken to keep the grains sufficiently distant from each other, or the flame will, at last, grow strong enough to cause an explosion, by extending the heat of the flame rising from each grain to those which are contiguous.

· The recoil of a gun always increases with the charge. The utility of different quantities of powder in actual service may be collected from the following experiments.

Mr. Robins tried an eighteen-pounder with one quarter of a pound of powder, in lieu of nine pounds, which was then its customary charge. The range was, in several experiments, from 220 to 250 yards. With half a pound of powder, it ranged 500 yards, and grazing, bounded on 300 yards farther. With one pound of pounder, and an elevation of near fifteen degrees, (the former elevations were a trifle less,) the bullet ranged from 1400 to 1600 yards; after which, the elevation being diminished to 5 degrees, it ranged from 550 to 630 yards.

With two pounds of powder, at $3\frac{1}{4}$ degrees, the range was from 900 to 1100 yards. At 15 degrees it would have ranged to a mile and a half.

With three pounds, and 6 degrees of elevation, it ranged from 1500 to 1650 yards; with $3\frac{1}{2}$lb. of powder and the same elevation, it ranged twice for exactly an English mile, or 1760 yards. At 15 degrees, Mr. Robins concludes that it would have flown about 3000 yards, or more. The ranges in the two last trials would not, he thinks, be increased more than 200 yards, by an addition of 7 pounds of powder.

The VELOCITY is according to the *square root* of the weight of powder (the reader will remember that the ranges are not even in proportion to the increased velocity) to about the charge of eight ounces, according to the statement of Dr. Hutton; and so it would continue for all charges, were the guns of an indefinite length; but, as the length of the charge is increased in proportion to the length of the bore, the velocity falls short of that pro-portion.—The velocity of the ball increases with the charge to a certain point, peculiar to each gun, where it is the greatest ; and, by farther increasing the charge, the velocity diminishes, until the bore is filled with powder. The part of the bore filled with powder, to produce the greatest velocity, bears a lesser proportion to the whole in long guns than in short ; being nearly as the square root of the empty part.

TABLE OF CHARGES PRODUCING THE GREATEST VELOCITY.

	Length of the bore.	Ditto in calibers.	Part of the whole filled.	Length.	Powder.
Gun No. 1	28.2 inches	15	3 tenths	8.2 inches	12 oz.
No. 2	38.1	20	3 twelfths	9.5	14
No. 3	57.4	30	3-16ths	10.7	16
No. 4	79.9	40	3-20ths	12.1	18

The velocity increases in a ratio less than the square root of the length of the bore, and somewhat greater than the cube root : too inconsiderable for any practical advantage. Dr. Hutton, indeed, is of opinion, that a double length of gun does not give above one seventh part more range.

The TIME of the BALL'S FLIGHT is nearly as the range : the gun and elevation being the same : and the velocity is not sensibly affected by the use of wads, of different degrees of ramming, or by firing the powder in different places.

Mr. Robins has given his opinion that no field-piece should be loaded with more than one fifth of the weight of the bullet in powder, nor any battering piece with more than one third.—The promptitude and facility of the service will, in his judgement, more than compensate for the inferiority of *impetus* against any rampart.

The PENETRATION of balls, with different charges of powder, is more than in proportion to the increased velocity. It appears, from the authority of Mr. Robins, that an eighteen-pound shot, with a velocity of 400 feet per second, penetrated $3\frac{1}{4}$ inches into a butt of seasoned oak ; and, with three times the velocity, to 34 inches. A bullet of 5 inches diameter will penetrate nearly fifteen times as deep as one of three quarters of an inch. A bullet from a common musket, with one twenty-fourth part of its weight in powder, will go through a plank of fir above an inch thick. Mr. Robins also tried some four-pounders, weighing two, three, and four, hundred weight ; the last of which he thinks fully sufficient for service, and concludes that the weight of artillery might be reduced with advantage. His maxim that the penetration is in proportion to the square of the velocity is disputed by Dr. Hutton, from the result of experiments recorded in his own tracts.

In fact, the penetration must be considerably influenced by the resistance of the air, as a 24 lb. ball, on first issuing from the piece, is opposed by a re-action equal to 24 times its own weight ; and (we have again to repeat) as the resistance increases in a far greater ratio than the increasing velocities arising from augmented charges, the force which a bullet retains, on arriving at its object, will be affected thereby.

On loading an eighteen-pounder with six pounds of powder, Mr. Robins found that it penetrated into several beams of timber firmly compacted, from 37 to 46 inches deep, in several trials.— With 3 lb. 33 inches ; $2\frac{1}{2}$ lb. 28 inches ; 1 lb. $14\frac{1}{4}$ to $15\frac{1}{2}$ inches.

From the series of facts which we have detailed, the Gunner will be enabled to perceive that the theories on which his art has hitherto been grounded are of no farther use in practice than to augment his ingenuity in devising experiments, and to strengthen his faculties by the mixture of science which he may imbibe from the perusal of books on those branches of the mathematics more immediately connected with Gunnery, in forming accurate deductions from those experiments which have been already made, or which a course of actual service may afford him the opportunity of observing.

It remains for us only to observe here, that the preceding GENERAL EXPLANATION is to be considered only as *Introductory* to the particulars which are explained in the following Section. These particulars are arranged alphabetically for more convenient reference, and will be found to be much more distinctly treated on under the respective heads ; as CANNON ; CARRONADES ; GUNS ; ORDNANCE ; SHOT ; RANGE ; VELOCITY ; &c. &c.

SECTION V.

MISCELLANEOUS INFORMATION

AND

INSTRUCTIONS;

ALPHABETICALLY ARRANGED.

₊ ALTHOUGH, for convenient reference, the articles in this
section are arranged dictionary-wise, or alphabetically, we are
anxious that the young Gunner should understand that he will
find it advantageous to peruse every subject regularly throughout; then take a re-perusal of the preceding section, and ad-
vert once again to the leading articles in the following one.
By this mean, it is presumed, he will acquire sufficient information to enable him to practise every particular that can be
required in actual service at sea; and many particulars, also,
which may be occasionally required in conjunct expeditions on-
shore.

Aᴮꜱᴏʟᴜᴛᴇ GRAVITY. A term which signifies the whole force
by which a body, shell, or shot, is impelled towards the surface
and centre of the earth. See GRAVITY.

ACCELERATION. The increase of velocity in moving bodies.
Falling bodies, as shot or shells, obtain their accelerated motion
by the impulse of GRAVITY, which produces an augmentation of
motion in every successive instant: for, the velocity acquired by a
falling body, from this impulse, is proportional to the time in
which it is produced; so that, if a body falls through a certain
number of feet during a first instant of time; it will fall through
twice that number of feet during the second instant; thrice that
number during the third instant, &c.

We have already stated, in the preceding section, that, by the laws of Gravity, all objects suspended in the air are drawn towards the centre of the earth with a velocity whose ratio increases in proportion to the square of the time; falling through 16 feet in one second, 64 in two, and so forth. Hence will appear the necessity of pointing guns with at least a small elevation of angle, otherwise the action of gravity would draw the shot to the ground, &c. But see also, the article GRAVITY hereafter.

ACTION, PREPARATION FOR. In coming into action at night, or on a sudden, it will be best, if the enemy be to leeward, or an inferior sailing ship, to lie by till every thing is properly prepared, during which time the ship should be well barricadoed, every kind of lumber cleared off the deck, and the quarters well lighted up.—When this necessary preparation is finished, the private signal, whilst standing towards the stranger, should be made; and now proceed, within hail, fully prepared for either alternative. Let the men at their quarters be cautioned not to fire a gun until they are ordered. Should the strange ship prove that of an enemy, direct the first broadside with the utmost precision, with the guns rather depressed than otherwise. Have two or three guns with skilful men at them, to fire at the masts and rigging only, for this will probably be found very serviceable.

A platform must be made, either in the tiers or after hold, with the awnings spread over it, for wounded people.

The decks to be wet, and sand strewed over them.

The lanterns hung up in their places.

The top-sail yards slung and top-sail sheets stoppered.

Buckets filled with water in the chains, ready to extinguish any fire; the engine filled and placed on the poop of a line-of-battle-ship, and on the quarter-deck of a frigate.

Preventer-braces led along.

Salt-boxes filled and match-tubs in their places; the fire-screens hung round the hatchways.

The spare tiller ready to ship. Locks on the guns; vent-stoppers to every man.—Spare breechings, trucks, and tackles, distributed at the different hatchways, ready to supply the place of those which may be carried away.

A sufficient number of pistols, and pistol cartridge boxes filled and at hand. The half-pikes, tomahawks, &c. ready at hand.

The boarders to have their belts and cutlasses at their quarters.

The firemen a bucket and swab at each gun.

The powder horns to be all filled.

In pricking the cartridges; it has been observed, that, ramming the wire hard occasions a great part of the powder and the end of the cartridge to remain in the gun : of this circumstance every seaman should be cautioned, as likewise that very dangerous consequences have resulted from not ramming the cartridge home, and putting in too many shot. See ENGAGEMENT.

THE FOLLOWING REGULATIONS ARE TO BE OBSERVED IN THE MANAGEMENT OF THE GREAT GUNS IN TIME OF ACTION.

The people are to be equally divided, with a captain to each division, who, upon being ordered to quarters, the first division, with its captain, are to repair to their gun, clear and prepare it for action ; the second captain and his division to provide the necessary materials, viz. crows, handspecs, spunge, vent, powder-horns, match-tubs, shot, &c. ; and, when all is provided, he and his people are to repair to their quarters.

The first captain is to pick the cartridge, prime, and direct the gun ; the second captain is to fire and put in the vent; a man to be employed to sponge and load. The boarders to manage the crows and handspecs, and the rest of the people to attend the gun and follow their occasional employment when called.

A certain number of men are to be selected from each gun and appointed *Boarders, Sail-trimmers, Fire-men,* and *Powder-men* ; and the person who supplies the powder should be a steady attentive man.

If the starboard guns are engaged and the larboard guns ordered to be cleared, the second captain, with his division, are to clear them ; but if the larboard guns be engaged, and the starboard ordered to be cleared, then the first captain and his division go to the starboard, and the second, with his division, to the larboard, guns. The first division to be at the fore part of the gun, and the second at the after part.

In time of exercise the officers should be particularly careful that the people be successively changed in the different parts of the exercise ; that every man may know how to perform every manœuvre, as well as he who is particularly charged in time of action to perform it.

IN SHIPS OF THREE DECKS, where there are three magazines, the fore magazine is to supply the lower deck, the midship magazine is to supply the middle deck, and the powder to come up the main hatchway by the powder-whips; the after magazine to supply the upper deck, and the powder to come up the after hatchways by the whips. By each magazine supplying a different deck the mixture and confusion of cartridges will be avoided.

IN SHIPS OF TWO DECKS, the fore-magazine to supply the lower deck, forecastle, and quarter deck, guns; the powder for the forecastle and quarter deck to come up the fore hatchway by whips; the after magazine to supply the main deck, and to come up the after-hatchways.

IN A FRIGATE, with two magazines, the fore magazine to supply the main deck; the after magazine to supply the forecastle and quarter deck.

A man at the four after guns, on the lower deck, to be appointed to attend tiller-tackles, if necessary.

AIM. The act of bringing a gun or other missile weapon to a proper line of direction with the object intended to be struck. See POINTING.

'ALTITUDE. The perpendicular or angular height of any object. Hence the altitude of any shot or shell is the perpendicular height of the vertex or top of the curve in which it moves above the horizon.

AMBER-LIGHTS. A species of artificial fire-works, driven and contained in small cases for illuminations. The composition is, meal-powder nine ounces, and amber three ounces.

Lights of another kind may be made with saltpetre 3lb. sulphur 1lb. meal-powder 1lb. antimony 10½ ounces. All these to be mixed with the oil of spike. See COMPOSITION.

AMMUNITION. All sorts of powder and ball, shells, bullets, cartridges, grape-shot, tin and case shot, carcasses, grenades, &c. *Fixed Ammunition* comprises loaded shells, carcasses, and cartridges filled with powder; also shot fixed to powder, &c. *Unfixed Ammunition* means those unfilled or unfixed, &c. Ammunition for the navy is generally unfixed, when first sent on-board, except it may be the hand-grenades; and when on-board the gunner receives directions to keep a certain number of cartridges, filled with powder, for immediate service.

ANGLE. See Definitions in Geometry, pages 18 and 19.

An ANGLE OF ELEVATION, in Gunnery, is that angle which the axis of the hollow cylinder, or barrel of the gun, makes with the line of the horizon. See ELEVATION.

An ANGLE OF INCIDENCE is that angle which the line of direction of a projectile makes with the surface of the object on which it impinges or strikes. The force or effect of a shot striking a wall or other obstacle, in an oblique direction, is to its force, if it had struck the same obstacle in a perpendicular direction, as the angle of incidence is to radius. Hence the impulsive forces of the same shot, fired in different directions, are to each other as the respective angles of incidence of these directions.

An ANGLE OF REFLECTION is an angle intercepted between the line of direction of a body rebounding, after it has struck against another body, and a perpendicular proceeding from the point of contact; as the angle DBE.

Or, if the projectile strikes on a plane surface, it is, more properly the angle DBC, opposed to the angle of incidence as above defined.

APRON. The square plate of lead that covers the vent of a cannon, to keep the charge dry, and the vent clean and open.

· The dimensions are as follow : for 42, 32, and 24, pounders, 15 inches by 13; for 18, 12, and 9, pounders, 12 inches by 10; for 6 and 3 pounders, 10 inches by 8. Each is tied on by two pieces of marline, the length of which, for 42 to 12 pounders, inclusive, is 18 feet, or 9 feet each; for 9 pounders, and under, 12 feet, or 6 feet each.

ARMED. A cross-bar shot is said to be armed when some rope-yarn, or the like, is rolled about the end of the iron bar which runs through the shot.

ARMS. All kinds of weapons, used for offence or defence. Fire-arms are great guns, fire-locks, carbines, guns, pistols, &c. The ARMS, in Artillery, are the two ends of an axle-tree. See CARRIAGE.

Arms, small. See SMALL ARMS.

ARRANGEMENT OF GUNS. The gun number 1 is the foremost gun on the larboard side, and the numbers increase thence aft, and to the starboard side forward; the numbers regularly continuing through the whole number of one species.

ARTILLERY. The heavy equipage of war; comprehending all sorts of large fire-arms, with their appurtenances; as cannon, mortars, howitzers, carronades, balls, shells, &c. being what is otherwise called ORDNANCE.

The term Artillery or Royal Artillery is also applied to the persons employed in that service; and likewise to the art or science of Gunnery itself.

AVOIRDUPOIS WEIGHT, by which all gun-stores are weighed, is as follows:

16 drams are equal to one ounce, marked..............oz.
16 ounces..........one pound.....................lb.
28 pounds.........one quarter of a hundred weight...qr.
4 quarters........one hundred weight of 112lb......cwt.
20 hundred weight...one ton.......................T.
90 pounds of powder are equal to one whole barrel.
45 ditto.....................one half barrel.

AXIS OF A GUN. An imaginary line, passing through its centre, from one end to the other.

AXLE-TREE. A transverse beam supporting a carriage, and on the ends of which the wheels revolve.

BALLS. All sorts of bullets for fire-arms, from the pistol up to the largest cannon. Cannon balls are made of cast iron; but the musket and pistol balls of lead, as these are both heavier under the same bulk, and do not furrow the barrels of the pieces.

CANNON BALLS are distinguished by their respective calibers, and are in diameter as follows:

A 42-pound ball, or 42-pounder, 6.684 inches; a 32-pounder, 6.105 inches; a 24-pounder, 5.547 inches; an 18-pounder, 5.04 inches; a 12-pounder, 4.403 inches; a 9-pounder, 4.0 inches; a 6-pounder, 3.498 inches; a 3-pounder, 2.775 inches; a 2-pounder, 2.423 inches; a 1-pounder, 1.923 inch.

BALLS OF LEAD, or BULLETS, of the different species, are as follow:

F

Species of bullet.	Number to one pound.	Diameter in parts of an inch.	Number made from one ton of lead.
Wall-pieces	64	.89	14,760
Muskets	14½	.68	32,480
Carbines	20	.60	44,800
Pistols	34	.51	78,048

Leaden balls are packed in boxes containing each one cwt. See BULLETS.

FIRE and LIGHT BALLS.—Balls composed of, or filled with, an illuminating or inflammable composition.

The *Light Ball* is for giving a strong light on objects at a distance; and is made with mealed powder, 2 parts; sulphur, one; resin, one; turpentine, 2½; and saltpetre, 1½. Tow is then taken, dipped and mixed in this composition, till of a proper size, and then a coat of mealed powder is applied. A stone may be made use of covered with several coats of the composition, until it has acquired the size intended: the last coat should be of grained powder.—The best sort of light ball is, however, said to be made of thick brown paper, to the size of the mortar, filled with a composition consisting of an equal quantity of sulphur, resin, and mealed powder; which, being well mixed, and put in warm, will produce a clear fire, and burn for some time.

Of *Fire Balls*, which are used to set fire to buildings, &c. the composition is, mealed powder 10 parts; saltpetre, 2; sulphur, 4; and resin, 1: or it may rather be, mealed powder, 48; saltpetre, 32; sulphur, 16; resin, 4; steel or iron filings, 2; sawdust of fir, boiled in a ley of saltpetre, 2; charcoal of birch-wood, one.

With either of these compositions, a thick bag or sack is to be filled; ramming it, if possible, as hard as a stone; putting in the opening a fuse, and about the same an iron ring one fifth of the ball's diameter wide; and, on the opposite end, another ring, of one sixth of the ball's diameter: then, with a strong cord, of a quarter of an inch in diameter, lace round the hoops, or rings, from one end of the ball to the other, as often as is requisite: this is called the *Ribbed-Coat:* then lace it again the contrary way, which is called the *Check-Coat.*

Between each square cord, iron barrels are driven in, one third of which are filled with powder, and a bullet; at the end of each a small vent is made, so that the composition may inflame the powder, and drive the balls out on every side, which not only destroys whatever lies within the extent of its explosion, but prevents any one from extinguishing it. The balls, when finished, are dipped in a composition of melted pitch, resin, and turpentine oil, which fastens the whole together.

SMOKE-BALLS are a species of ball, contrived to give an uncommon smoke, and so annoy an enemy. They are thrown from mortars, and continue to smoke from 25 to 30 minutes. The preparation is similar to those above described, but with 5 parts to 1 of pitch, resin, and saw-dust; this is put into shells made for the purpose, having 4 holes to let out the smoke. These balls serve to conceal a design or project, answer as signals, &c.

STINK-BALLS, for the annoyance of an enemy, are similar to the former, but prepared by a composition of mealed powder, resin, saltpetre, pitch, sulphur, rasped horses and asses hoofs, burnt in the fire, assa-foetida, and other ingredients of a similar nature.

These balls may be formed of two half-globes made of coarse paper, glued together until half an inch thick; then filled and covered over with a net.

CHAIN-BALLS or SHOT are formed by two balls, linked together by a chain 8 or 10 inches long, or of greater length. They are particularly useful in destroying the rigging of ships.

STANG-BALLS, or BAR-SHOT, otherwise called DOUBLE-HEADED SHOT, are made either of two half balls connected by a bar of iron, from 8 to 14 inches long, or of two whole balls, connected in the same manner. They answer the same purpose as chain-balls.

BALLOONS. GRENADE BALLOONS are bags made of thick canvas, and filled with gunpowder and grenades. First, put two pounds of powder at the bottom, and a loaded grenade over it; then more powder and more grenades; after the bag is entirely filled, excepting to leave a sufficiency to tie, introduce a fuse into its mouth, which is to be tied in as closely as possible. The bag is then to be well pitched all over, with hot pitch; and may be thrown by hand or as required.

BALLOONS for MORTARS are made in the same manner; and STONE Balloons also, excepting that the latter are loaded with stones, made so as to burst in the air, so that the stones fall like hail upon the enemy.

Another sort of Balloon has been made of tin cases, filled with pieces of canvas, well pitched and dipped in sulphur and resin; the box covered with wood, and a fuse introduced as described before, so that the canvas may take fire so soon as the canister is fired. They may be of infinite use in setting fire to an enemy's ship, on its running on-shore, &c.; for, if one of the pieces of canvas should fall on the sails or rigging, it would inevitably set them on fire.

There is another invention, though of antient date, for setting buildings, &c. on fire, which is a bearded dart, armed with iron, below the beard of which is moused on with matches, a quantity of combustibles, which will continue burning with violence for some minutes, wherever it catches. This sort of fiery darts was used by the antients, before the use of fire-arms, and were usually projected from bows, but may easily be adapted to musketry, by setting fire to the matches, and then firing them out of the muskets as one would a ram-rod or any other piece of stick.

BARREL, Beer. An English vessel or cask, containing 36 gallons of beer measure, or 32 gallons of ale measure. The barrel of beer, vinegar, or of liquor intended for vinegar, ought to contain 34 gallons, according to the standard of the ale quart.

BARRELS made to contain Powder, will contain 100 pounds, and half-barrels 50 pounds, but of late only 90 pounds have been put up into the barrels, 45 into half-barrels, and 22½ in quarter-barrels; which, by leaving the powder-room to be shifted, preserves it better.

Dimensions of Barrels for Powder.

	Whole barrels. Ft. In. Pts.	Half-barrels. Ft. In. Pts.	Quarter-barrels. Ft. In. Pts.
Depth	1 9 61	1 2 51	1 2 25
Diameter at top	1 3 61	1 0 37	0 9 35
Ditto at bulge	1 5 36	1 3 0	0 10 71
Ditto at bottom	1 3 51	1 0 31	0 9 41

BUDGE BARRELS, copper hooped, are used in bomb-vessels, and hold from 40 to 60 pounds of powder; at one end is fixed a leather bag, with brass nails. They are also used in service on batteries, for loading guns and mortars, to keep the powder from firing by accident.

BATTERY. Any place raised to plant cannon upon, in order to play with the more advantage on the enemy. It generally consists of an *epaulement*, parapet, or breastwork, about 8 feet high, and 18 or 20 feet thick.

In all batteries, the open spaces through which the muzzles of the cannon are pointed, are called *Embrasures*, and the distances between the embrasures, *Merlons*. The guns are placed upon a platform of planks, &c. ascending a little from the parapet, to check the recoil, and that the gun may be the more easily brought back again to the parapet: they are placed from 12 to 16 feet distant from each other, that the parapet may be strong and the gunners have room to work.

A BARBET BATTERY is a battery having its breast-work only 3 feet high, so that the guns may fire over it without embrasures. The guns are then said to fire *en barbet*.

MORTAR BATTERIES differ from others, in that the slope of the parapet is inwards, and it is also without embrasures, the shells being fired quite over the parapet, commonly at the elevation of 45 degrees.

An OPEN BATTERY is nothing more than a number of cannon ranged in a row abreast of one another, commonly on some little elevation.

A COVERED or MASKED BATTERY is a bank or breast-work commonly made of brushwood, faggots, and earth, formed to cover the gunners, &c.

A SUNK or BURIED BATTERY is formed by having its platform sunk or let down into the ground, so that trenches must be cut in the earth opposite the muzzles of the guns, to serve as embrasures to fire through. This sort of battery is mostly used on the first making of approaches in besieging, &c.

CROSS BATTERIES are batteries playing athwart each other upon the same object, forming an angle there, and battering to more effect, because what one shakes the other beats down.

- An HORIZONTAL BATTERY is one which has a parapet and ditch; the platform being only the surface of the ground made level.

There are various batteries which differ either in formation or position from either of those above described, the names of which are of consequence only to the army on shore. We shall, there-therefore, only add that a

BLOCK-BATTERY is a wooden battery for two or more small pieces, mounted on wheels, and moveable from place to place; very ready to fire *en barbet*, in places where room is wanted.

To BEAR. A cannon, &c. is said to *bear* or *come to bear*, when pointed directly so as to hit an object.

BEDS, MORTAR. See MORTAR.

BLANKETS. Combustibles used in fire-ships, and made of coarse paper steeped in a solution of saltpetre; which, when dry, are again dipped in a composition of tallow, resin, and sulphur.— See FIRE-SHIP.

BLOWING of a GUN. An expression signifying that the vent or touch-hole is run or gullied and become wide, so that the powder will flame out.

BLUE LIGHTS. A species of useful artificial fire-works, well known.—The composition is as follows: Saltpetre, 1 lb. 4 oz.— sulphur, 5 ounces, antimony, 7 ounces; mealed powder, one ounce.

To make blue-lights; provide, in the first instance, a piece of trunnel, about 10 inches long, boring a hole at one end, about 3 inches deep, and three-quarters of an inch in diameter; then would it with a rope-yarn, while loading it with the composition; putting in a tea-spoon-full at a time; and, with an iron rammer to fit the hole, striking it hard with a wooden mallet, five or six times, till it is filled up. At the top put a small quantity of mealed powder, as priming, tying a piece of paper over it. Thus it will be fit for use, as signals, by night.

BOARDING. The art of approaching the ship of an enemy so near, that you can easily, and in spite of him, throw on-board the graplings, which are fixed on the lower yard-arms, at the forecastle, gangways, &c. for the purpose of being thrown into the enemy's ship, so soon as along-side, in order to confine the vessels together, and give the people an opportunity of getting on-board, to carry the adverse ship sword in hand.

Copious instructions for boarding ships, under various circumstances and in different situations, may be found in Steel's— " *System of Naval Tactics,*" published by the proprietors of the present work.

It has been recommended, by an experienced officer, that the second and junior lieutenants, in large ships, and the junior only, in small ones, should have the command of the boarders, who ought to constitute at other times a small-arm party, regularly trained to the uses of musketry, the pike, and cutlass. If cudgel-sticks could be provided, to teach the boarders the sword-exercise, it might prove of the greatest advantage against an enemy. The first lieutenant commonly commands all the boarders, unless they land, and then they are commanded by their respective officers. At these times an uniform made of canvas, in a jacket and trowsers, edged with blue cloth, and a cap of the same kind, with the ship's name painted on it, would add to regularity of appearance, and serve other useful purposes *.

BOARDERS, SAIL-TRIMMERS, and FIRE-MEN.—Number of, in EACH RATE.

FIRST RATE OF 100 GUNS.—*Boarders;* four men from each gun on the lower deck, three from each gun on the middle deck, and two from each upper deck gun; in all, 145. To be commanded by the first and seventh lieutenants, with two mates and four midshipmen.

Sail-trimmers; two men from each gun on the middle deck, and two from each gun on the upper deck; in all, 70 men, under the direction of the second lieutenant, one mate, and three midshipmen.

Fire-men; one man from every gun; in all, 50 men, under the direction of the third lieutenant, one mate, and two midshipmen.

SECOND RATE OF 90 GUNS.—The same as in a first rate.

AN 80-GUN SHIP.—*Boarders* 125, under the direction of the first and fifth lieutenants, one mate, and four midshipmen.

Sail-trimmers, 65, under the direction of the second lieutenant, one mate, and two midshipmen.

Fire-men, 40, under the direction of the third lieutenant, one mate, and two midshipmen.

A 74-GUN SHIP.—*Boarders,* 116, under the direction of the first and fifth lieutenants, one mate, and three midshipmen.

Sail-trimmers, 63, under the direction of the second lieutenant, one mate, and three midshipmen.

Fire-men, 40, under the direction of the third lieutenant, one mate, and two midshipmen.

* See " *Observations and Instructions for Officers of the Royal Navy,*" &c. &c. Published by Steel and Co.

A 64-GUN SHIP.—*Boarders*, 105, under the first lieutenant, one mate, and three midshipmen.

Sail-trimmers, 64, under the second lieutenant, one mate, and two midshipmen.

Fire-men, 40, under the third lieutenant, one mate, and two midshipmen.

A 50-GUN SHIP.—*Boarders*, 74, under the first lieutenant, one mate, and two midshipmen.

Sail-trimmers, 50, under the second lieutenant, one mate, and two midshipmen.

Fire-men, 30, under the third lieutenant and two midshipmen.

FORTY-FOUR, 38, AND 36, GUN SHIPS.—*Boarders*, 65, under the first lieutenant, one mate, and two midshipmen.

Sail-trimmers, 40, under the second lieutenant, one mate, and two midshipmen.

Fire-men, 30, under the third lieutenant and two midshipmen.

THIRTY-TWO AND 28 GUN SHIPS.—*Boarders*, 50, under the first lieutenant, one mate, and two midshipmen.

Sail-trimmers, 30, under one mate and one midshipman.

Firemen, 23, under the second lieutenant and two midshipmen.

A 24-GUN SHIP.—*Boarders*, 35, under the first lieutenant, one mate, and one midshipmen.

Sail-trimmers, 25, under one mate and one midshipman.

Fire-men, 20, under two midshipman.

BOMB. A globe or shell of cast iron, having a vent to receive a wooden fuse. The shell being filled with powder, the fuse is fastened with a cement. This tube is filled with combustible matter, which burns when the bomb is fired off, and at last communicating with the gunpowder, the bomb explodes with great violence. See SHELL, FUSE, and MORTAR.

BOMBARDMENT. The act of assaulting a place by throwing shells into it, in order to set fire to and ruin the buildings, &c. See MORTAR.

BOMBELLES. *(French.)* Diminutive bombs or shells, which are used against a besieged place, for the purpose of creating confusion, &c.

BOMB-VESSEL. A vessel of war, of peculiar strength, and particularly designed for throwing shells from mortars. It was invented by the French, and said to have been first used in the bombardment of Algiers. Prior to that time the throwing of shells from sea was supposed impossible.

A complete description of the methods of fitting this vessel, which is a ketch, equipped with two masts, may be found in Steel's " *Elements and Practice of Naval Architecture.*" For a description of the Mortar, with its bed, see MORTAR.

The general dimensions, &c. of a modern bomb-vessel, are as follow :

Length on the range of the deck, 91 ft. 6 in. Length of keel, for casting the tonnage, 74 ft. 1¼ in. Breadth extreme, 27 ft. 6 in. Depth in hold, 12 ft. 1 in. Burthen in tons, 298. Load draught of water 12 ft. 3 in. Height of the lower ports, above the water in midships, 4 ft. 8 inches.

The bomb ketches upon the old establishment carry one thirteen-inch and one ten-inch mortar ; with eight six-pounders, besides swivels, for their own immediate defence. The modern bomb-vessels carry two ten-inch mortars, four 68-pounder, and six 18-pounder, carronades ; and the mortars may be fired at as low an angle as 20 degrees. These mortars are not, however, intended to be used at sea, unless on urgent occasions ; they are more particularly for the purpose of covering the landing of troops, and protecting harbours, &c.

The following are the Instructions given for the management and security of Bomb-vessels, during action.

1. A Dutch pump, filled with water, must be placed in each round top, one upon the forecastle, one on the main deck, and one on the quarter-deck ; and furnished with leather buckets, for a fresh supply of water.

2. The booms must be wetted by the pumps before the tarpaulins and mortar hatches are taken off ; and a wooden screen, 5 feet square, is to be hung under the booms, over each mortar, to receive the fire from the vents.

3. The embrasures being fixed and properly secured, the port must be let down low enough to be covered by the sole of the embrasure. Previous to its being let down, a spar must be lashed across it, to which the tackle for raising it again must be fixed : this spar serves to project the tackles clear of the explosion.

4. The mortars must not be fired through the embrasures at a

Q

lower angle than 20 degrees, nor with a greater charge than 5 lbs. of powder.

5. Previous to firing, the doors of the bulk-head, under the quarter-deck, must be shut, to prevent the cabin being injured by the explosion.

6. The bed must be wedged in the circular curb, so soon as the mortar is pointed, to prevent re-action; the first wedge being driven tight before the rear ones are fixed, in order to give the full bearing on the table, as well as the rear of the bed.—The holes for dog-bolts must be corked up, to prevent the sparks falling into them.

7. When any shells are to be used on-board the bomb, they must be fixed on-board the tender *, and brought thence in boxes in her long-boat; and kept along-side the bomb-ship till wanted, carefully covered up.

8. In the old-constructed bomb-vessels it is necessary to hoist out the booms; and raft them along-side previous to firing; but, in the new ones, with embrasures, only the boats need be hoisted out; after which the mortars may be prepared for action in 10 minutes.

Proportion of Ordnance and Ammunition for a Bomb-Vessel, carrying two 10-inch mortars, to fire at low angles, and at 45 degrees, four 68-pounders, and six 8-pounders, carronades.

Species.	Quantity.
Mortars, sea-service, with beds, &c. 10-inch	2
Coins for do.—2 for 45°—2 for 20° elevation.	4
Cap-squares, with keys, &c. spare....................	2
Handspikes or handspees, large......................	4
Sponges, with rammer heads	4
Handscrews ....small.....................	2
Hand-crow levers, 6 feet............................	4
Handspikes or handspecs, common.	6
Linstocks, with cocks..............................	4
Powder-horns............new pattern...............	4
Match...................................cwt.......	1

* The use of the bomb-tender is now discontinued; although generally used when these instructions were originally given.

Proportion of Ordnance, &c. for a Bomb-vessel.—Continued.	Quantity.
Marline..skeins.....	12
Budge-barrels ....copper hooped.............	2
Lanterns, Muscovy.......................................	4
Lanterns, dark..	4
Carronades, 68-pounders..............................	4
————, 18-pounders..............................	6
having sliding carriages, elevating screws, sponges, rammers, &c. complete.	
Gun-tackles, complete for traversing mortars, 12-pounders	4
Wads 68-pounders	540
——— 18-pounders	660
Muskets.............. { Bright...............	32
{ Black...............	8
Pistols....................pairs	15
Swords...	40
Pole-axes...	6
Pikes..	40
Musketoons...	2
Flints............. { Musket...............	900
{ Pistol...............	150
Ball-cartridges .... { Musket...............	2000
{ Pistol...............	2000
Shot.................. { Musket, cwt. qrs. lbs....	1.0.0
{ Pistol...............	0.1.1
Round carcasses, fixed....................10-inch. ..	200
Empty shells...........................10-inch. ..	400
Iron shot ....1 lb.	5000
Fixed shells ....10-inch. ..	48
Case-shot ....68-pounders, carronades ...	40
Empty shells .... 8-inch. for carronades.....	152
Shot, round.............68-pounders..............	100
Carcasses, ditto..........68-pounders..............	200
Shot, round ....18-pounders..............	300
Case-shot.............18-pounders.............	60
Carcasses, ditto, fixed......18-pounders.............	300
Hand-shells, fixed, sea service	150
Fuses for ditto, spare.............................	15

Proportion of Ordnance, &c. for a Bomb-vessel.—Continued.　　Quantity.

Paper covers for cartridges, 10-inch....................	715
————————————, 68-pounders..............	594
————————————, 18-pounders.............	726
Flannel cartridges, empty, for 10-inch { to hold 5lbs..	106
mortars .... ⎩ ditto　10lbs..	609
Flannel cartridges, empty, for 68-prs. ⎰ to hold 5lbs.. ⎱	
carronades. .... ⎱ ditto .. 4lbs.. ⎰	594
Flannel cartridges, empty, for 18-prs., .. to hold 1¼lbs..	726
Paper cartridges for bursting, 10-inch, empty	352
————————————, 8-inch, empty	100
Ditto, filled with 2lb. 10oz. for 10-inch..............	48
———————— 1lb. 14oz. for 8-inch..............	52
Fuses, drove. .... { 10-inch................	440
⎩ 8-inch................	167
Valenciennes ⎰ 200 for 10-inch shells, at 14oz. each...lbs.	175
composition. ⎱ 768 for 10-inch shells, at 2oz. each...lbs.	42
Tube-boxes, tin....................................	12
Fuse composition, for priming carcasses..............	10
Powder-bags	6
Port-fires	200
Quick-match, cotton......................lbs	20
Spirits of wine...........................gallons....	4
Kitt.....................................lbs	30
Bottoms of wood.........................10-inch ...	50
Signal-rockets, 1lb.......................dozens	2
Blue-lights..............................ditto......	3
Gunpowder for the mortars and carronades ..half-barrels	222
Powder for priming ....ditto......	1
Powder for bursting.....................ditto......	28

with all the articles which usually attend mortars on
every service; and the articles necessary for the service of carronades at sea.

Laboratory-chests.......................4 feet.....	2
———————— ....3 feet.....	2
Hand-pumps for wetting the rigging, &c...............	6
Leather buckets	24

BOOM. A long beam or beams of timber, connected by chains,

or a strong chain or cable, floated with wood, used to prevent an enemy entering a harbour, river, &c.

BORE or CALIBER OF A GUN. The cylinder or hollow part, which contains the powder, shot, &c.

BOW-CHASERS. The cannon situated in the fore part of a ship to fire upon any object a-head of her.

BREECH OF A GUN. The hinder part, from the cascabel or pomilion to the lower part of the bore. See CANNON.

BREECHINGS. The ropes used to secure the cannon on-board, and prevent them from recoiling too much in time of action. See GUN-TACKLES.

BROADSIDE. The whole discharge of the artillery on one side of a ship of war, above and below ; as,

'We poured a broadside into the enemy's ship,' that is, discharged all the cannon on one side upon her. 'She brought her broadside to bear upon the castle;' that is, disposed the ship so as to point all her cannon to it, within point-blank range. 'A squall laid the ship on her broadside;' that is, pressed her down in the water, so as nearly to overturn her.

BUDGE-BARRELS.—See BARRELS.

BULLETS. Balls of lead, with which small arms are loaded, &c. Bullets, balls, or shot, have different denominations according to the use that is made of them ; viz.

HOLLOW BULLETS, or SHELLS, which are of a cylindrical shape, and have an opening and a fuse at the end, by which fire is communicated to combustibles within, when the shell bursts with a destructive explosion.

CHAIN-BULLETS. Two balls connected by a chain, at any given distance.

BRANCH-BULLETS. Two balls connected with an iron bar.

TWO-HEADED BULLETS, or ANGLES. Two halves of a bullet connected by a chain or bar.

The diameter of a common leaden bullet is found by dividing 1.6706 by the cube root of the number contained in one pound.

The diameter of musket bullets differs but one fiftieth part from that of the musket bore; for if the shot but just rolls into the barrel it will be sufficient.

BURR. A round iron ring, which serves to rivet the end of a bolt, so as to form a round head.

BURREL-SHOT. Small bullets, nails, and stones, discharged from a piece of ordnance.

BUTT. A solid parapet of earth, to fire against in the proving of guns, or in practice.

BUTTON. That part of the cascabel or pomilion of a cannon, &c. which is the hinder-part, and made in form of a ball. See CANNON.

CALIBER or **CALIPER.** The thickness or diameter of any round body, as the bore or width of a piece of ordnance, or that of its ball.

CALIBER or **CALIPER COMPASSES.** An instrument used for measuring the diameter of shot, shells, guns, &c. They are formed as other compasses, excepting that the legs are formed of wood, and arched so that the points may touch the extremities of the arch required. These legs are so broad as to contain a variety of scales, tables, proportions, &c. necessary to be known to gunners, and of which a description is generally given with the instrument. To show the diameter of a circle, a quadrant is fastened to one leg, which passes through the other, and is marked with inches and parts which exhibit the diameter required. The length of each rule or leg is generally between 6 and 12 inches.

Plate II.   Page

The Twenty-four Pounder Sea Gun-Carriage.

FIG. I.   FIG. 2.

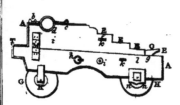

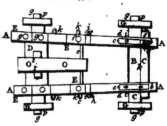

The Carronade Carriage.

FIG. 3.   FIG. 5.

The Carriage between Decks

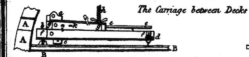

FIG. 4.   FIG. 6.

The Common Carriage

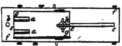

FIG. 7.

The GUNNER'S   QUADRANT.

LONDON
Publish'd Apn 30th 1819 by Steel & Co. Chart-sellers to the Hon.e Board of Admiralty at their Navigation Warehouse, &c.

CANNON. An engine of war, too well known to require description, and the names of the exterior parts of which, for sea-service are exhibited in the margin. In addition to these names are to be added several others, viz.

The Mouth or *entrance of the bore,* which is that part wherein both powder and ball are put, or the hollow part that receives the charge.

The Vent or *touch-hole* is the small hole pierced at the end, or near it, of the bore or chamber, to prime the piece with powder and admit fire to the charge.

The Chamber is the place wherein the powder is lodged, which forms the charge.

Muzzle ring.

Neck ring.

Trunnion ring.
Trunnion.

Reinforce ring.

Fuse ring.

Base ring.

Cascable or Pomilion.

The *Breech* is the solid metal behind, between the vent and the extremity of the base-ring, and which terminates the hinder part of the gun, exclusive of the cascable. *See the respective terms in the alphabetical arrangement.*

The names of the different parts and particulars of the carriage, represented in plate II. figures 1 and 2, are

A. The Cheeks.—B. Transom.—C. Fore Axle-tree.—D. Hind Axle-tree.—E. Steps.—F. Quarter-round.—G. Fore-trucks.—H. Hind-trucks.—I. Horns.—K. Fore axle-tree clout.—L. Hind axle-tree clout.—M. Side-clouts.—N. Trunnion-holes.—O. Stool-bed.— a. Cap-square.—b. Eye-bolts.—c. Joint-bolt.—d. Transom-bolt.— e. Bed-bolt.—f. Bracket-bolt.—g. Hind axle-tree bolts.—h. Breeching-bolt rings.—i. Burrs.—k. Loops.—l. Dowel-pins.—m. Square rivetting-plates.—n. Rings with keys.—p. Linch-pins.—q. Axle-tree hoops.—r. Axle-tree stay.—s. Keys, chains, and staples.—t. Bed-stool bolts.

For the number of Cannon of the various sizes on each deck of every rate, see the article Gun hereafter. The dimensions and weight of Carriages for Ships' Guns are as follow.

NAMES OF THE SEVERAL PARTS OF GUN-CARRIAGES.		32-Pounders.		24-Pounders.		18-Pounders.		12-Pounders.		9-Pounders.		6-Pounders.	
		Ft.	In.	Ft.	In.	Ft.	In.	Ft.	In.	Ft.	In.	Ft.	In.
Width	Before......	1.	6	1.	5	1.	3	1.	2	1.	1	1.	0
	Behind.....	2.	2	1.	11	1.	9	1.	7½	1.	7	1.	5
Fore axle-tree length		4.	9	4.	7	4.	3	3.	9½	3.	6½	3.	4
Body of the fore axle-tree.....	Length	3.	0	2.	11	2.	9	2.	6	2.	3½	2.	0½
	Height......	0.	10¼	0.	10	0.	10	0.	10	0.	9¾	0.	9
	Breadth.....	0.	6¾	0.	6¼	0.	6	0.	5½	0.	5¼	0.	5
Arms.....	Length	0.	10½	0.	9¾	0.	9½	0.	8	0.	7½	0.	7
	Diameter....	0.	6⅛	0.	6¼	0.	5¾	0.	5¼	0.	5	0.	4½
Hind axle-tree length.....		4.	9	4.	7	4.	3	3.	9½	3.	6½	3.	4
Body of the hind axle-tree.....	Length	3.	0	2.	11	2.	9	2.	6	2.	3½	2.	8¼
	Height	0.	6¾	0.	6¾	0.	6	0.	5½	0.	5¼	0.	5
	Breadth.....	1.	0	1.	0	1.	0	1.	0	1.	0	1.	0
Fore-trucks	Diameter...	1.	7	1.	6	1.	6	1.	4	1.	4	1.	2
	Thickness...	0.	6	0.	5½	0.	5	0.	4½	0.	4	0.	3½
Hind ditto	Diameter...	1.	4	1.	4	1.	3	1.	2	1.	2	1.	0
	Thickness...	0.	6	0.	5½	0.	5	0.	4½	0.	4	0.	3½
Side-pieces	Heighth, fore	2.	2	2.	0	1.	10	1.	8	1.	6	1.	4
	Length	6.	4	6.	0	5.	9	5.	6	5.	3	5.	0
	Breadth.....	0.	6	0.	5½	0.	5	0.	4½	0.	4	0.	3½
Trunnions from the head..		0.	8	0.	8	0.	8	0.	6¾	0.	6¾	0.	6¾
Whole height to the beds of the trunnions.........		2.	9	2.	7	2.	6	2.	3	2.	1	2.	0
Weight of the carriages, beds, and coins		cwt.	qs.	cwt.	qs.	cwt.	qs.	cwt.	qs.	cwt.	qs.	cwt.	qs.
		9.	0	8.	0	7.	0	6.	0	3.	3	2.	3

The cheeks, transoms, and trucks, of the gun-carriages are made of elm; the axle-trees of oak.

The LENGTH and WEIGHT of CANNON, or *Long Iron Guns*, in the *Royal Navy*.

Prs.	Ft.	In.	Cwt.	qrs.	lb.
32....	9	6....	55	2	0
24..⎰	9	6....	50	2	0
⎱	9	0....	47	3	0
18..⎰	9	0....	42	2	0
⎱	8	0....	37	3	0
12..⎧	9	0....	34	3	0
⎨	8	6....	33	1	0
⎨	7	6....	29	1	0
⎩	7	0....	21	0	0
9..⎧	9	0....	31	0	0
⎨	8	6....	29	2	0
⎨	7	6....	26	2	0
⎩	7	0....	25	1	0
6..⎧	8	6....	22	1	0
⎪	8	0....	21	2	0
⎨	7	6....	20	1	0
⎨	7	0....	19	1	0
⎪	6	6....	18	2	0
⎩	6	0....	17	2	0
4....	5	6....	11	3	0
3....	4	6....	7	1	0

THE DIAMETER of CANNON, Diameter of Shot, and Proportion of Powder for Service to be used with the same, in the Royal Navy.

Species	32	24	18	12	9	6	4	3	2	1	½
Diam. Guns. (In. th.)	6 4/10	5 8/10	5 3/10	4 7/10	4 2/10	3 7/10	3 2/10	2 9/10	2 5/10	2 0/10	1 6/10
Diam. Shot. (In. th.)	6 2/10	5 6/10	5 1/10	4 5/10	4 0/10	3 5/10	3 1/10	2 8/10	2 4/10	1 9/10	1 5/10
Pro. Powder. (lbs. oz.)	10 10	08 08	06 06	04 04	03 03	02 5½	01 5½	01 01	0 10½	0 5	0 2½

For the quantity of powder to be used for salutes and scaling, and with two shots, &c. see POWDER.

For the Range of Shot, from the different species of cannon, see RANGE.

The IMPLEMENTS for LOADING and FIRING CANNON are Rammers, Sponges, Ladles, Worms, Hand-spikes, Wedges, and Screws.

Coins, Quoins, or Wedges, are to lie under the breech of the gun, in order to elevate or depress it.

Hand-spikes are to move and lay the gun.

Ladles are used to load a gun with loose powder.

Rammers are cylinders of wood, whose diameters are equal to those of the shot: they are used to ram home the wads put upon the powder and shot.

The Sponge is fixed at one end of the rammer. It is covered with lamb-skin, and used to clean the gun when fired.

The TOOLS required for PROVING CANNON are, a searcher with a reliever, and a searcher with one point.

The *Searcher* is an iron, hollow at one end to receive a wooden handle, and the other end has on it from four to eight flat springs of about 8 or 10 inches long, pointed and turned outwards at the ends.

The Reliever is a flat iron ring, with a wooden handle, at right angles to it. When a gun is to be searched, after it has been fired, the searcher is introduced, and turned every way, from end to end; and, if there be any hole, the point of one or other of the springs, gets into it, and remains till the reliever, passing round the handle of the searcher, and pressing the springs together, relieves it.

If any hole or roughness be found in the gun, its distance from the mouth is marked on the outside with chalk.

The other searcher has a wooden handle, as the former, with a point at the fore end, of about an inch long, at right angles to the length; about this point is affixed some wax, mixed with tallow, which, when introduced into the hole or cavity, is pressed in; the impression upon the wax then shows its depth, and the length is known by the motion of the searcher backwards and forwards: if the fissure be one ninth of an inch deep, the gun is rejected.

To CANNONADE. To exercise or apply cannon, in the purposes of war, against an enemy.

CAPS. Leather caps, used for the purpose that tompions were, to prevent dirt or rain from falling into the bore of guns, &c. Canvas caps, for a similar purpose, are used for mortars.

CAP-SQUARES. The strong iron plates, placed over the trunnions of a gun, to keep it in its carriage.

CARBINE. A kind of short musket, which carries a ball of 20 in the pound: its barrel is 3 feet long, and the whole length, including the stock, 4 feet. It is used, chiefly, by the cavalry.

CARCASS. A hollow case, formed of ribs of iron, and covered over with pitched cloth, &c.; or made wholly of iron, excepting several holes for the fire to blaze through : being filled with various combustibles, to set fire to and destroy buildings, &c.

The Carcasses for sea-service differ from a shell only in the composition, and the four holes from which the fire issues when let off. The composition is, pitch, 2 parts ; saltpetre, 4 ; sulphur, 1 ; and corned powder, 3. The pitch is melted in an earthen pot ; and, when the pot is taken off, the ingredients, first well mixed, are put in ; then the carcass is filled with as much as can be pressed in. They are primed with fuse composition ; pitched over until used.

Another composition for Carcasses is, saltpetre, 50 parts ; sulphur, 25 ; antimony, 5 ; resin, 8 ; pitch, 5. See Composi-TION.

The VALENCIENNES COMPOSITION, so called from its having been used by the Austrians at the siege of that place, has the effect of making shells answer the purpose of carcasses after they burst. This is formed of saltpetre, 50 parts ; sulphur, 28 ; antimony, 18 ; resin, or Swedish pitch, 6.

This composition is cast in copper cylindric moulds, 6 inches long, and of different diameters according to the shell in which it is to be used. It is put in along with the bursting powder, in pieces as large as the shell will admit, without preventing the fuse's being driven down.

DIMENSIONS, WEIGHT, &c. of CARCASSES.

Species..		Weight empty.			Weight of composition.			Weight complete.			Time each will burn.
For	In.	lbs.	oz.	drs.	lbs.	oz.	drs.	lbs.	oz.	drs.	Minutes.
Mortars	13	194	10	11	18	14	0	213	8	16	11
and	10	89	13	11	7	8	11	97	6	11	8½
Howitzers	8	44	9	5	4	4	11	48	14	0	5½
	Prs.										
	42	27	3	0	2	7	11	29	10	11	5
	32	20	13	5	1	14	5	22	11	11	4¼
Guns ...	24	14	12	0	1	9	11	16	5	11	4
	18	11	13	11	1	1	5	12	15	0	4
	68	—	—	—	—	—	—	—	—	—	—
For	42	26	0	0	2	7	0	28	7	0	4¼
Carronades	32	21	10	0	1	13	0	23	7	0	4
	24	14	5	0	2	5	0	16	10	0	3½
	18	10	4	0	1	2	0	11	6	0	3

Oblong Carcasses, formerly used, are now obsolete in the British service.

CARRIAGE of a Gun. The machinery upon which it is mounted; serving to point or direct it for firing, and to convey it from place to place. See CANNON and CARRONADE.

The Gun-carriage invented by Mr. Gover, of Rotherhithe, is a machine whose peculiar excellencies will be found described in the following explanation.

General advantages of this over the common Gun-carriage.

1st. It may be worked with one third the number of men that are required to work the common gun-carriage, and with much more ease and safety to those who work it.

2dly. Its motion in traversing is so easy, that it may be always thrown fore and aft, and loaded within board, (if approved of,) clear of the port-hole; which will preserve the men from the enemy's small arms; it is, also, when loaded, readily run out again and pointed to the object with ease and certainty.

3dly. As the gun, with its carriage, moves on an inclined plane, which may be raised or lowered, as the situation of the ship, or object to be fired at requires, by means of a jack, which enables the captain of the gun to run the gun out himself, by giving the plane a sufficient inclination; the same mean which produces this effect also retards the counteraction of the gun, which moreover eases the breechings as well as the ship's sides greatly, when the gun recoils.

Advantages over the common carriage when the lee-guns are engaged.

When the lee-gun is discharged upon the common carriage, and recoils to the extent of the breeching, if the men are not very attentive to the relieving tackles, which at all times they cannot be, the ship at the same time having a heel, the gun immediately returns to the port, so that the men upon the old plan are obliged to bowse the gun in again before it can be loaded, which makes it as difficult in fighting the lee-guns as the weather-guns; but the difficulties are obviated in the new carriage by its having a pole, which, when the lee-guns are discharged, drops and prevents the gun's returning to the port until loaded again; this, also, obviates the necessity of relieving tackles.

Advantage arising from securing the guns fore and aft, when at sea or out of action.

When guns are secured fore and aft they stow snugly and closely to the ship's side, resting upon two or three beams, and afford more room within board to work and manage the ship, especially on the upper deck; it gives the advantage of keeping all the ports close shut, and the guns dry on the lower deck; it also conceals them from the enemy until it be necessary to use them; they can be got ready for action much sooner than in the old way, when secured athwart-ship, by the breechings and tackles being strapped together, and muzzle-lashed over the port. When a gun is. secured athwartship, the muzzle of the gun rests entirely against the short timbers over the port, being the weakest part of the ship's side; and it is the opinion of many experienced mariners, that several ships have foundered, that may have proved very leaky and become damaged from the working of the guns against the sides, when bowsed. in that manner, and often break loose by the strain and working of the ship beyond what the breeching and tackles will allow.

Advantages of the new carriage over the common one in pointing the gun.

The captain of the gun will be capable of running the gun to the port without any. assistance, whether to windward or to leeward, by means of the jack, as above-mentioned; he will also be able to traverse it fore and aft, elevate and depress the gun himself, with much more ease and certainty of doing execution than in the common carriage, from the following reasons; the captain of the gun standing at the train of the carriage with a laniard of the lock in one hand, and the handle of the screw in the other, he traverses, elevates, or depresses, the gun, without depending upon the other men, and the moment it is pointed at the object, he discharges it, and consequently is the more sure of doing execution; so that, at a proper distance for a ship to engage, he must be a very indifferent gunner to miss striking the object; whereas, upon the common plan, in action, great part of the powder and shot is expended without doing any execution whatever.

The inventor of this carriage observes, that, during the last war, in his Majesty's service, he has seen men in action take nearly five minutes to point the gun, and perhaps not near the object at last; for it must be observed, that, before the train of a common carriage can be moved, you must entirely relieve the trucks from the deck: and the men who perform this service, not standing at the breech of the gun, but at the side of the carriage, cannot see the object they are directing at: and this accounts for the great uncertainty of the gun's doing execution.

If the ship has a pitching motion, it will be necessary to apply tackles to steady the gun; one man to each tackle-fall will be sufficient for this purpose. The captain of the gun will stand at the train of the gun, with the handle of the screw in his hand, directing these men to train the gun until it comes to the object he is aiming at; he then immediately discharges the gun, without being under the necessity of giving these men any signal to drop the tackle-falls. The tackles, however, being hooked to the traversing carriage, are not affected by the recoil of the gun, therefore the men would not be injured if they had the tackle-falls in their hands when the gun is discharged; neither are they in the least danger of being injured by the projection of the trucks or ropes that are applied to the common gun-carriage, as this new carriage acts without those projections.

Directions how to manage the Carriage, in order to point the gun with greater certainty,

In order to attain the true level of the gun, with the surface of the water, when the ship or the object of its attack should happen to be surrounded with smoke, and the gunner consequently deprived of any certain mode of pointing the gun by his eye, it will be proper to observe the following rule: let the gunner, when the ship is in smooth water, and the carriage is consequently upon a level with its surface, place the inclined plane in a horizontal position, and the gun point-blank; then let him wind up the jack till the plane has inclined enough to give the gun motion towards the port, and observing the number of turns the jack requires for that purpose, which will not exceed three; he will turn the same back again, which brings the gun point-blank, and consequently certain of doing execution.

The common carriages, possessing no such mechanical principles to ascertain the level of the gun, with the surface of the water, when the object is obscured from the sight, can be under no certainty (but quite the reverse) of the effect of the shot ; whereas, within a moderate distance for ships to engage, this principle insures nearly the certain effect of striking the object, and therefore the proportion of this effect is reasonable, and moderately calculated at three to one in favor of the new carriage. Thus, also, a considerable saving, in the expense of powder and shot is produced.

Disadvantages that attend pointing a gun, mounted on the common gun-carriage.

In training the common gun-carriage, iron crows and hand-spikes must be applied, which are very dangerous in action ; and, although you are obliged to apply these instruments for the sake of their great power, it must be considered as a very uncertain way of pointing a gun. Suppose the captain of the gun directs these men with crows and handspikes to train the gun fore and aft, as occasion may require, it is probable they may train the gun too far, then it must be trained back again; and, after the captain of the gun has laid it, as he supposes, to do execution, it is his duty to see the breeching, tackle-falls, and men, clear, before he discharges the gun, as many accidents happen from want of strict attention to the clearing of the tackles, ropes, &c. that are applied to the common carriage, and, too often, while the captain of a gun is taking these precautions, the position of the ship may be so altered as to make the shot go wide of the object.

Another material advantage which the new gun-carriage possesses, is the preservation of the ship's decks, which, by the use of iron crows and handspikes to the common carriage, are very much damaged and torn, particularly in ships that go to sea short-handed, as it is impossible to traverse the guns, or bowse them to the port, if a weather gun, without the assistance of these prejudicial instruments ; therefore a considerable expense will be saved in the preservation of ships' decks by the principles of this invention.

The newly invented carriage would cause a considerable saving by the reduction of men, or an advantage in short complements ; as the proportion of 250 men, on the old plan, would not require 100 on the new ; and a ship would go to sea much better prepared for fighting than they do with the common carriage with 250 men.

Comparative statement of the advantages of the patent gun-carriage over the common one in point of expense.

The *common gun-carriage*, used on board a ship of war or India-man carrying (upon supposition) 40 guns and 160 men, will require of that number, to be properly managed, 140 men to work her full broadside of 20 twelve-pounders, at the rate of 7, the usual complement of men, to each gun; in which case there are only 20 left to manage the ship.

With the patent gun-carriage on-board, carrying the same number of guns, and 100 men only, the full complement of men to each gun being three, it will require only 60 men to work her broadside, consequently 40 will be left to work the ship; but if necessity should require both sides of the ship to be engaged at the same time, then the complement of three may, with propriety, be reduced to two, who will, with greater ease and expedition, and considerable more certainty of effect, work the gun than the full complement to the common carriage. In this case the whole 40 guns may be worked with 80 men, and 20 are left to work the ship. Thus, it appears, that a ship carrying 100 men, with the use of this new carriage, will have considerable advantages over one with 160 men upon the common plan.

Allowing, therefore, the superior advantage of the ship with 100 men over the 160, and so in proportion, the complement of men is reduced to 60; and calculating the expense of that number for 18 months, at $5l.$ per month, it will be found to amount to $5400l.$; from which, deducting the first additional expense of fitting out a ship of 40 guns with carriages of this construction, amounting to $400l.$ there will remain a saving of $5000l.$

Advantage the patent gun-carriage possesses over the common one in throwing the guns overboard.

The last, though not the least important advantage that the patent carriage possesses over the common one, is the ease with which the gun may be dismounted and thrown overboard in stress of weather, or to avoid an enemy of superior force, which is sometimes the only expedient left to save the lives of the people as well as the ship. This service is effected in the following manner.

The carriage, which is supposed to be secured, must be cast loose, and trained athwartship, square with the ship's sides, and in the centre of the part fore and aft; the jack must then be shipped, and the gun run out, (and in case the motion of the ship should be so violent as to cause the gun to run backwards and forwards on the inclined plane, it will be necessary to stop the gun out,) the bed and coin must then be taken out, and the cross bar which supports the inclined plane when the gun is secured, must be laid across the graduations of the upper carriage, resting on the two sides of the same, so as to depress the muzzle of the gun as much as possible; the bed should then be placed upright, with the thick end bearing on the sill of the port, and the thin end to receive the underside of the gun as near the centre as possible; the cap-squares must then be turned back to let the gun rise; the plane, which is now wound down as low as the train of the carriage will admit, must be wound up as high at the train, as the length of the rack of the jack will allow, which raises the body of the gun considerably above the carriage; and the gun which now rests with its breech on the cross bar, and the centre of the metal on the bed, may, by two men pinching at the breech with a handspike, be thrown overboard, without the assistance of tackles or any thing else but what belongs to the gun. If a roller were laid on the port-sill within the bed, that would facilitate the rolling of the gun out of the port when the bed falls; this service is performed by four men only, being the number quartered to the gun in action, and in the short space of five minutes.

A comparative statement of the two plans, with their full complement of men to each gun.

Old Plan.		New Plan.	
Guns.	Men.	Guns.	Men.
32-Pounder	18	32-Pounder	6 or 5
24 ——	15	24 ——	5 or 4
18 ——	12	18 ——	4 or 3
12 ——	9	12 ——	3
9 ——	7	9 ——	5 to 2 guns
6 ——	5	6 ——	2
4 ——	4	4 ——	2
Total	70	Total	27

Comparative statement of arming a frigate's main-deck with 28 twenty-four pounders, weight 48 cwt. mounted on common car-

s

riages; and one with 28 twenty-four pounders, medium guns, weight 31 cwt. mounted on patent carriages, together with the number of men necessary to each plan, when either the broadside or the whole of the guns are engaged; to which are added the charges of powder to each gun, and the expense incurred by each mode of arming.

	With heavy guns and common carriages.	Medium guns and patent carriages.
Number of guns to main deck	28	28
Species of gun.	24 Pr.	24 Pr.
Weight of gun.	48 Cwt.	31 Cwt.
Number of men to each gun.	12	4
Number of men to broadside of 14 guns	168	56
Number of men to both sides	336	112
Charge of powder.	8 lbs.	4 lbs.
Expense of each gun and carriage	58l.	60l.
Total expense	1624l.	1680l.
Extra expense		56l.

It is proper to observe that the 24-pounder, sea-service gun, weighing 48 cwt. is the lightest 24-pounder at present in his Majesty's service.

By the above statement it appears that a frigate carrying 28 twenty-four pounders (heavy guns and common carriages) on her main deck, will, if both sides are engaged, require 336 men, which exceeds the complement generally allowed to ships of that force; consequently there is not a man left for other services; whereas, a ship carrying the same number of guns on her main deck, 24-pounders, of a medium species, but equally effectual, mounted on patent carriages, would require but 112 men to fight both sides: there are then 224 men left for other purposes of war, two thirds of which might be spared, if found necessary, for manning the prizes, or for other services; and the frigate thus reduced in men, would be able to make a better defense with her great guns than she could with her full complement on the common plan. The additional expense incurred by arming a ship with medium guns and patent carriages will be about 56l.; but if the usual complement of men were reduced ten, that reduction could not be felt, and would lessen the annual expense of a frigate about 700l. There will also be a considerable saving in the expense of gunpowder, the medium gun requiring but one sixth of the shot's weight; whereas the heavy gun requires one third, being double the quantity.

Thus it appears, that a ship armed with medium guns and patent carriages will have considerable advantages over one armed on the common plan ; and, from the facility and accuracy with which they are worked, would have a double effect ; and by the proposed reduction of men it will be found that a considerable saving would be obtained by this mode of arming ships.

CARRONADE. A species of short sea-ordnance, originally made at Carron, in Scotland, in 1774,

It differs from other ordnance in having no trunnions, and being elevated upon a joint and bolt. The lengths are as shown in the next page ; and, by reason of the shortness of the peace a thin projection of metal is cast upon the muzzle, to carry the explosion of the charge clear of the ship's sides and rigging. All carronades have chambers, and much less windage than guns, by which they make a considerable range, and a recoil that is almost ungovernable.

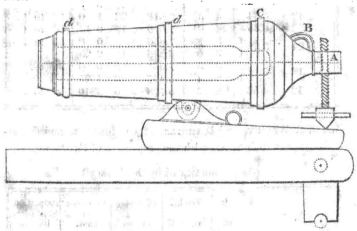

REFERENCES.—A. Solid metal, instead of the button of a gun, through which a screw passes, to serve as a levelling-screw.— B. Metal to confine the rope or hawser.—C, d, d. Small knobs which mark the *line of metal*, and by which the carronade is levelled.

The particulars of a CARRONADE-CARRIAGE are exhibited in

s 2

plate II, figures 3, 4, 5, 6. Figures 3, 4, and 5, are those of a carriage under deck; being the elevation, plan, and front view, the reference to which are as follow:

a g. Two pieces of iron, serving as trunnion-beds.—*g g.* A piece of wood on which they are fixed.—*i k.* Rings and bolts.—*h.* Levelling-screw.—*f.* Platform.—*e e.* Handle.—*a.* A wheel on which the hinder part may be moved round *b.*—*b.* Nail fixing the platform to the deck B B.—A the side of the ship.

Figure 6, represents the carronade-carriage used on deck, in firing over the sides of a ship, and which traverses on the centre *b.*

DIMENSIONS AND WEIGHT OF CARRONADES.

(As given by Captain Adye, R. A.)

Species.	Diameter of bore in inches.	Length in		Weight.			Proportion between the shot and carronade.
		Ft.	In.	Calibers.	Cwt.	qrs.	lbs.	

Species.	Diameter of bore in inches.	Ft.	In.	Calibers.	Cwt.	qrs.	lbs.	Proportion between the shot and carronade.
Pdrs. 68	8.05	5	2	7.702	36	0	0	59 to 1
— —	— —	4	0	5.962	29	0	0	
42	6.84	4	$3\frac{1}{2}$	7.518	22	1	0	58 to 1
32	6.35	4	$0\frac{1}{4}$	7.679	17	0	14	62 to 1
24	5.68 {	3	$7\frac{1}{2}$	7.656	13	0	0	56 to 1
		3	0	6.336	11	2	25	
18	5.16 {	3	3	7.587	9	0	0	56 to 1
		2	4	5.447	8	1	25	
12	4.52	2	2	5.778	5	3	10	56 to 1

LENGTH, WEIGHT, and DIAMETER, of CARRONADES, and Diameter of their SHOT, with the proportion of POWDER.

(As communicated by the Author.)

Species.	Length in Ft. In.		Weight. Cwt. qr. lb.			Diameter in inches.	Diameter of shot.	Proportion of powder. lb. oz.	
Pounders 68	5	2	36	0	0	$8\frac{2}{10}$	8	0	5	10.
42	4	5	22	0	0	$6\frac{9}{10}$	6	$\frac{7}{10}$	3	8
32	4	0	17	3	0	$6\frac{7}{10}$	6	0	2	10
24	3	8	13	0	0	$5\frac{7}{10}$	5	$\frac{4}{10}$	2	0
18	3	6	10	0	0	$5\frac{9}{10}$	5	0	1	8
12	2	9	6	2	0	$4\frac{6}{10}$	4	$\frac{4}{10}$	1	0

THE FULL PROPORTION of POWDER, for CARRONADES of all Species, in from two to 100 CARTRIDGES.

Species.	2	3	4	5	10	20	30	40	50	100
	lb. oz.	lb. oz.	lb. oz.	lb. oz.	lb. oz.	lb. oz.	lb. oz.	lb. oz.	lb. oz.	lb. oz.
Pdrs. 68	11 8	17 4	23 0	28 12	57 8	115 0	172 8	230 0	287 8	573 0
42	7 0	10 8	14 0	17 8	35 0	70 0	105 0	140 0	175 0	350 0
32	5 4	7 14	10 8	13 2	26 4	52 8	78 12	150 0	131 4	262 8
24	4 0	6 0	8 0	10 0	20 0	40 0	60 0	80 0	100 0	200 0
18	3 0	4 8	6 0	7 8	15 0	30 0	45 0	60 0	75 0	150 0
12	2 0	3 0	4 0	5 0	10 0	20 0	30 0	40 0	50 0	100 0

REMARKS made on CARRONADES, by EXPERIMENT, in the year 1798.

In proceeding with the experiment, it was, in the first instance, observed that the breechings, particularly if new, should be seized so short at first as only to admit the carronade to recoil sufficiently within the port for loading.

The whole of the present experiment was pursued without any unusual or improper stretch of the breechings, or any risk of dismounting the carronades, or damaging the transom of the slide; whence the committee conceived, that, if carronades were loaded with the charge recommended of one twelfth of the weight, and fired with only one shot at each round, prejudice would never arise from the strain to which carronades are subject. The lightness and particular construction of them, together with the short check of breeching, always occasion it to fall on the muzzle in the act of firing; and, upon the re-action of the breeching, the elevating screw, by bearing the first blow or strain against the bed of the carriage, may, therefore, in a quick repetition of fire, be liable to damage: and, should it so appear, a small coin under the breech will be necessary to relieve the elevating screw upon this re-action.

The committee, on this consideration, recommended the propriety of loading carronades with only one shot, of the species of the piece, at each round: this restriction is the more important to be observed with carronades than it may be with guns; where it is said, that, at particular moments, in a close action, some rounds are permitted with double or two shot at a charge, although a certain hazard must attend that practice even with guns. For it is clear that the discharging a double portion of iron, at each round, must occasion a very great addition of strain upon the piece of ordnance.

When we consider that the weight of metal and the construction of carronades are about one fourth less in proportion than is established for guns, the consequence is, that the effect of a double charge in carronades must produce an action and strain upon every fixture ; and the restraint from the deduction of powder, according to the charge of a gun of the same caliber does in no measure compensate. It should, also, be recollected, that, when two shots are fired at one round, the decrease of velocity, and, consequently, of the range, together with the additional irregularity that must attend the flight of the shot, will considerably lessen the chance of striking any determinate objects unless it be very close.

For the Range of Carronades, see RANGE.

DIMENSIONS FOR FITTING CARRONADE-PORTS.

	Carronade-ports for			
	32 Pounders.	24 Pounders.	18 Pounders.	12 Pounders.
	Feet. Inch.	Feet. Inch.	Feet. Inch.	Feet. Inch.
Width of the port, fore-and-aft, in the clear............	3. 4	3. 2	3. 0	2. 10
Height of the port in the clear, generally termed day-light ..	2. 9	2. 7	2. 5	2. 3
Length of the slide ...	6. 0	6. 0	6. 0	6. 0
Depth of the breast of the slide.	0. $9\frac{1}{3}$	0. $9\frac{1}{3}$	0. $9\frac{1}{3}$	0. $9\frac{1}{3}$
Thicknes of the chock	0. 5	0. 4	0. 4	0. 4
Opening above the deck	0. 5	0. 4	0. 3	0. 3

OBSERVATIONS.—The opening above the decks may be more or less, so as the height or day-light is preserved.—The slide must lie three inches above a level in its length to midship.—The breadth of the chock must be determined by the tumble-home of the side, as the pivots must drop down, when the slide is home against the side.—The iron plates in the chock are four inches

broad, and three eighths of an inch thick; they are rivetted together; one let in on the upper side, the other on the under side, very
exactly, so that the side may traverse freely, when the pivot is in
its place.

As the iron-work for securing the slides and carriages is subject to contract wet from salt-water, which may rust and corrode
it, the pins, keys, &c. should be frequently taken out, scraped,
and examined, being lightly greased with a mixture of sweet-oil and
tallow, before they are replaced.

Less windage being allowed to carronades than to guns, and
their shot being sent on-board separately, should be kept in a
locker by themselves, and particular care taken that they be not
mixed with the others.

The cartrides being of flannel, and consequently exposed to
moths or vermin, should be aired in fine weather, and darned, if
necessary, with worsted and needles allowed for that purpose.

The carronades and 18-pounders supplied for arming the launch,
together with the round shot, grape, and case, should be kept in
readiness for immediate service, and the iron-work kept in good
order in a basket.

CARRONADE FOR THE LAUNCH, &c.

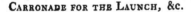
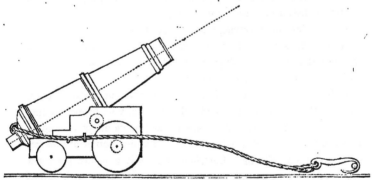

This carronade, as above noticed, should be particularly attended to; and, if required, be ready for any other service, at a
moment's notice. It has therefore been found necessary to mount
it on a small carriage, as shown above, for annoying the enemy's
tops when in action; to be placed where found most convenient,
either on the poop or quarter-deck. The breeching to be of a

greater length than usual, to allow for recoiling, with a hook at each end, so that it may be hooked to a ring-bolt, round the capstan, or any other place most convenient, on the side opposite to that which you engage on.

The highest charge for carronades is one eighth of the weight of the shot ; the lowest, one sixteenth.

OBSERVATIONS at QUARTERS ON THE CARRONADES.

It is necessary to have the spare breechings and tackles at hand, in case of any being shot or carried away by the recoil of the piece, which is violent in proportion to the increase of heat by frequent firing. Examine the iron-work of the carriage and slide, as well as the navel trunnion-bolt, to see that the pins are well in and keyed.

Train your slide as nearly as you can in the direction in which you would point, and mind that your carronade is run quite out at each discharge, as far as the slide will admit, since it will act with less force at the breeching, besides throwing the fire more clear of your hammock-cloth, rigging, &c. which, from the nature of the bore will expand very much when fired. From their being so short, and admitting so much air at the muzzles, it is necessary to be careful in stopping the vent, and sponging well at each fire, besides frequently worming.

If you find your carriage and slide strain very much, your breeching to snap, and other accidents of a similar nature, it is a proof that you are using too great a proportion of powder, which must be reduced accordingly.

CARTRIDGE. A case of paper or flannel, or partly of both, fitted to the bore of a gun, and holding exactly its proper charge. Musket and pistol cartridges are always made of strong paper ; between 30 and 40 of which are made from one pound of powder, including their priming. Cartridges for heavy guns are now made partly of cured paper only, and partly of cured paper with flannel bottoms. Those for field ordnance and carronades are all of flannel, and suited to the bore or chamber of the pieces for which they are intended.

The Ball-cartridges for wall-pieces, muskets, carbines, and pistols, are made of whited-brown-paper, on formers of wood. The quantity of powder contained in these cartridges is, for wall-pieces, 10 drams ; musket, 6 ; carbine, 4 ; and pistol, 3. Blank-cartridges for muskets, carbines, and pistols, are made of blue paper, to preserve a distinction between ball and blank, and to prevent the possibility of accidents happening from one being mixed with the other.

Flannel is used in preference to paper, because when cartridges of the latter have been used it has been commonly found that the bottoms remain in the piece, and accumulate so much that the priming cannot reach the powder. When the flannel cartridge is made up, a paper cylinder or cap is put over it to preserve the powder, and prevent its dust from getting through. The cartridges made with cured paper and flannel bottoms are for battering-ordnance.

The best way of making flannel cartridges is, to boil the flannel in size ; which will prevent the powder-dust from passing through, and render it more stiff and manageable ; for, without this precaution, cartridges are so pliable, from their size and the quantity they contain, that they are not gotten into the piece without difficulty.

NUMBER of MUSKET and PISTOL CARTRIDGES made from one sheet to one and two quires of paper.

	Cartridges.	Sheets.	Quires.
MUSKET	16	1	0
	384	24	1
	768	48	2
PISTOL	24	1	0
	576	24	1
	1152	48	2

WEIGHT, LENGTH, AND TONNAGE, OF CARTRIDGES.

Paper.	Weight of one dozen.			Length.		Tonnage. No. packed in ¾ ton vat.
Pounders.	lb.	oz.	dr.	Feet.	In.	Number.
42	3	0	0	2	4	1000
32	3	0	0	2	4	1100
24	3	0	0	2	4	1400
18	2	14	0	2	4	1500
12	2	4	0	2	4	1600

T

Weight, Length, and Tonnage, of Cartridges, continued.

Of paper.	Weight of one dozen.			Length.		Tonnage. No. packed in ¼ ton vat.
Pounders.	lb.	oz.	dr.	Feet.	In.	Number.
9	2	4	0	..2	4..	 1800
6	..1	5	0	..2	0..	 2000
4	..1	1	0	..1	7..	 2200
3	..1	1	0	..1	7..	 2200
OF FLANNEL.						
42 and 32	..2	2	0	..2	3	The tonnage of flannel cartridges is one fifth more than that of paper.
24 { Heavy	..1	12	0	..1	10	
24 { Medium	..1	6	0	..1	5	
24 { Light	..1	1	8	..1	0	
18	..1	6	0	..2	3	
12 { Heavy	..1	3	0	..1	6	
12 { Medium	..0	11	0	..1	2	
12 { Light	..0	8	0	..0	10	
9	..0	10	0	..1	4	
6 { Heavy	..0	14	0	.1	1	
6 { Medium	—	—		—	—	
6 { Light	..0	5	0	..0	9¼	
3	..0	6	0	..0	1	
13-inch mortar	..1	2	8	..1	6	
10	..0	10	8	..1	1	
8	..0	7	0	..1	0	
5¼	..0	4	0	..0	9	
4¾	..0	3	0	..0	7	
8-inch howitzer	..0	10	8	..1	1¼	
5½	..0	4	8	..0	9¼	
4¾	..0	4	0	..0	9¼	

CASCABEL or POMILION of a GUN. The knob or button of metal behind the breech of a cannon ; serving as a kind of handle by which to direct and elevate the piece. See CANNON.

CASE-SHOT, or CANISTER-SHOT. A species of shell, containing a number of small balls, which are inclosed in a round tin case, or canister, and so prepared as to be shot out of great guns, to the great annoyance and destruction of the enemy. These have superseded and been substituted for grape-shot, formerly used.

The tin case which contains the shot is cylindric, in diameter a little less than the caliber of the gun or howitzer, in which they are to be used. It is filled with iron balls, so as to make up the weight of the shot. These balls are seldom less than one ounce and a quarter in weight.

The whole charge of this shot takes effect on the enemy at any distance; and it may be fired with an effect equally close and collected, to any distance within the range of the piece. The artillery need not advance within musket-shot of the enemy to make use of this kind of fire with its full effect, and are not so subject to have their guns charged either by cavalry or infantry.

It requires less precision to point a piece of ordnance charged with spherical case shot than with round shot; because case-shot is a wide and dispersed fire, and the difficulty in elevation consequently less.

Its comparative destruction with that of round shot will be, generally, as the number of shot within the shells is to one; that is to say, a three-pounder, twenty-two to one in its favour; a six-pounder fifty to one, &c. in which calculation is not enumerated any effect from the splinters of the shell.

Small balls cannot be projected to very considerable distances, unless inclosed in heavy spherical cases, which from their form and weight, are not much influenced by the resistance of the air, or diverted from their direction.

The explosion of the shell makes no change in the direction of the shot within it; they, consequently, complete the curve of the shell, which has sometimes been observed to be 400 yards.

For a more enlarged explanation of this subject, see the valuable and excellent 'Military Dictionary' by Major Chas. James, of the Royal Artillery.

CASES for CARTRIDGES. Vehicles made of wood, to the exact size of the different species of cartridges, for the purpose of carrying them, in safety, from the magazine to the different guns on-board.

CENTRE of GRAVITY. That point in any substance or body about which its several parts balance each other, in every situation.

CHAIN-SHOT. Two balls, or bullets, connected by a strong chain, 8 or 10 inches long, and used, chiefly, to cut in pieces the rigging, &c. of an enemy.

CHAMBER of a GUN. That part of the bore which receives the powder. See CANNON and CARRONADE.

CHARCOAL. A kind of artificial coal, consisting of wood half burnt; and well known as a component part of gunpowder. The process in making it is simple. The wood is cut into pieces nearly of the same size, then disposed in heaps and covered with earth so as to prevent all communication with the air, except what is necessary to make the wood burn, and to drive off the oil and water formed during the combustion; they are then kindled, and when they have burnt a sufficient time, the fire is extinguished by stopping the holes through which the air was admitted.

Charcoal made purely from beech-wood is brittle, burns in the air without any flame, and leaves few ashes. It is neither soluble in water or in acids, and attracts water when exposed to the air. It is six times lighter than water; looks black, shining, and transparent, sounds hollow when held loosely, and burns with a crackling noise.

The best charcoal is from beech, birch, oak, and fir; the oak-coal, however, frequently does not become white hot. The coal for gunpowder ought to possess its native gloss, and before made use of, should be carefully sifted and separated from any small stones, sand, &c.

CHARGE. The quantity of ball, powder, &c. with which a gun is loaded. The weight of the powder is commonly one third that of the ball; but the allowance for 32-pounders is seven sixteenths of the same weight. The charge for battering-guns is one third of the weight; for round shot, as above; and one fourth of it for case-shot. That for carronades is usually one twelfth of the weight of the shot. The highest one eighth, and the lowest one sixteenth. See CANNON, CARRONADES, &c.

CHASE or CHACE of a Gun. The length of its bore or cylinder.

COIN or QUOIN. The wedge laid under the breech of a gun, for the purpose of elevating or depressing it.

COMPOSITION. The compounded ingredients of which gun-powder, fire-works, &c. are made. It, also, particularly signifies a mixture of bees-wax, with pitch and tar, used in making up fuses and shells.

All dry compositions must be well mixed; first by the hands, and then passed several times through fine hair sieves, that the ingredients may be thoroughly incorporated. In mixing compositions which require fire, the greatest precautions are necessary; particularly in those wherein gunpowder enters. The dry part of the composition may, in general, be mixed together first, and put by degrees into the cauldron, where the other ingredients are fluid, being well stirred all the time of putting in. When the dry ingredients are inflammable, the cauldron must not only be taken off the fire, but the bottom must be dipped in water, to prevent the possibility of accidents while mixing them.

For some general remarks on the composition of artificial fireworks, see FIRE-WORKS.

The composition for BENGAL LIGHTS is, saltpetre, 7lb.; sulphur, 1lb. 12oz.; and red orpiment, 8oz.: or, saltpetre, 2lb. 4oz.; sulphur, 8oz.; antimony, 4oz., and orpiment, 1½oz.

For CHINESE or WHITE LIGHTS, the composition is, nitre, from 50 to 60 parts; sulphur, 16 to 20; antimony, 5; orpiment, 8 to 10.

For FIRE-BALLS, &c. see BALLS, and the respective articles in the alphabetical arrangement.

CONIC. A gun or piece of ordnance is said to be conic when it is wider towards the mouth than about the breech.

CROSS-BAR SHOT. Shot having iron bars crossed through them, and sometimes projecting 6 or 8 inches out from each side. They are used for destroying rigging, clearing away palisades, &c.

CUBE. A regular or solid body, consisting of six equal sides or faces, which are squares. CUBIC NUMBERS are those which are formed by multiplying any numbers twice by themselves. So the cubes of 1, 2, 3, 4, 5, 6, &c. are

1, 8, 27, 64, 125, 216, &c. and the first quantity, or basis, is called the ROOT. For a Table of Cubes, with their corresponding roots, see SQUARE. For the methods of extracting the cube-root, see page 12.

DEPRESSION. The inclination of a gun downwards, so that its shot may strike beneath the line of point-blank. The gun thus inclined is therefore said to be depressed.

DETONATION. The noise from explosion which any substance makes upon the application of fire, as gunpowder, &c.

DIAMETER. *Rule to find the diameter of shot or shell's.* For an iron ball, whose diameter is given, supposing a nine-pounder, which is nearly 4 inches, say, the cube-root of 2.08 of 9 pounds, is to 4 inches as the cube-root of the given weight is to the diameter sought. Or, if 4 be divided by 2.08, the cube-root of 9, the quotient 1.923 will be the diameter of a one-pound shot;

which, being continually multiplied by the cube-root of the given weight, gives the diameter required.

DISMANTLE. To dismantle a gun is to render it unfit for use, by capsising it, &c.

DISPART. The dispart of a gun is the medium or half-difference between the two diameters, at the muzzle-ring and base-ring. It is, in general, one fifty-sixth part of the length.

To DISPART is to set a mark on the muzzle-ring, so that it may be of equal height with the base-ring : hence a line drawn from one to the other will be parallel to the axis of the cylinder, for the gunner to take aim by, so as to hit the mark intended. For, the bore and dispart-line being parallel, an aim so taken will be true. This exactness can, however, be seldom obtained during an engagement, when practice and the eye must be the best guides.

If a cannon be not truly bored, the dispart line will be false; and the visual ray will not be parallel to the direction of the ball, so long as it continues in a straight direction. By the following rule the dispart may be found when the chase lies equally and tend upward or downward.

RULE. Take half the diameter of the chase at the breech, and add to it the thickness of the metal at the base-ring; take, likewise, the diameter of the chase, at the muzzle-ring, and add to it the thickness of the metal there; the difference between these is the true dispart.

ELEVATION. The angle comprehended between the horizon and the line of direction of an elevated gun, &c.; or that which the chase of a piece, or its axis, makes with the plane of the horizon.

EMERY. Ground iron ore, very serviceable for cleaning small arms, &c.

ENGAGEMENT. A battle at sea, either between single ships or squadrons.

The whole œconomy of a naval engagement may be ranged under the following heads, viz. the PREPARATION; the ACTION; and the REPAIR, or refitting for the purposes of navigation.

The PREPARATION is begun by issuing an order to clear the ship for action, which is repeated by the boatswain and his mates at all the hatchways leading to the different decks. As the cannon cannot be worked while the hammocs are suspended in their usual situations, it becomes necessary to remove them as quick as possible. By this circumstance a double advantage is obtained: the batteries of cannon are immediately cleared of an incumbrance, and the hammocs are converted into a sort of parapet, to prevent the execution of small shot on the quarter-deck, tops, and fore-castle. At the summons of the boatswain, *Up all hammocs!* every sailor repairs to his own, and, having stowed his bedding properly, he cords it firmly with a lashing, or line, provided for that purpose, he then carries it to the quarter-deck, poop, or fore-castle, or wherever it may be necessary. As each side of the quarter-deck and poop is furnished with a double net-work, supported by iron cranes fixed immediately above the gunnel, or top of the ship's side, the hammocs thus corded are firmly stowed by the quarter-master between the two parts of the netting, so as to form an excellent barrier. The tops, waist, and fore-castle, are then fenced in the same manner.

Whilst these offices are performed below, the boatswain and his mates are employed in securing the sail-yards, to prevent them from tumbling down when the ship is cannonaded, as she might thereby be disabled, and rendered incapable of attack, retreat, or pursuit. The yards are now likewise secured by strong chains, or ropes, additional to those by which they are usually suspended. The boatswain also provides the necessary materials to repair the rigging, wherever it may be damaged by the shot of the enemy, and to supply whatever parts of it may be entirely destroyed. The carpenter and his crew in the meanwhile prepare the shot-plugs and mauls, to close up any dangerous breaches that may be made near the surface of the water; and provide the iron work necessary to refit the chain-pumps, in case their machinery should be wounded in the engagement. The gunner, with his mates and quarter-gunners, is busied in examining the cannon of the different batteries; to see that their charges are thoroughly dry and fit for execution: to have every thing ready for furnishing the great guns and small arms with powder, so soon as the action begins: and to keep a sufficient number of cartridges continually filled, to supply the place of those expended in battle. The master and his mates are attentive to have the sails properly trimmed, according to the situation of the ship; and to reduce or multiply them, as occasion requires, with all possible expedition. The lieutenants visit the different decks, to see that they are effectually cleared of all incumbrance, so that nothing may retard the excution of the artillery ; and to enjoin the other officers to diligence and alertness, in making the necessary dispositions for the expected engagement, so that every thing may be in readiness at a moment's warning.

When the hostile ships have approached each other to a competent distance, the drums beat to arms. The boatswain and his mates pipe, *all hands to quarters !* at every hatchway. All the persons appointed to manage the great guns immediately repair to their respective stations. The crows, handspecs, rammers, sponges, powder-horns, matches, and train-tackles, are placed in order by the side of every cannon. The hatches are immediately laid, to prevent any one from deserting his post by escaping into the lower apartments. The marines are drawn up in rank and file on the quarter-deck, poop, and fore-castle. The lashings of the great guns are cast loose, and the tompions withdrawn. The whole artillery, above and below, is run out at the ports, and levelled to the point-blank range ready for firing.

The necessary preparations being completed, and the officers and crew ready at their respective stations, to obey the order, the commencement of the action is determined by the mutual distance and situation of the adverse ships, or by the signal from the commander-in-chief of the fleet or squadron. The cannon being levelled in parallel rows, projecting from the ship's side, the most natural order for battle is evidently to range the ships a-breast of each other, especially if the engagement is general. The most convenient distance is properly within the point-blank range of a musket, so that all the artillery may do effectual execution.

The ACTION usually begins with a vigorous cannonade, accompanied with the whole efforts of the carronades, swivel-guns, and small arms. The method of firing in platoons, or vollies of cannon at once, appears inconvenient in the sea-service, and perhaps should never be attempted, unless in the battering of a fortification. The sides and decks of the ship, although sufficiently strong for all the purposes of war, would be too much shaken by so violent an explosion and recoil. The general rule observed on this occasion throughout the ship, is to load, fire, and sponge, the guns with all possible expedition, yet without confusion or precipitation. The captain of each gun is particularly enjoined to fire when the piece is properly directed to its object, that the shot may not be fruitlessly expended. The lieutenants, who command the different batteries, traverse the deck to see that the battle is prosecuted with vivacity; and to exhort and animate the men to their duty. The midshipmen second these injunctions, and give the necessary assistance, wherever it may be required, at the guns committed to their charge. The gunner should be particularly attentive that all the artillery is sufficiently supplied with powder, and that the cartridges are carefully conveyed along the decks in covered boxes. The havock produced by a continuation of this mutual assault may readily be conjectured by the reader's imagination. The defeated ship having acknowledged the victor, by striking her colours, is immediately taken possession of by the conqueror, who secures her officers and crew as prisoners in his own ship, and invests his principal officer with the command of the prize until a captain is appointed by the commander-in-chief.

The engagement being concluded, they begin the REPAIR: the cannon are secured by their breechings and tackles with all convenient expedition. Whatever sails have been rendered unserviceable are unbent, and the wounded masts and yards struck upon the deck, and fished or replaced by others. The standing rigging is knotted, and the running rigging spliced wherever necessary. Proper sails are bent in the room of those which have been displaced as useless. The carpenter and his crew are employed in repairing the breaches made in the ship's hull, by shot-plugs, pieces of plank, and sheet-lead. The gunner and his assistants are busied in replenishing the allotted number of charged cartridges, to supply the place of those which have been expended, and in refitting whatever furniture of the cannon may have been damaged by the late action.

Such are the usual process and consequences of an engagement between two ships of war, which may be considered as descriptive of a general battle between fleets or squadrons. The latter, however, involves a greater variety of incidents, and necessarily requires more comprehensive skill and judgement in the commanding-officer.

For a more enlarged detail of preparation for action, see ACTION; and see, also, the article QUARTERS, hereafter.

EXERCISE. The preparatory practice of managing the ordnance and small arms, in order to make the ship's company perfectly skilled therein, so as to direct its execution successfully in time of battle.

For the exercise of small arms, see SMALL-ARMS.

The EXERCISE OF THE GREAT GUNS is as follows:

Upon beating to arms (every person having immediately repaired to his quarters) the midshipman, commanding a number of guns, is to see they are not without every necessary article, as (at every gun) a sponge, powder-horn, with its priming wires, and a sufficient quantity of powder, shot, crow, handspec, bed, coin, train-tackle, &c. sending, without delay, for a supply of any thing that may be missing; and, for the greater certainty of not overlooking any deficiency, he is to give strict orders to each captain under him, to make the like examination at his respective gun, and to take care that every requisite is in a serviceable condition, which he is to report accordingly. And, for the still more certain and speedy account being taken upon these occasions, the midshipman is to give each man his charge at quarters, (as expressed in the form of the monthly-report) who is to search for his particular implements, and, not finding them, is immediately to acquaint his captain, that, upon his report to the midshipman, they may be replaced.

The man who takes care of the powder is to place himself on the opposite side of the deck from that where we engage; except when fighting both sides at once, when he is to be amidship. He is not to suffer any other man to take a cartridge from him but he who is appointed to serve the gun with that article, either in time of a real engagement, or at exercise.

Lanterns are not to be brought to quarters in the night, until the midshipman gives his orders for so doing to the person he charges with that article. Every thing being in its place, and not the least lumber in the way of the guns, the exercise begins with,

1st. SILENCE.—At this word every one is to observe a silent attention to the officers.

2d. Cast loose your guns.—The muzzle lashing is to be taken off from the guns; and, being coiled up in a small compass, is to be made fast to the eye-bolt above the port. The lashing-tackles at the same time to be cast loose, and the middle of the breeching seized to the thimble of the pomilion. The sponge to be taken down, and, with the crow, handspec, &c. laid upon the deck, by the gun.

When prepared for engaging an enemy, the seizing within the clinch of the breeching is to be cut, that the gun may come sufficiently within-board for loading, and that the force of the recoil may be more spent before it acts upon the breeching.

3d. Level your guns.—The breech of your metal is to be raised so as to admit the foot of the bed being placed upon the axle-tree of the carriage, with the coin upon the bed, both their ends being even one with the other.

When levelled for firing, the bed is to be lashed to the bolt which supports the inner end of it, that it may not be thrown out of its place by the violence of the gun's motion, when hot with frequent discharges.

4th. Take out your tompions.—The tompion is to be taken out of the gun's mouth, and left hanging by its laniard.

5th. Run out your guns.—With the tackles hooked to the upper bolts of the carriage, the gun is be bowsed out as close as possible, without the assistance of crows or handspecs; taking care at the same time to keep the breeching clear of the trucks, by hauling it through the rings; it is then to be bent so as to run clear when the gun is fired. When the gun is out, the tackle-falls are to be laid along-side the carriages in neat fakes, so that, when the gun, by recoiling, overhauls them, they may not be subject to get foul, as they would if in a common coil.

6th. Prime.—If the cartridge is to be pierced with the priming-wire, and the vent filled with powder, the pan also is to be filled; and the flat space, having a score through it at the end of the pan, is to be covered, and this part of the priming is to be bruised with the round part of the horn. The apron is to be laid over, and the horn hung up out of danger from the flash of the priming.

7th. Point your guns.—At this command the gun is, in the first place, to be elevated to the height of the object, by means of the side-sights; and then the person pointing is to direct his fire by the upper-sight, having a crow on one side, and a hand-spec on the other, to heave the gun by his direction till he catches the object.

The men who heave the gun for pointing are to stand between the ship's side and their crows or handspecs, to escape the injury they might otherwise receive from their being struck against them, or splintered by a shot; and the man who attends the captain with a match is to bring it at the word, " POINT YOUR GUNS ;" and, kneeling upon one knee opposite the train-truck of the carriage, and at such a distance as to be able to touch the priming, is to turn his head from the gun, and keep blowing gently upon the lighted match to keep it clear from ashes. And, as the missing of an enemy in action, by neglect or want of coolness, is most inexcuseable, it is particularly recommended to have the people thoroughly instructed in pointing well, and taught to know the ill-consequences of not taking proper means to hit their mark; wherefore they should be made to elevate their guns to the utmost nicety, and then to point with the same exactness; and, having caught the object through the upper-sight, at the word—

8th. FIRE.—The match is instantly to be put to the bruised part of the priming; and, when the gun is discharged, the vent is to be closed on the words " STOP YOUR VENTS," in order to smother any sparks of fire that may remain in the chamber of the gun; and the man who sponges is immediately to place himself by the muzzle of the gun in readiness.

9th. WORM AND SPONGE YOUR GUNS.—The sponge is to be rammed down to the bottom of the chamber, and then twisted round, to extinguish effectually any remains of fire; and, when drawn out, to be struck against the outside of the muzzle, to shake off any sparks or scraps of the cartridge that may have come out with it; and next, its end is to be shifted ready for loading; and, while this is doing, the man appointed to provide a cartridge is to go to the box, and by the time the sponge is out of the gun, he is to have it ready.

10th. LOAD WITH CARTRIDGE.—The cartridge (with the bottom end first, seam downwards, and a wad after it) is to be put into the gun, and thrust a little way within the mouth, when the rammer is to be entered; the cartridge is then to be forcibly rammed down, and the captain at the same time is to keep his priming-wire in the vent, and, feeling the cartridge, is to give the word *home*, when the rammer is to be drawn, and not before. While this is doing, the man appointed to provide a shot is to provide one (or two, according to the order at that time) ready at the muzzle, with a wad likewise, and when the rammer is drawn, at the words—

11th. LOAD WITH SHOT, and WAD TO YOUR SHOT.—The shot and wad upon it are to be put into the gun, and thrust a little way down, when the rammer is to be entered as before.

12th. RAM HOME WAD AND SHOT.—The shot and wad are to be rammed down to the cartridge, and there have a couple of forcible strokes, when the rammer is to be drawn, and laid out of the way of the guns and tackles, if the exercise or action is continued; but, if it is over, the sponge is to be secured in the place it is at all times kept in.

13th. PUT IN YOUR TOMPIONS.—The tompions to be put into the muzzle of the cannon.

14th. HOUSE YOUR GUNS.—The seizing is to be put on again upon the clinched end of the breeching, leaving it no slacker than to admit of the guns being housed with ease. The coin is to be taken from under the breech of the gun, and the bed, still resting upon the bolt, within the carriage, thrust under, till the foot of it falls off the axle-tree, leaving it to rest upon the end which projects out from the foot. The metal is to be let down upon this. The gun is to be placed exactly square, and the muzzle is to be close to the wood, in its proper place for passing the muzzle-lashings.

15th. SECURE YOUR GUNS.—The muzzle-lashings must first be made secure, and then with one tackle (having all its parts equally tight with the breeching) the gun is to be lashed. The other tackle is to be bowsed tight, and by itself made fast, that it may be ready to cast off for lashing a second breeching.

Care must be taken to hook the first tackle to the upper bolt of the carriage, that it may not otherwise obstruct the reeving of the second breeching, and to give the greater length to the end part of the fall.

No pains should be spared in bowsing the lashing very tight, that the gun may have the least play that is possible, as their being loose may be productive of very dangerous consequences.

The coin, crow, and handspec, are to be put under the gun, the powder-horn hung up in its place, &c.

Being engaged at any time when there is a large swell, a rough sea, or in squally weather, &c. as the ship may be liable to be suddenly much heeled, the port-tackle-fall is to be kept clear, and (whenever the working of the gun will admit of it) the man charged with that office is to keep it in his hand; at the same time the muzzle-lashing is to be kept fast to the ring of the port, and being hauled tight, is to be fastened to the eye-bolt over the port-hole, so as to be out of the gun's way, in firing, in order to haul it in at any time of danger.

This precaution is not to be omitted, when engaging to the windward, any more than when to the leeward, those situations being very subject to alter at too short a warning.

A train-tackle is always to be made use of with the lee guns, and the man stationed to attend it is to be very careful in preventing the gun's running out at an improper time.

The WORDS OF COMMAND in the SHORT EXERCISE are as follow : every sentence of which should be explained as above.

Silence.

1. The guns are now loaded.
2. Cast loose the guns.
3. Prime.
4. Point your guns to the object.
5. Fire.
6. Sponge and load.
7. Run out your guns.

FACE of a GUN. The superficies of the metal at the extremities of the muzzle.

FALSE FIRES and LIGHTS. By FALSE FIRE is meant any fire or light which is made use of for the purpose of deceiving an enemy. FALSE LIGHTS, likewise, are those which may be used as signals of deception for the same purpose. See LIGHT and FIRE COMPOSITION, hereafter.

FIRE-ARROW. A small iron or steel dart, formerly used by privateers and pirates, to fire the sails of an enemy in battle. It was furnished with springs and bars, together with a match, impregnated with powder and sulphur, wound about its shaft, and then fired from a swivel-gun or musketoon. The match, being kindled by the explosion, communicates the flame to the sail against which it is directed, where the arrow is fastened by means of its bars and springs. As this is peculiar to hot climates, particularly the West-Indies, the sails being extremely dry, are instantly inflamed, and of course convey the fire to the masts and rigging, and finally to the vessel itself.

FIRE-PAN. The receptacle in a gun for the priming powder.

FIRE-POT. A small earthern pot, into which is put a charged grenade, and over that powder enough to cover the grenade; the whole covered with a piece of parchment, and two pieces of quick-match across, lighted. This fires the powder; and, consequently, the grenade, which has no fuse, that its operation may be the quicker.

FIRE-MEN. See BOARDERS.

FIRE-SHIP. A fire-ship is generally an old vessel, peculiarly fitted up, and having its greater part filled with combustible materials. It is fitted with sheer-hooks to the yard-arms, and grappling-irons, for the purpose of hooking and setting fire to the enemy's ships in battle, &c.

There is nothing materially different in the construction of fire-ship's from that of other vessels, excepting what relates to the fitting of that part of the ship where the combustibles are inclosed, and the apparatus by which the fire is instantly conveyed from one part to another, and thence to the enemy. A description of this may be found in Steel's " Elements and Practice of Naval Architure."

The proportion of combustible stores for a fire-ship of 150 tons is as follows:

	No.
Fire-barrels, filled with composition	8
Iron-chambers, to blow open the ports........	12
Composition for priming. ....barrels.....	$3\frac{1}{4}$
Quick-match. ....ditto. .....'.	1
Curtains, dipped.	48
Reeds, long, single dipped.................	150
Ditto, short.... { double dipped	75
{ single dipped..............	75
Bavins, single dipped.....................	250

The fire-barrels are about two feet four inches high, and one foot six inches diameter.—Each barrel must have four holes of about six inches square cut in its sides; and these holes must have a square piece of canvas nailed over them quite close. They are then filled with the same composition as for carcasses, and four plugs, of about one inch diameter and three inches long, and well greased, are thrust into the top, and then left to dry. When dry these plugs are taken out, and the holes filled with fuse-composition, and quick-match at the top; which goes from one hole to the other; after this the top is smeared over with mealed powder mixed up with spirits of wine.—When dry again, a sheet or two of brown paper is laid over the top, and then one of the canvas covers, which is made secure by the upper hoop of the barrel.

The composition for dipping reeds, bavins, and curtains, is,

Resin ....120lb.
Coarse sulphur............................. 90
Swedish pitch............................. 60
Tallow 6
Mealed powder 12

This proportion will dip about 100 reeds and 25 bavins.

Each curtain contains one square yard of barras.

Each cover for fire-barrels one ditto of sacking.

Immediately that the curtains, covers, &c. are dipped, they are to be strewed over with fine brimstone, before the composition grows cold.

The iron chambers, for blowing open the ports, hold from nine to eleven ounces of powder. They are fixed in such a manner as to prevent their recoil, and to ensure the ports being blown open. The vents are generally corked up, and covered with a piece of barras, till required to be primed.

To fit out a Fire-ship.—The whole breadth of the fire-room is to be divided into nine parts, and troughs laid the whole length of the room. Cross troughs of communication are laid between them, about 20 in each row, perpendicular to the long troughs.— These troughs are usually four inches wide, and four deep. There are two fire-trunks and two fire-scuttles on each side, under which the eight fire-barrels are to be placed.

The reeds and bavins are to be tied down in the troughs.—The curtains are to be nailed up to the beams, equally through the fire-room. The ship is not to be primed when fitted out, but only when intended to be fired.

To Prime.—Composition for priming.

Saltpetre pulverised.................22 lbs. 8 oz.
Resin............................. 2   11
Sulphur 18   0
Mealed powder 45   0
Linseed oil .... 1 pint.

All the reeds and bavins are to be taken up, and a little of the above composition sprinkled in the bottom of the troughs ; the reeds, &c. to be then gently tied down again.—Quick-match of six or eight threads doubled, must be laid along on the tops of all the reeds, &c. and the priming composition strewed over it, and over all the fire-room.—The covers of all the fire-barrels must be cut open, and made to hang down on the sides of the barrels.—Leaders of strong quick-match must be laid from the reeds to the barrels and to the chambers ; and must be tied down to the vents to insure its not falling off.—Strong leaders of quick-match, four or five times doubled, must be laid from the reeds to the sally-ports, and the sally-ports must be connected by quick-match, that the whole may take fire at once.

The following method is now adopted of producing an external fire, in addition to the internal fire, before gained by the fire-room.

Fire-boxes, filled with the carcass composition, are distributed in the following manner, in a ship of three masts :

One suspended from each side of the catheads and davits,
   on each side the boy.   4
Eight slung across the bowsprit   8
Four across each of the out-riggers abaft   8
Two from the grapplins of each of the lower yard-arms ., 12
One from the dead-eyes on each side of the three round-
   tops..   6
One from the middle of the inside of the main, fore, and
   mizen, shrouds..   6
                                                            ———
                                                             44
                                                            ═══

The boxes are suspended by chains and hooks, and those slung across the bowsprit and out-riggers are fixed by staples. The two

x

inner ones are laid with leaders of quick-match, which fire instantly, or with portfires, which burn a given time; they communicate with the outer ones by reeds, which are tied down on
the bowsprit and out-riggers.—The boxes hanging from the dead-
eyes and shrouds, are fired by curtains suspended from the shrouds,
the lower one of which hangs immediately over one of the large
fire-barrels. The two boxes on each yard-arm are hung one over
the other; the upper one having a leader of quick-match carried
along the yard from the shrouds; and, in burning, will no doubt
fire the lower one. Besides the boxes, there are fire-barrels arranged as follows : two half-barrels on the forecastle; two abaft
the main-deck, and four on the main-deck; two in each round-
top, placed against the masts ; and four large fire-barrels under
fire-trucks, to convey fire to the curtains on the shrouds. All
these fire-barrels and boxes are to be fired by separate leaders of
quick-match or port-fire, in order that any part of the ship may
be fired, to cover its approach by the smoke ; and the remaining
part instantaneously upon quitting the ship. It has been found
by experiment, that two men with lighted port-fires can set fire
to the whole of the leaders on the deck, bowsprit, catheads, out-
riggers, &c. in less than a minute; therefore the risk of trusting
to one main leader to the whole, may be avoided.

The leaders are laid in painted canvas hose, made for the purpose.—*(Adye's Bombardier.)*

FIRE-WORKS, ARTIFICIAL. For the composition of artificial
Fire-works, as Rockets, Blue-lights, &c. see the respective articles. In the composition of Fire-works, generally, it is to be
observed—1. That *Mealed powder* does not contribute most effectually to *expedite* effect. 2. *Nitre*, or saltpetre, used for these
purposes, should be as pure as possible : this article causes a slow
fire. 3. *Sulphur* tends to prolong a fire. 4. *Charcoal*, if well
pulverized, is of great use, and maintains the fire. 5. *Tar, pitch,*
and *colophony*, or *black resin*, kindle easily, and render a composition slower in its operation. 6. *Antimony* renders a composition
quicker, and contributes to produce a greater explosion. 7. *Cam-
phor* causes a beautiful white flame. 8. *Iron filings* make a spark-
ling fire. 8. *Oil* and *fat* feed a fire, and render its operation
slower. 10. *Spirits of wine, brandy,* and other spirits, are used
to moisten a composition when mixing it. 11. *Gums* serve to

glue or stiffen a composition when mixing it. Several other articles, as *mercury*, *potass*, *saffron*, *acids*, &c. are also used in making artificial fire-works. In all cases it is to be observed, that the strength of the composition does not more depend on the ingredients than on the effectual manner in which they are blended and the mode in which they are made up for service.

FLAG. The colours or ensigns of a ship, &c. Flags in the Royal Navy are either red, white, or blue, and are hoisted either at the head of the main-mast, fore-mast, or mizen-mast. When a flag is displayed on the main-mast, it is the distinguishing mark of an admiral; when on the fore-mast, of a vice-admiral; and when on the mizen-mast, of a rear-admiral.

The highest flag in the navy is the *anchor and cable*, which is displayed only when the lord-high-admiral, or the lords commissioners of the admiralty, is or are on board; the next is the *union*, the distinction peculiar to the second officer, called the admiral of the fleet; and the lowest is the *blue* at the mizen-mast.

FLINT. A well-known hard and semi-pellucid stone, of the chrystal kind, made use of to strike fire with steel. They are usually packed for service in half-barrels, and one half-barrel contains, of

Musket	2000	in weight	2 qrs.	14 lb.
Carbine	3000		2	10
Pistol	4000		3	15.

The most transparent and free from veins are esteemed the best.

In tonnage, 28 kegs of musket-flints are equal to 18 cwt; and 10 kegs of pistol, 3 cwt. 2 qrs.

FOOT. A measure of length, divided into twelve equal parts or inches, each of which are generally subdivided into eight parts, but frequently into ten.

The following table will be found useful for the more easy calculating the contents of a superficies or solid, the dimensions of which are given in feet, inches, and eighths of an inch; as it exhibits the corresponding fraction of a foot to every eighth of an inch, and thereby saves the trouble of working that problem by the complex rule of *duodecimals*, which can be so much more readily performed by simple decimals. The first two figures of the decimal will be sufficiently exact for common purposes, and thus the operation will be facilitated.

In.	8ths.	Decim.	In.	8ths.	Decim.	In.	8ths.	Decim.	In.	8ths.	Decim.
			3	0....	.250	6	0....	.500	9	0....	.750
0	1....	.010		1....	.260		1....	.510		1....	.760
	2....	.020		2....	.271		2....	.521		2....	.771
	3....	.031		3....	.281		3....	.531		3....	.781
	4....	.041		4....	.292		4....	.542		4....	.792
	5....	.052		5....	.302		5....	.552		5....	.802
	6....	.062		6....	.312		6....	.562		6....	.812
	7....	.072		7....	.323		7....	.573		7....	.823
1	0....	.083	4	0....	.333	7	0....	.583	10	0....	.833
	1....	.094		1....	.344		1....	.594		1....	.844
	2....	.104		2....	.354		2....	.604		2....	.854
	3....	.115		3....	.365		3....	.614		3....	.864
	4....	.125		4....	.375		4....	.625		4....	.875
	5....	.135		5....	.385		5....	.635		5....	.885
	6....	.146		6....	.396		6....	.646		6....	.896
	7....	.156		7....	.406		7....	.656		7....	.906
2	0....	.167	5	0....	.417	8	0....	.667	11	0....	.917
	1....	.177		1....	.427		1....	.677		1....	.927
	2....	.187		2....	.437		2....	.687		2....	.937
	3....	.198		3....	.448		3....	.698		3....	.948
	4....	.208		4 ..	.458		4....	.708		4....	.958
	5....	.219		5....	.469		5....	.719		5....	.968
	6....	.229		6....	.479		6....	.729		6....	.979
	7....	.239		7....	.489		7..	.739		7....	.989

FORMERS. Round pieces of wood, fitted to the diameter of the bore of a gun, and round which the cartridge, paper, or cotton, is rolled before it is sewed or fastened.

To FUMIGATE. To medicate or heal by vapours; to clear or purify the air of any infected place, by smoke, &c. The frequent fumigation of ships is highly necessary, in order to prevent diseases produced by confined or infected air. The materials may be brimstone with saw-dust, or brimstone thrown over hot coals. Nitre, to which a little vitriolic acid is added; or common salt, with the same addition of vitriolic acid. Gunpowder wetted, or the heated loggerhead in the pitch-pot. The operation should always be performed under the eye of a medical officer, to prevent an improper expenditure of the respective articles applied.

Dr. James Carmichael Smyth's method of fumigating with nitrous acid, as published by order of the Admiralty, is as follows:

Such a number of pipkins as may be necessary are to be two thirds filled with sand previously heated. In this heated sand is to be immersed a gallipot, into which is to be poured one measure of concentrated vitriolic acid, when it has acquired some degree of heat: a measure of the pure nitre, in powder, is then to be gradually added, and the mixture stirred with the glass spatula until the vapour arises in considerable quantity. The pipkins are then to be carried to every part of the ship where foul air is expected to lodge.

FUSES. Wooden tubes, made use of to fire the charge of a shell. They are filled with combustible composition, and furnished at the end with a quick-match. The composition is, saltpetre, 3lb. 4oz.; sulphur, 1lb.; and mealed powder, 2lb.

DIAMETERS OF FUSES AND COMPOSITION.

Species.	Diameter of fuse.			Composition.			Drove by 1 man in 1 day.
	Below the cup.	At the bottom.	At the cup.	Diameter.	Length.	Time it burns.	
Inches.	Inch.	Inches.	Inches.	Inches.	Inches.	Seconds.	No.
13	2.1	1.575	2.49	.5	8.4	35	25
10	1.8	1.35	2.13	.438	7.2	33	25
8	1.3	1.25	1.78	.375	6.37	29	30
5½	1.1	.825	1.3	.275	4.4	18	50
4⅖	1.0	.75	1.18	.25	3.5	15	700
Grenades.	0.8	.6	.9	.2	2.25		1000

The Diameter inside the cup is three diameters of the bore.

Depth of the cup .... 1¼ ditto.

Thickness of the wood at the bottom of the bore, 2 diameters.

The 13 and 10-inch fuses of the same length burn so nearly equal, that one common length answers both, as do the 8-inch, 5½, and 4⅖.—Therefore, to find the length of fuse for any range, multiply the time of flight by .22 for the 13 and 10-inch, and .24 for the 8, 5½, and 4⅖; which is the decimal part of an inch a fuse burns in a second. Fuses are thought to keep better by being painted; and, for field-service are often marked off with black lines into seconds and half seconds.

GRAPE-SHOT. A combination of small shot, included in a thick canvas bag, and corded strongly together, in a cylindrical form, equal in diameter to that of a ball adapted to a cannon.

The bag is made exactly to hold a bottom which is put into it;

as many shot are then thrown in as the grape is to contain. The whole is next quilted over with strong pack-thread, to keep the shot from moving. When finished, the bags are put into boxes for the purpose of being conveniently carried.

The number of shot in a grape varies according to the size of the guns; in sea-service nine is always the number; but for land it is increased to any number or size, from an ounce and a quarter in weight to four pounds. It forms the thickest fire that can be produced in the same space; and can be exceeded in effect only by the CASE-SHOT, already noticed.

The following statement exhibits the number and sorts of shot contained in the grapes, for guns of the different species.

GUNS.	Species of shot in grape.	Number in each.	Number in each box.
42-Pounders	4 lb.	9	4
32 ————	3	9	4
24 ————		9	6
18 ————	$1\frac{1}{4}$	9	8
12 ————	1	9	10
9 ————	13 ounces	9	12
6 ————	8	9	20
4 ————	6	9	20

GRAPPLING-IRONS. Implements of iron, composed of 4, 5, or 6, branches, bent round and pointed, with a ring at the root, to which a rope is fastened to hold by, when the grappling is thrown upon any thing, in order to bring it near, or to lay hold of it.

A FIRE-GRAPPLING nearly resembles the above, but is fitted with strong barbs instead of flukes, and is fixed at the yard-arms of a fire-ship, to grapple her adversary, and set her on fire. See FIRE-SHIP.

GRAVITATION. The exercise of gravity, or the pressure that one body exerts on another by the power of gravity.

GRAVITY. The cause by which all bodies tend towards a centre, or towards each other. The most familiar effect of this power is the WEIGHT of bodies, or their tendency towards the centre of the earth.

Gravity equally affects all bodies, without regard to bulk, figure, or matter; so that, abstracting from the resistance of the medium, as air, the most compact and the most loose the greatest and the smallest bodies would all descend through an equal space in the same time, as appears from the quick descent of every light body in an exhausted receiver. The space which bodies fall through in vacuo is $16\frac{1}{12}$ feet in the first second of time, in the latitude of London.

This power is the greatest at the earth's surface; whence it decreases both upwards and downwards: but not both ways in the same proportion; for, upwards the force of gravity is less, or decreases as the square of the distance from the centre increases; so that, at a double distance from the centre, above the surface, the force will be only one fourth of what it is at the surface; but, below the surface, the power decreases in the direct ratio of the distance from the centre. See ACCELERATION.

By SPECIFIC GRAVITY is meant the comparative difference in the weight or gravity of two bodies of equal bulk; hence called also relative or comparative gravity, because we judge of it by comparison.

The absolute gravity of a body is the force with which it tends downwards; and is always proportional to the density of the body without any regard to its magnitude; so that a pound of cork is as heavy as a pound of gold. But the specific gravity of bodies are their relative weights under the same magnitude, and are proportional to their density. Thus a cubic foot of lead is heavier than a cubic foot of fir; for lead, being more dense than fir, contains, under the same bulk, a greater quantity of matter.

LAWS OF THE SPECIFIC GRAVITY OF BODIES.

1. If two bodies be equal in bulk, their specific gravities are to each other as their weights, or as their densities.

2. If two bodies be of the same specific gravity or density, their absolute weights will be as their magnitudes.

3. In bodies of the same weight, the specific gravities are reciprocally as their bulks.

4. The specific gravities of all bodies are in a ratio compounded of the direct ratio of their weights and the reciprocal ratio of their magnitudes. And hence, again, the specific gravities are as the densities.

5. The absolute gravities or weights of bodies are in the compound ratio of their specific gravities and magnitudes or bulks.

6. The magnitudes of bodies are directly as their weights, and reciprocally as their specific gravities.

7. A body specifically heavier than a fluid, loses as much of its weight when immersed in it, as is equal to the weight of a quantity of the fluid of the same bulk or magnitude.

Hence, since the specific gravities are as the absolute gravities under the same bulk; the specific gravity of the fluid will be to that of the body immersed, as the part of the weight lost by the solid is to the whole weight.

And hence the specific gravities of fluids are as the weights lost by the same solid immersed in them.

In the following table of specific gravities, the numbers express the number of avoirdupois ounces in a cubic foot of each body; that of common or rain water being just 1000 ounces. To determine, therefore, the specific gravity of any substance heavier than water, weigh any given quantity of that substance in air, in a common balance, and afterwards weigh it in water, carefully noting the loss of weight; divide its whole absolute gravity, or weight of the substance in air by its loss of weight in water, and you will have its true specific gravity.

A TABLE OF SPECIFIC GRAVITIES.

Lead	11325	Ebony	1177	Rain-water	1000
Fine copper	9000	Pitch	1150	Oak	925
Gun metal	8784	Resin	1100	Ash	800
Fine brass	8350	Mahogany	1063	Beech	700
Iron from 7827 to 7645		Box wood	1030	Elm	600
Cast iron	7425	Sea-water	1030	Fir	548
Sand	1520	Tar	1015	Cork	240
Lignum vitæ	1327	River-water	1009	Common air	1.232

These numbers being the weight of a cubic foot, or 1728 cubic inches, of each of the bodies in avoirdupois ounces; by proportion, the quantity in any other weight, or the weight of any other quantity, may be readily known.

PROBLEM 1. *To find the Magnitude of any Body from its Weight.*

RULE. As the tabular specific gravity of the body
Is to its weight in avoirdupois ounces;

So is one cubic foot, or 1728 cubic inches,

To its content in feet or inches, respectively.

EXAMPLE 1. Required the content of an irregular piece of dry oak, which weighs 234 lb. or 3744 ounces. ?

Sp. gr. oz.   Oz.   Cub. In. Cub. In.
As 925 : 3744 :: 1628 : 6994¼ or 4 feet 8 inches, the cubic content.

EXAMPLE 2. How many cubic feet are there in a ton weight of dry elm, of which the specific gravity is 600oz. or 37½lb.?

lb. lb. in a ton. ft.   ft.
37½ : 2240 :: 1 : 59.73, the content.

PROBLEM 2. *To find the Weight of a Body from its Magnitude.*

RULE. As one cubic foot, or 1728 cubic inches,

Is to the content of the body,

So is its tabular specific gravity

To the weight of the body.

EXAMPLE. Required the weight of a piece of dry fir timber, 25 feet long, and 1 foot 6 inches square ?

The length 25 ft. × 1 ft. 6 in. × 1 ft. 6 in. = 56ft. 3 in. the content.

ft.   ft.   Tab. gr.
Therefore, as 1 : 56¼ :: 550 : the weight; or 1934 lbs. = 17 cwt. 30 lbs.

PROBLEM 3. *To find the Specific Gravity of a Body.*

1. If the body be heavier than water, weigh it both in water and out of water, and take the difference, which will be the weight lost in water. Then state the question thus :

As the weight lost in water

Is to the whole weight,

So is the specific gravity of water

To the specific gravity of the body.

A piece of fine copper weighed 9lb. but in water only 8lb. Required its specific gravity ?

lb. lb.   oz.   oz.
As 1 : 9 :: 1000 (the spec. grav. of water) : 9000 the specific gravity required.

2. If the body be lighter than water, so that it will not wholly sink, affix to it a piece of another body heavier than water, so that

Y

the whole may sink together. Then weigh them both together and separately, in water and out of it. Next find how much each loses in water, by subtracting its weight in water from its weight when out of it. Subtract the lesser of these remainders from the greater; then say,

As the last remainder
Is to the weight of the light body in air,
So is the specific gravity of water
To the specific gravity of the body.

Suppose a piece of cork weighs 25lb. in air, and that a piece of lead, which weighs 100lb. in air and 91.17 in water is affixed to it; and that the compound weighs 12lb. in water. Required the specific gravity of the cork.

Lead.		Compound.
100	in air	125
91.17	in water	12
8.83		113
		8.83

Then, as the last remainder........104.17 : 25 :: 1000 : 240, the specific gravity required.

GRENADES, GRANADES, or GRANADOES. Hollow balls or shells, of iron or other metal, which, being filled with fine powder, are fired by means of a small fuse, made of well-seasoned beech wood, and thrown either by the hand or a piece of ordnance. So soon as it is kindled, the case flies in pieces, to the great danger of all who stand near it.

There is a sort of Grenade which is thrown out of a mortar, which differs from the bomb or shell only by not having any handles to it.

HAND-GRENADES may be thrown to the distance of 13 fathoms. For their dimensions, see the word SHELL.

GUN. The word Gun includes most of the species of fire arms; mortars and pistols being almost the only kind excepted from this denomination. In the Navy, however, GUN is generally considered as synonimous with CANNON, which has been already described. See CANNON.

Under the present head we subjoin some general remarks on the mode of ascertaining the condition of the guns, as to their

defects; the preparation for throwing them overboard in bad
weather; and the number of them on each deck of every rate in
the Royal Navy, with their respective weights, &c.

CONDITION OF GUNS, remarks on. 1. A Gun sets rightly in
the carriage when you perceive the same distance between the gun
and carriage at the trunnion on one side as the other; and the
carriage is of a proper length when the pomilion comes over with
the end, or train, of the carriage, which measures five eighths
of the length of the bore of the piece.

2. SUPPOSE A SHOT SHOULD FETCH WAY in a gun when it is
secured, in bad weather? Observe, when a gun is properly housed,
half the tompion generally comes below the upper sill of the port,
which must be cut away; and then thrust in pieces of rope, or
rope sponge, and secure the shot; but, if no part of the tompion
comes below the upper sill of the port, drown the powder with
vinegar.

3. TO ASCERTAIN IF A GUN BE CRACKED or not :—Lay it as free
or hollow as possible, and ring it with a hammer; if suspected to
be cracked, smoke it; first stopping the vent as closely as possible. Then take a piece of lighted touch-wood, put it in the gun,
and put in the tompion closely. If the piece be sound the fire
will extinguish; but, if otherwise, will keep burning, and the
smoke will make its appearance through the crack.

4. TO CLEAR A GUN, WHEN THERE IS A BITT BROKEN IN BORING
DOWN :—Draw the charge, then put vinegar to the vent, and
keep it supplied till the vinegar is gone down; then take a large
priming-wire, press on the bitt, and it will go down into the
chamber.

5. THE QUANTITY OF METAL AT THE BREECH of a gun, greater
than that at the muzzle, is, in the first instance to obviate the
danger of its bursting; secondly, to prevent its recoiling too
violently; thirdly, that it may not heat too quickly in frequent
firing. The breech, also, meets the greatest resistance when the
piece is discharged.

6. PREPARATION FOR THROWING GUNS OVERBOARD in bad weather.—1. In the first place you are to cast loose the tackle-falls
from the guns, and secure the carriages to the ship's side with
them.

2. Then cast off your breechings, unreeve them from the

breeching-rings, and raise the guns, with the coins on edge, so that the outer part may take the sill of the port.

3. Have the forelock-keys ready to be taken out at a moment's notice, in order to throw back the capsquares.

4. Then, with two capstan-bars, one at each side of the gun fixed under and between the fuse and reinforce-rings, take great care at the same time to heave up the guns very briskly with the lee-roll of the ship, and the guns will then go clear of the ship's side overboard.

5. Those on the lower deck, are to be treated in the same manner as those on the upper deck, excepting that, in casting them loose, be very careful to have two tackles hooked as train tackles, in order to bear the weight of the guns, when bowsed from the ship's side, after the muzzle-lashings are cast loose, in order to lay the guns on their beds and coins, to ease them to the ship's side.

6. Be careful to have a man placed at the port-tackle-falls to let the ports down the moment the guns are out of the port-holes, to prevent the water coming into the ship.

For instructions on the arrangement of the tackles, &c. see GUN-TACKLES.

GUNS AND CARRONADES ON EACH DECK OF EVERY RATE.

NAMES OF THE DECKS. N.B. The length of a gun or carronade is reckoned from the face of the piece to the back part of the base-ring.	110 GUNS.					100 GUNS.					98 GUNS.				
	Number.	Species.	Length.	Mean weight of each gun.	Average weight of all the metal.	Number.	Species.	Length.	Mean weight of each gun.	Average weight of all the metal.	Number.	Species.	Length.	Mean weight of each gun.	Average weight of all the metal.
	No.	P.	ft.	Cwt.	Tons.	No.	P.	ft.	Cwt.	Tons.	No.	P.	ft.	Cwt.	Tons.
Guns on the Gun deck	30	32	9½	55¾		28	32	9½	55¾		28	32	9½	55¾	
Guns on the Middle deck	30	24	9½	50½		28	24	9½	50½		30	18	9	43	
Guns on the Upper deck	32	18	9	43	255¼	30	12	9	34	221	30	12	9	34	208¼
Guns on the Quarter deck	14	12	7½	29½		4	12	8½	32		0	0	0	0	
Guns on the Forecastle	4	12	8½	32		10	12	7½	29½		10	12	7½	29½	
Total of guns	110				255¼	100				221	98				208¼
Carronades on the Forecastle	2	32	4	17¼		2	32	4	17¼		2	32	4	17¼	
Carronades on the Round house	7	24	3½	13	6¼	6	24	3⅔	13	5½	6	18	3⅓	10	4¾
Carronades on the Quarter deck	0	0	0	0		0	0	0	0		0	0	0	0	
Total number and weight of guns and carronades	119				261½	108				226½	106				213
Total value of metal, at £20 per ton	£5230 0 0					£4530 0 0					£4260 0 0				

Guns and Carronades on each Deck of every Rate, continued.

NAMES OF THE DECKS.	90 GUNS. Number.	90 GUNS. Species.	90 GUNS. Length.	90 GUNS. Mean weight of each gun.	90 GUNS. Average weight of all the metal.	80 GUNS. Number.	80 GUNS. Species.	80 GUNS. Length.	80 GUNS. Mean weight of each gun.	80 GUNS. Average weight of all the metal.	74 GUNS (large.) Number.	74 GUNS (large.) Species.	74 GUNS (large.) Length.	74 GUNS (large.) Mean weight of each gun.	74 GUNS (large.) Average weight of all the metal.
	No.	P.	ft.	Cwt.	Tons.	No.	P.	ft.	Cwt.	Tons.	No.	P.	ft.	Cwt.	Tons.
Guns on the Gun deck	28	32	9½	55¾	208½	26	32	9½	55¼	167¼	30	32	9½	55¾	160
Guns on the Middle deck	30	18	9	43		26	18	9	43		0	0	0	0	
Guns on the Upper deck	30	12	9	34		24	9	9	29		30	18	9	43	
Guns on the Quarter deck	8	12	7½	29½		0	0	0	0		4	18	8	38	
Guns on the Forecastle	2	12	8½	32		4	6	7½	20½		2	18	9	43	
Total of guns	98				208½	80				167¼	66				160
Carronades on the Forecastle	2	32	4	17¼	4¾	2	32	4	7¼	4¾	2	32	4	17¼	13¼
Carronades on the Round house	6	18	3⅓	10		6	18	3⅓	10		6	18	3⅓	10	
Carronades on the Quarter deck	0	0	0	0		0	0	0	0		10	32	4	17¼	
Total number and weight of guns and carronades	106				213¼	88				172	84				173¼
Total value of metal at £20 per ton	£4265 0 0					£3440 0 0					£3465 0 0				

Guns and Carronades on each Deck of every Rate, continued.

NAMES OF THE DECKS.	74 GUNS (*small*).					.64 GUNS.					50 GUNS.				
	Number.	Species.	Length.	Mean weight of each gun.	Average weight of all the metal.	Number.	Species.	Length.	Mean weight of each gun.	Average weight of all the metal.	Number.	Species.	Length.	Mean weight of each gun.	Average weight of all the metal.
	No.	P.	ft.	Cwt.	Tons.	No.	P.	ft.	Cwt.	Tons.	No.	P.	ft.	Cwt.	Tons.
Guns on the Gun deck	28	32	9½	55¾		26	24	9½	50½		22	24	9	48	
Guns on the Middle deck	0	0	0	0		0	0	0	0		0	0	0	0	
Guns on the Upper deck	28	18	9	43.	152	26	18	9	43	137¼	22	12	8½	32	94¼
Guns on the Quarter deck	4	9	8½	27½		2	9	8½	27½		2	6	8	21½	
Guns on the Forecastle	14	9	7½	26		10	9	7½	26		4	6	7½	20½	
Total of guns	74				152	64				137¼	50				94¼
Carronades on the Forecastle	2	32	4	17¼		2	24	3⅔	13		2	24	3⅔	13	
Carronades on the Round house	6	18	3⅓	10	4¾	6	18	3⅓	10	4¼	6	12	2¾	6¼	5¾
Carronades on the Quarter deck	0	0	0	0		0	0	0	0		4	24	3⅓	13	
Total number and weight of guns and carronades	82				156¾	72				141½	62				100
Total value of Metal at £20 per ton	£3135 0 0					£2830 0 0					£2000 0 0				

Guns and Carronades on each Deck of every Rate, continued.

NAMES OF THE DECKS.	44 GUNS. Number.	Species.	Length.	Mean weight of each gun.	Average weight of all the metal.	38 GUNS. Number.	Species.	Length.	Mean weight of each gun.	Average weight of all the metal.	36 GUNS. Number.	Species.	Length.	Mean weight of each gun.	Average weight of all the metal.
	No.	P.	ft.	Cwt.	Tons.	No.	P.	ft.	Cwt.	Tons.	No.	P.	ft.	Cwt.	Tons.
Guns on the Gun deck	20	18	9	43		0	0	0	0		0	0	0	0	
Guns on the Middle deck	0	0	0	0		0	0	0	0		0	0	0	0	
Guns on the Upper deck	22	12	7½	29½	80½	28	18	8	38	65½	26	18	9	43	68
Guns on the Quarter deck	4	6	6	17		8	9	7	24½		10	9	7	24½	
Guns on the Forecastle	2	6	6½	18		2	9	7½	26		0	0	0	0	
Total of Guns	48				80½	38				65½	36				68
Carronades on the Forecastle	2	24	3⅔	3		0	0	0	0		2	32	4	17¼	
Carronades on the Round house	0	0	0	0	5¼	0	0	0	0	7	0	0	0	0	7
Carronades on the Quarter deck	6	24	3⅔	13		8	32	4	17¼		6	32	4	17¼	
Total number and weight of guns and carronades	56				85¾	46				72½	44				75
Total value of metal at £20 per ton	£1715 0 0					£1450 0 0					£1500 0 0				

Guns and Carronades on each Deck of every Rate, continued.

NAMES OF THE DECKS.	32 GUNS. Number.	32 GUNS. Species.	32 GUNS. Length.	32 GUNS. Mean weight of each gun.	32 GUNS. Average weight of all the metal.	28 GUNS. Number.	28 GUNS. Species.	28 GUNS. Length.	28 GUNS. Mean weight of each gun.	28 GUNS. Average weight of all the metal.	24 GUNS. Number.	24 GUNS. Species.	24 GUNS. Length.	24 GUNS. Mean weight of each gun.	24 GUNS. Average weight of all the metal.
	No.	P.	ft.	Cwt.	Tons.	No.	P.	ft.	Cwt.	Tons.	No.	P.	ft.	Cwt.	Tons.
Guns on the Gun deck	26	18	8	38	$54\frac{1}{2}$	24	9	7	$24\frac{1}{2}$	$32\frac{3}{4}$	22	9	7	$24\frac{1}{2}$	$27\frac{1}{2}$
Guns on the Quarter deck	6	6	6	17		4	6	6	17		2	6	6	17	
Guns on the Forecastle	0	0	0	0		0	0	0	0		0	0	0	0	
Total of guns	32				$54\frac{1}{2}$	28				$32\frac{3}{4}$	24				$27\frac{1}{2}$
Carronades on the Forecastle	2	24	$3\frac{2}{3}$	13	4	2	24	$3\frac{2}{3}$	13	4	2	24	$3\frac{2}{3}$	13	$4\frac{1}{4}$
Carronades on the Round house	0	0	0	0		0	0	0	0		0	0	0	0	
Carronades on the Quarter deck	4	24	$3\frac{2}{3}$	13		4	24	$3\frac{2}{3}$	13		6	18	$3\frac{1}{3}$	10	
Total number and weight of guns and carronades	38				$58\frac{1}{2}$	34				$36\frac{3}{4}$	32				$31\frac{3}{4}$
Total value of Metal at £20 per ton	£1170 0 0					£735 0 0					£635 0 0				

Guns and Carronades on each Deck of every Rate, continued.

NAMES OF THE DECKS.	20 GUNS.					18 GUNS.					16 GUNS.				
	Number.	Species.	Length.	Mean weight of each gun.	Average weight of all the metal.	Number.	Species.	Length.	Mean weight of each gun.	Average weight of all the metal.	Number.	Species.	Length.	Mean weight of each gun.	Average weight of all the metal.
	No.	P.	ft.	Cwt.	Tons.	No.	P.	ft.	Cwt.	Tons.	No.	P.	ft.	Cwt.	Tons.
Guns on the Gun deck	20	9	7½	26		18	6	6	17		16	6	6	17	
Guns on the Quarter deck	4	6	6	17	29½	0	0	0	0	15¼	0	0	0	0	13½
Guns on the Forecastle	0	0	0	0		0	0	0	0		0	0	0	0	
Total of Guns	24				29½	18				15¼	16				13½
Carronades on the Forecastle	2	12	2¾	6¼		2	12	2¾	6¼		0	0	0	0	
Carronades on the Round house	0	0	0	0	⅝	0	0	0	0	2½	0	0	0	0	0
Carronades on the Quarter deck	0	0	0	0		6	12	2¾	6¼		0	0	0	0	
Total number and weight of guns and carronades	26				30⅛	26				17¾	16				13½
Total value of metal at £20 per ton	£602 10 0					£355 0 0					£270 0 0				

GUNNER. Having already shown at large, in a preceding section, the duty of a master-gunner in the Royal Navy, we shall subjoin under the present head only a series of general orders which have been recommended to be issued by the captain to this officer.

1. The magazine is never to be opened without an express order of the commanding-officer; and then to be attended by the gunner, the master-at-arms, or ship's corporal, and a midshipman in the light-room.

2. No cartridges containing powder, or powder horns, are to be kept in the store-rooms or passages.

3. Every opportunity is to be taken in airing the store-rooms; at which time application is to be made for sentinels to be placed at the doors.

4. When at sea, the gunner is to examine the guns every morning and evening, and report their being secure to the first lieutenant.

5. No spirit or wine is to be kept in the passages or storeroom.

6. When the decks are washed, the gunner is to appropriate a part of his crew to clean the passages and store-rooms.

7. The gunner is to be very careful that the small-arms, and locks for the guns, are kept in good order, and with proper flints in them.

8. The gunner is to be very particular in turning the cartridges frequently, and likewise the powder-barrels.

9. A sufficient number of wads is to be always kept complete; but the gunner is to instruct the people at their quarters, not to put more than one wad into each gun.

10. The gunner is to use great pains in instructing the people at their quarters with the exercise of their guns, and the manner and intention of elevating and depressing them.

11. The gunner is to represent the necessity of getting his stores upon deck to air, whenever they require it.

12. No fire-arms, powder, or ammunition, is ever to be taken out of the ship without the orders of the commanding-officer.

13. The lower-deck guns are never to be loaded on going to sea without express orders.

GUNNER'S CREW. An intelligent officer has remarked that

z 2

the gunner's crew in a ship appears to be a class much neglected; for, instead of making them skilful artillery-men, and retaining them principally for that service, they are too often suffered to remain totally ignorant of it, and only perform that part of the duty of seamen which is attached to their station. As gunners, it was certainly intended, from the name they bear, that they should be acquainted with some part of the art of gunnery; and, if this were the case, they ought first to be well acquainted with it themselves, that it may become their duty to instruct the raw hands in the knowledge of it afterwards.

The Gunner's Yeoman ought to know where all the gunner's stores are to be found in the dark; and it will be considered as an instance of great negligence if the gunner is obliged to leave his quarters under the intention or pretence of looking after any of his stores.

GUN-POWDER. A composition of saltpetre, sulphur, and charcoal, well mixed together and granulated, which readily takes fire and explodes with amazing force, being one of the strongest propellants known. To make the powder, take the three articles above-mentioned, reduce them to a fine powder, and beat them for some time in a stone mortar with a wooden pestle, wetting the mixture occasionally with water, so as to form the whole into an uniform paste, which is afterwards reduced to grains by passing it through a sieve of copper wire; and, in this form, being carefully dried it becomes the common powder. For great quantities, mills are used, by which more work may be done in one day than a man can do in a hundred.

Proportions of the different ingredients for making Gunpowder, by different powers in Europe.

	England.	France.	Sweden.	Poland.	Italy.	Russia.
Saltpetre......	75	75	75	80.5	$76\frac{1}{4}$	70
Sulphur........	10	$9\frac{1}{2}$	9	8	11	$11\frac{1}{4}$
Charcoal......	15	$15\frac{1}{4}$	16	12	$12\frac{1}{2}$	$13\frac{1}{4}$
	100	100	100	100	100	100

Proofs of Powder.—The first examination of powder in the king's mills, is by rubbing it in the hands, to find whether it contains any irregular hard lumps. The second is by blasting two drachms of each sort on a copper-plate, and in this comparing it with an approved powder : in this proof it should not emit any sparks, nor leave any beads of foulness on the copper. It is then compared with an improved powder, in projecting an iron ball of 64lbs. from an 8-inch mortar, with a charge of two ounces. The best cylinder powder generally gives about 180 feet range, and pit 150 ; but the weakest powder, or powder that has been re-dried, &c. only from 107 to 117 feet.

The merchant's powder, before it is received into the king's service, is tried against powder of the same kind made at the king's mills ; and it is received if it gives a range of one twentieth less than the king's powder with which it is compared.—In this comparison both sorts are tried on the same day, and at the same time, and under exactly the same circumstances.

The proof of fine grained, or musket-powder, is with a charge of four drachms from a musket-barrel, to perforate, with a steel ball, a certain number of half-inch wet elm boards, placed three quarters of an inch asunder, and the first 39 feet 10 inches from the barrel : the king's powder generally passes through 15 or 16, and re-stoved powder from 9 to 12.—The last trial of powder is by exposing about one pound of each sort, accurately weighed, to the atmosphere for 17 or 18 days ; during which time, if the materials are pure, it will not increase any thing material in weight, by attracting moisture from the atmosphere.

In this exposure 100lbs. of good gunpowder should not absorb more than 12oz. or somewhat less than one per cent.

TABLE showing the QUANTITIES of GUNPOWDER in good condition, appointed to be used with the different species of ordnance, &c. on-board his Majesty's ships.

Cylindric Powder.		For service.		For salutes and scaling.
		With one shot; being one third of the weight of one shot.	With two shots; being one fourth of the weight of one shot.	
			lb. oz.	lb. oz
Cannon or Guns.	42-Pounders .	0	10 8	3 4
	32.........	10 10	8 0	2 12
	24.........	8 0	6 0	2 0
	18.........	6 0	4 8	1 8
	12.........	4 0	3 0	1 0
	9.........	3 0	2 4	0 12
	6.........	2 0	1 8	0 8
	4.........	1 5	1 0.	0 6
	3.........	1 0	0 12	0 4
	2.........	0 10	0 8	0 3
	1.........	0 5	0 4	0 1
	½.........	0 2	0 2	0 1
Carronades	68-Pdrs...	5 10	....	2 0
	42........	3 8	....	1 8
	32........	2 10	....	1 4
	24........	2 0	....	1 0
	18........	1 8	....	1 0
	12........	1 0	....	0 12

For wall-pieces....proof..2oz. 8dr.   Service..0oz. 10dr.
Muskets.............0   12   ——   0   6
Pistols.............0   6   ——   0   3

It is recommended by the admiralty that the use of two shots for each round in guns should be restrained as much as possible, it having appeared, from various experiments which have been made with different species of sea-service ordnance, that, after firing twenty rounds repeatedly at only the interval of five minutes between each round, the gun has become so violently heated as to render it extremely hazardous to continue the firing at that rate.

It is also suggested, that the rule which captains of ships of war have hitherto practised, in reducing the charges of powder for carronades as well as for cannon, when the pieces become warm in a long engagement, may be rigidly attended to.

The proportion of gunpowder delivered to his Majesty's navy consists of the following quantities and descriptions, viz.

For foreign service .. $\begin{cases} \text{5-7ths of red L. G.} \\ \text{2-7ths of white L. G.} \end{cases}$

For Channel service . $\begin{cases} \text{4-7ths of red L. G.} \\ \text{3-7ths of white L. G.} \end{cases}$

It is to be understood that the red L. G. gunpowder is to be used for distant engagements, and the white L. G. gunpowder for close engagements; and that the white L. G. gunpowder only be used for scaling or salutes.

For an explanation of the marks on the powder-barrels, see MARKS.

TABLE showing the FULL PROPORTION of POWDER for GUNS, in from 5 to 100 cartridges.

Guns.	Cart. 5		Cart. 10		Cart. 20		Cart. 30		Cart. 40		Cart. 50		Cart. 100	
Pounders.	lb.	oz.	lb.	oz.	lb.	oz.	lb.	oz.	lb.	oz.	lb.	oz.	lb.	oz.
3	5	0	10	0	20	0	30	0	40	0	50	0	100	0
4	6	14	13	12	27	4	41	0	54	12	68	8	138	0
6	10	0	20	0	40	0	60	0	80	0	100	0	200	0
9	15	0	30	0	60	0	90	0	120	0	150	0	300	0
12	20	0	40	0	80	0	120	0	160	0	200	0	400	0
18	30	0	60	0	120	0	180	0	240	0	300	0	600	0
24	40	0	80	0	160	0	240	0	320	0	400	0	800	0
32	53	7	106	14	213	12	320	0	427	12	534	12	1069	12

PROPORTIONS of POWDER for the supply of the different classes of ships in his Majesty's Navy; for foreign and Channel service.

Rates of ships.	Total quantity of barrels.		
	Whole Barrels.	Half Barrels.	Half Barrels for priming.
100 { Foreign	479		5
{ Channel	431		5
98 { Foreign	402		5
{ Channel	356		5
90 { Foreign	355		5
{ Channel	320		5
80 { Foreign	292		4
{ Channel	257		4

Proportión of Powder, &c. continued.

Rates of ships.	Total quantity of barrels.		
	Whole Barrels.	Half Barrels.	Half Barrels for priming.
74 { Foreign	30		4
{ Channel	295		4
64 { Foreign	256		3
{ Channel	232		3
50 { Foreign	194		3
{ Channel	174		3
38 { Foreign	147		2
{ Channel	128		2
36 { Foreign	138		2
{ Channel	120		2
32 { Foreign		182	2
{ Channel		154	2
28 { Foreign		140	1
{ Channel		122	1
14 { Foreign		55	1
{ Channel		49	1

To restore damaged Gunpowder to its proper strength.

If powder be kept long in a damp place, it will become weak, and be formed partly into hard lumps, a sure sign of its being damaged. When powder is thus found, you will see at the bottom of the barrel some saltpetre, which, by being wet, will separate from the sulphur and coal, and fall to the bottom of the vessel, settling there in the form of white downy matter. The only method to prevent this is, to move the barrels as often as convenient, and place them on their opposite sides or ends ; but, though the greatest care be taken, length of time will greatly lessen the primitive strength.

If it be supposed that the powder has received but little damage, spread it on canvas or dry boards, and expose it to the sun ; then add to it an equal quantity of good powder, and mix them well ; and, when thoroughly dry, barrel, and put it in a dry place. But, if the powder be found entirely bad, first ascertain what it weighed when good ; then, by weighing it again, you will find how much it has lost by the separation and evaporation of the saltpetre ; then add to it as much refined saltpetre as it has wasted ; but, as a large quantity of this would be difficult to mix,

it will be best to put a proportion of nitre to every 20lb. of powder; when done, put one of these proportions into a mealing
table, and grind it till you have brought it to an impalpable powder, then searce it with a fine sieve; but, if any remain in the
sieve that will not pass, return it to the table and grind it again,
until you have made it all fine enough to go through; being thus
well ground and sifted, it must be granulated thus; first you
must have some copper wire sieves, made to suit the required size
of the grains; (these are called corning sieves or grainers,) which
are to be filled with the composition; then shake them about, and
the powder will pass through, formed into grains. Having thus
corned it, set it to dry in the sun; and, when quite dry, searce
it with a fine hair sieve, to separate the dust from the grains.
This dust may, be worked with another mixture, so that none may
be wasted. Sometimes it may happen that the weight when good
cannot be known; in this case add to each pound one ounce or
one ounce and a half of saltpetre, according to the decay of the
powder; then grind sift and granulate it, as before.

If you have a large quantity that appears to be quite spoiled,
the best way is to extract the saltpetre from it , as it can scarcely
be worth while to attempt its recovery. See SALTPETRE.

GUN-TACKLES. ' Gun-tackling consists of ropes, blocks, &c.
and is to run the guns in and out, and to secure them to the
ship's side in bad weather. The BREECHING is a rope to secure
and prevent the gun from recoiling too much. It is formed with
a cont-splice in the middle, which passes over the pomilion, or
cascable, of the gun, and through ring-bolts in each side of the
carriage, and is clinched to large ring-bolts in the side of the
ship, on each side of the port. PREVENTER-BREECHING is similar
to the breeching, and is used for additional security. The PORT-
TACKLE is used to run the gun out of the port, and keep it in a
situation for firing. It has a single block that hooks to the eye-
bolts in the sides of the carriage, and a single or double block,
for 32 pounders, that hooks to other ring-bolts by the sides of
the ports. RELIEVING or TRAIN-TACKLES are to run guns in, and
so retain them, by hooking the double block of the tackle to an
eye-bolt in the train of the carriage, and its single block to another eye-bolt in the deck; one of which is fixed opposite to every
gun. COINS, or QUOINS, (besides those used to elevate and de-

press the gun,) are tapered pieces of wood, like wedges, that are thrust under the trucks of the carriages, and there kept by being nailed to the deck; they are used in keeping the gun securely housed.

Guns are housed or secured by taken out the coins and lowering the breech, so that the muzzle may take the upper part of the port. When thus placed, the two sides of the breeching are frapped under the gun at the muzzle near the breast part of the carriage. The muzzle of the gun is confined by several turns of a rope, or gasket, made fast to it, and the eye-bolts that are fixed in the ship's side, over the midship of the port.

The lower-deck guns are usually kept housed and secured when at sea.

It is requisite to keep your second set of breechings clenched and reeved through the proper ring-bolts before you come into action. In winter-time or stormy weather, coil them up and stop them to the ship's side.

In double breechings, take care to have your frapping of the second breeching bear equal strain with the first, that all the iron-work may bear an equal part.

If you have occasion to coin your guns with the new pattern coins, the weather ones are to be coined as close as possible to the trucks; but the lee ones must be an inch or two free, on account of the ship's side falling home in case of veering, or going on the other tack.

If a gun should break adrift, or draw the iron-work, from the violent rolling of the ship, cut down the hammocks and check her; then lash and secure it in the best manner you can, until the gale is over.

PROPORTIONS of BREECHINGS, TACKLE-FALLS, and MUZZLE-LASHINGS.

BREECHINGS. Three times the length of the bore of the gun is the length of a breeching.

TACKLE-FALLS. Six times the length of the bore of the gun is the length of a tackle-fall.

MUZZLE-LASHINGS. All muzzle-lashings are of five fathoms, each of 2½-inch rope.

Table showing the number and lengths of **Breechings, Tackles, Muzzle-lashings, Port-ropes,** and **port-tackle-falls,** for the different rates.

Rates of the ships.	Number of guns.	Pounders.	Length.	Number on each deck.	What decks they are on.	Breechings. Size on each deck.	Breechings. Length in feet.	Breechings. No. on each deck.	Tackles. Size on each deck.	Tackles. Length in fathoms.	Tackles. No. on each deck.	Muzzle lashings. Size.	Muzzle lashings. Length in fathoms.	Muzzle lashings. Number.	Port ropes. Size on each deck.	Port ropes. Length in feet.	Port ropes. No. on each deck.	Port ropes. Total for each ship.	Port tackle falls. Size on each deck.	Port tackle falls. Length in feet.	Port tackle falls. No. on each deck.	Port tackle falls. Total for each ship.
						In			In			In			In				In			
1st.	100	32	10	28	Lower....	6	30	28	2½	10	56	2½	4	28	3	21	32	76	2	24	32	72
		24	10	28	Middle...	6	30	28	2½	10	56	—	—	—	2½	16	26	—	2	21	16	—
		11	9½	28	Upper.. .	5	28	28	2	8	56	—	—	—	2	14	14	—	2	18	14	—
		6	9	16	Quart. & Forecast.	4	27	16	2	7	32	—	—	—	2	10	4	—	—	—	—	—
2nd	90	32	9½	26	Lower....	6	28	26	2½	10	52	2½	4	26	2½	21	32	74	2	24	32	70
		18	9½	26	Middle...	5	28	26	2½	9	52	—	—	—	2	16	24	—	2	21	24	—
		9	9½	26	Upper....	4	28	26	2	8	52	—	—	—	2	14	14	—	—	—	—	—
		6	9	12	Quart. & forecast.	4	27	12	2	7	24	—	—	—	2	10	4	—	—	—	—	—
3rd	80	32	9½	26	Lower....	6	28	26	2½	10	52	2½	4	26	2½	21	32	64	2	24	24	52
		12	9½	26	Middle...	5	28	26	2	8	52	—	—	—	2	16	24	—	2	21	24	—
		6	9½	28	Upper & Quarter.	4	27 25	28	2	7	56	—	—	—	2	10	8	—	—	—	—	—
3rd	74	24	9½	26	Lower....	6	28	26	2½	10	52	2½	4	26	2½	21	30	46	2	21	28	40
		12	9	26	Upper....	5	27	26	2	8	52	—	—	—	2	16	12	—	2	21	12	—
		6	9 8	18	Quart. & forecast.	4	27 24	18	2	7	36	—	—	—	2	10	4	—	—	—	—	—
4th	60	24	9½	24	Lower....	6	28	24	2½	10	48	2½	4	24	2½	21	28	42	2	21	28	38
		9	9	26	Upper....	4	27	26	2	8	52	—	—	—	2	16	10	—	2	28	10	—
		6	9 8	10	Quart. & forecast.	4	27 24	10	2	7	20	—	—	—	2	10	4	—	—	—	—	—
4th	50	18	9	22	Lower....	5	27	26	2½	9	44	2½	4	22	2½	21	24	40	2	18	24	24
		9	8½	22	Upper....	4	25	22	2	7	44	—	—	—	2	16	12	—	—	—	—	—
		6	9 8	6	Quart. & forecast.	4	27 24	6	2	7	12	—	—	—	2	10	4	—	—	—	—	—
5th	40	12	9	20	Lower....	5	27	20	2	8	40	2½	3	20	2	18	22	30	2	18	20	20
		6	8½	20	Upper....	4	25	0	2	7	40	—	—	—	2	10	8	—	—	—	—	—
	32	9	8½	8	Lower....	4	25	8	2	7	16	2½	3	8	2	18	10	18	2	18	8	8
		6	8	20	Upper....	4	24	20	2	7	40	—	—	—	2	10	8	—	—	—	—	—
		4	7½	2	Quarter....	4	22	2	2	6	4	—	—	—	—	—	—	—	—	—	—	—
6th	20	6	7	20	Upper....	4	22	20	2	6	10	—	—	—	—	10	20	20	2	18	20	20

The length of carronade-breechings and port-tackle-falls is left to the discretion of the gunner.

HAND-GRENADES. Small grenades, of from two to three inches diameter, calculated to produce much effect upon an enemy, though but seldom used. See GRENADE.

HAND-SPEC, or HAND-SPIKE, used in gunnery, is a wooden lever, five or 6 feet long, flattened at the lower end and tapering towards the other, useful in moving guns to their places after having been fired and loaded again, &c.

To **HANG-FIRE.** A gun is said to hang fire when the flame does not instantly communicate from the pan to the charge; which defect may arise from the powder's being damp or the vent foul.

HARDENING. Imparting a greater degree of hardness to metals, &c. more than they originally possessed.

There are several ways of hardening iron or steel, as by hammering them, quenching them when red-hot in oil, cold water, &c.

CASE-HARDENING is a superficial conversion of iron into steel, as if it were casing it with a thin coat of harder matter. It is thus performed:—Take cow-horn or hoof, dry it well in an oven, and beat it to powder; put equal quantities of this powder and of bay-salt into stale urine, or white-wine-vinegar, and mix them well together; cover the iron or steel all over with this mixture, and wrap it up in loam or plate iron, so as the mixture touch every part of the work: then put it in the fire, and blow the coals to it, till the whole lump have a blood-red heat, but no higher; lastly, take it out and quench it.

HEAD. The fore part of the cheeks of a gun or howitzer carriage.

HONEY-COMB. A cavity or flaw in a gun, resembling a cell in the honey-comb of a bee. The board of ordnance rejects all guns having an honey-comb of one ninth of an inch deep, as being unfit for service.

To find if a piece of ordnance be honey-combed; take a looking-glass and reflect the beams of the sun into the chase, which will illuminate and render visible the pores in the concave superficies: but if the sun does not shine, put a candle upon the end of a half-pike, and thrust it into the chase, and that will show the pores. This method is used chiefly in examining mortars. For Cannon, see CANNON. See, also, the words GUN and PROOF.

HORIZON. The circle which divides the visible from the invisible part of the earth. Hence HORIZONTAL; signifying parallel to the horizon, or on a level: also, HORIZONTAL-RANGE, or level range of a piece of ordnance, being the line it describes when directed parallel to the horizon.

HOWITZER or HOWITZ. A kind of small mortar, or short gun, mounted upon a field-carriage, like a gun; but differing from the latter in having the trunnions at the middle instead of the end. It has been superceded in the sea-service by the carronade.

INCIDENCE. The direction by which one body strikes upon another. See ANGLE, page 104.

To INDENT. To draw or value upon. To *Indent* for supplies therefore signifies to draw or give an order for such, &c.

INITIAL VELOCITY. A term frequently occurring in this work, and signifying the velocity acquired by a ball or shot in the first instant of its motion, from the explosion.

KEYS of GUN-CARRIAGES, are those denominated *Fore-lock Keys, Spring Keys,* &c.

FORE-LOCK KEYS serve to pass through the lower end of bolts, in order to fasten them.

SPRING KEYS are those which may be used in the same manner, but differently made, being formed of two pieces like two springs, one laid over the other. When put into the eye-bolts they are pinched together at the ends, so that, when in, they open again; and the motion of the carriage cannot disturb or put them out.

KEYS with *Chains* and *Staples* are fixed on the side pieces of a carriage or mortar-bed, to fasten the cap-square, by passing through the eyes of the eye-bolts.

KIT. A composition made of resin, 9lb. pitch, 6lb. and tallow, 1lb. used for the last covering of carcasses. To apply it, first break it into small pieces, and put it into an iron pot over a fire, where it must be kept in agitation until it be thoroughly dissolved. When very hot and completely liquid, it is fit for use.

LADLES, used in gunnery, are made of copper, to hold the powder for loading guns, with long wooden handles, when cartridges are not used.

LEVEL. The GUNNER's LEVEL, for levelling pieces of ordnance, consists of a triangular brass plate, of a radius of about four inches, at the lower part of which is a portion of a circle, divided into 45 degrees; which angle is sufficient for the highest elevation of guns, &c. : on the centre of this segment is screwed a piece of brass, by means of which it may be fixed at pleasure ; the end of this piece of brass is made so as to serve for a plummet and index, in order to show the degree of elevation. The instrument has also a brass foot, to set upon the piece, so that, when it is horizontal, the instrument will be perpendicular. The foot is to be placed on the piece to be elevated, in such a manner that the point of the plummet may fall on the proper degree, &c.

An improved and curious instrument of this description has been invented by Colonel Congreve, of the Royal Artillery, containing numerous particulars not shown on the common level, with various useful tables, &c.

LIGHT and FIRE COMPOSITION. *Light composition* consists of 8 parts of saltpetre, 4 parts of sulphur, and one part of antimony, or sometimes of other proportions, together with some mealed and grained powder.

The Fire composition contains 9 parts of pitch, 2 of tallow, 18 of powder, with some saltpetre and sulphur.

These compositions are mixed together, after the fusile ingredients have been melted over a fire : they are preserved, when prepared, in hard lumps. See COMPOSITION.

LINCH PINS. The pins which pass through the ends of the arms of an axle-tree to keep the trucks or wheels from slipping off.

LOOP, in a GUN-CARRIAGE. A ring made of iron, fastened one on the front of a fore axle-tree, and two on each side, through which the rope or tackle pass, whereby the guns are moved backwards and forwards.

MAGAZINE CHARGE. Remarks relative to :

1. Particular attention should be paid to the examination of the cases of wood, which are supplied to the Royal Navy, for conveying the cartridges of powder from the magazines to the guns, in order to ascertain that the cartridges may be easily admitted into the cases without forcing them down.

2. A supply of powder-barrels, water-tight, to be delivered for

the lower tier of ships' magazines, that the gunpowder may not be damaged by the bilge-water of the ships. The barrels containing red L. G. gunpowder are to be marked with the broad arrow in red paint, as large as the bouge of the barrel will admit ; and the barrels containing white L. G. gunpowder with white paint. Those barrels contain 80lbs. only, and half-barrels 40lbs.

3. Should your ship be stowed for foreign service, without having a very roomy magazine, it would be full, and you would be obliged to put as many of your barrels as you emptied at first under the palletting scuttles, towards the fore-peek. It will then be necessary to preserve the barrels from the wet, by dunnaging under them with the wooden hoops you strip off, or they would be otherwise thrown overboard.

4. We would also recommend that the tools for the magazine, such as adzes, drivers, and vises, be carefully hung up over the filling-room before the bitts, on wooden pegs, or copper nails, fixed for the purpose, before the powder is shipped. The copper funnels, shovels, and powder-measures, should also be kept ready for a minute's notice.

5. When your racks are complete with filled cartridges, and the barrels regularly and securely stowed, you can arrange your bundles of empty cartridges on the barrels, laying the tanned hides over them. This is a good expedient to keep them dry and ready to fill when required.

6. Twenty rounds of powder is a good proportion to keep constantly filled, besides what is in the cases of wood and salt-boxes. Five at full allowance always to be handed up first ; the other fifteen to be gradually reduced to what the metal will bear, which is two thirds and under.

7. Remember, before you go into the powder-room, that the people who assist you have nothing about them that can take fire, and see that they put on the slippers for that purpose.

8. When at work in the powder-room, never face the light when you offer any stroke to hoop or unhoop a barrel, lest the mallet should fly out of your hand towards the light. Be careful and place the driver on the hoops, striking it with the adze ; and put in the proper heads again when emptied, as it may be required to start the cartridges back again into the barrels.

9. When you have completed filling your cartridges with pow-

der, sweep well the flooring or palletting with a hair-broom, putting the sweepings into a basket lined with canvas, which should be sent up to the head to be thrown over-board by one of your mates or yeoman.

10. Then stow your powder-cases and salt-boxes, having good beckets and lanyards to them, all being filled with full allowance ready for handing up, keeping a sufficient number near the foot of the ladder for the use of the upper deck guns, as signals, &c. Come last out of the magazine, see your lights out safe, and be sure to make your people sweep and swab well the passage-ways. Return the keys yourself; and, if in health, always receive them in person from the commanding-officer.

11. You are to advise with your captain once a month, and to turn the cartridges which are filled with powder in the magazine, breaking the lumps with your hands. See that they are in a fit state to be handed on deck, and turn and examine the barrels.

12. If you suspect that any loose powder may have gone through the seams of the palletting of the magazine, acquaint your captain when the ship comes into harbour to refit or be paid off, in order that the palletting may be taken up, and the powder removed. Accidents may otherwise happen, as has been the case, when the ship is taken in hand by the artificers of the dock-yard.

MANUAL EXERCISE. See EXERCISE.

MARKS on the heads of the barrels, distinguishing the different sorts of gunpowder.

No. 1. L. G.	} Cylinder.	
No. 2. S. G.	} Cylinder.	} Marked in red.
No. 3. F. G.	} Cylinder.	

S. A.—The dust from No. 3, and F. G. Cyr.

½ Cylinder } Mixed—marked L. G.
½ Restoved }

L. G. or F. G. in blue, is powder made of pit-coal.

| R. S. | { No. ¼ L. G. { No. 3 F. G. | } Marked in yellow, is restoved. |

The red L. F. G. in S. G. denotes powder entirely made of the cylinder charcoal, and is that which is always used in service.

The white L. G. being a mixed powder, is not so uniform as the other, and is therefore generally used in filling shells, or for any such other purposes as do not require much accuracy. All powder for service is mixed in proportions according to the strength, so as to bring it as nearly as possible to a mean and uniform force.

MARLINES. Tarred skains, or long wreaths, or lines, of untwisted hemp, dipped in pitch or tar, with which ropes are encircled to prevent their fretting or chafing in blocks, &c. They are usually put up for service in small parcels called *Skains*.

MASTER-AT-ARMS. An officer appointed to teach the officers and company of a ship the exercise of small arms; also to confine prisoners and place sentinels over them, and to superintend whatever relates to them during their confinement. He is also to observe that the fire and lights are all extinguished, so soon as the evening gun is fired, excepting those that are permitted by proper authority, or are under the inspection of sentinels. It is likewise his duty to attend the gang-way, when any boats arrive, and search them carefully, together with their rowers, that no spirituous liquors may be conveyed into the ship unless by permission of the commanding-officer. In these several duties he is assisted by proper attendants, called *Corporals*, who also relieve the sentinels, and each other, at the regular periods.

MATCH. A kind of rope, slightly twisted, and prepared to retain fire for the use of the ordnance, &c. COMMON or SLOW MATCH is made of hemp or coarse flax, spun like cord, but very slack; it is composed of three twists or strands, which are again covered with tow so that the twists do not appear: lastly, it is boiled in the lees of old wine. This, when once lighted at the end, burns on gradually, without going out until the whole be consumed.

The Common Match may also be made by boiling the hemp for 24 hours in a ley of ashes, lime, and water; or merely of beech ashes and water. A good match ought to burn equally and gradually, and with a good hard point; to light with ease, and feel soft and dry. In order to be always fit for use, they should be carefully kept where they can imbibe no moisture.

B B

The slow match used by the English is made by contract : one yard of it will burn about eight hours.—The French slow match is usually made by soaking light twisted white rope for three days in a strong ley.—It burns about three feet in six hours.

Slow match was made at Gibraltar, during the last siege, in the following manner : eight ounces of saltpetre were put into a gallon of water, and just made to boil over a slow fire ; strong blue paper was then wetted with the liquor, and then hung to dry. When dry, each sheet was rolled up tight, and the outward edge pasted down, to prevent its opening : half a sheet, thus prepared, will burn three hours.

The French have lately made their slow-match by soaking the rope in a solution of sugar of lead and rain water : in the proportion of three fourths of an ounce of sugar of lead to one pint of water : and this they esteem as preferable to the old sort.

QUICK-MATCH is made of three cotton or worsted strands, drawn into lengths, and put into a kettle, just covered with white-wine-vinegar, and a quantity of saltpetre and mealed powder then added and boiled till well mixed ; or, sometimes saltpetre only is used ; taking the strands out hot and laying them into a trough with some mealed powder, moistened with spirits of wine, thoroughly wrought into the cotton by rolling it backwards and forwards with the hands : when this is done, they are taken out separately, and dried upon a line.

The cotton match is generally made of such cotton as is put in candles, of several sizes, from one to six threads thick, according to the pipes it is designed for. The composition is, cotton, 1lb. 12oz. ; saltpetre, 1lb. 8oz. ; spirits of wine, 2 quarts ; water, 2 quarts ; isinglass, 3 gills ; and mealed powder, 10lb. That for the worsted match is, worsted, 10oz. ; mealed powder, 10lb. ; spirits of wine, 3 pints ; and white-wine-vinegar, 3 pints.

The worsted or cotton may be laid evenly in an earthen or other pan, and the different ingredients poured over it, and about half the powder : being left a short time to soak ; afterwards wound smoothly on a reel, and laid to dry : the remaining half of the powder then sifted over it ; and it will be ready for use when dry.

MEALED. Pulverized, or reduced to fine powder.

MEASURES. A TABLE of those measures which are useful at sea.

WINE.

10	gallons, an anchor of brandy or rum.
18	gallons, a runlet.
31½	gallons, a half-hogshead.
42	gallons, a tierce or barrel.
84	gallons, a puncheon.
63	gallons, a hogshead.
126	gallons, a pipe or butt.
252	gallons, a tun.

DRY-MEASURES.

2 pints are equal to one quart.
4 quarts, one gallon.
2 gallons, one peck.
8 gallons, one bushel.

WINCHESTER MEASURE.

27	gallons, a half-hogshead	⎫
36	gallons, a barrel	⎪
54	gallons, a hogshead	Of beer.
168	gallons, a butt	⎪
72	gallons, a puncheon	⎪
216	gallons, a tun	⎭
8	gallons, a firkin	⎫
24	gallons, a half-hogshead	Of ale.
32	gallons, a barrel	⎪
48	gallons, a hogshead	⎭

LEAGERS.

The number multiplied by 3, and the quotient divided by 4, gives tuns and hogsheads.

1½ puncheons = 2 hogsheads.
3 barrels = 1½ puncheons = 2 hogsheads.
2 barrels = 1 puncheon.
1 barrel = ½ a puncheon.

2 butts.................	⎫
3 puncheons..............	⎪
4 hogsheads..............	Makeatun.
6 barrels................	⎪
8 half-hogsheads..........	⎭

MISSILE or MISSIVE. Any weapon thrown by hand or projected, and which strikes at a distance from the moving power; as a dart, &c.

MOMENTUM. The same with *impetus*, or the quantity of motion in a moving body; which is always equal to the quantity of matter multiplied into the velocity.

MORTAR. A piece of ordnance, shorter and wider than the cannon, and having a chamber different from, being smaller than, the size of its bore.

Mortars are used in the attack of a fortified place, by sea, to discharge bombs or carcasses amongst the buildings. The bomb or shell is a great hollow ball, filled with powder, which, falling into the works of a fortification, &c. destroys the most substantial buildings by its weight; and, bursting asunder, creates the greatest disorder and mischief by its splinters. See BOMB.

As the sea-mortars, or those which are fixed in the bomb-vessels, are generally fired at a much greater distance than is ever required ashore, they are made somewhat longer, and much heavier, than the land mortars.

The annexed figure represents a sea-mortar, the principal parts of which are, A, the chase; B, the re-inforce; C, the breech; and D, the trunnions. The interior part, comprehended between the dotted lines, is called the *bore*, wherein the powder is lodged; and the inner part of the bore, which is diminished towards the breech, and contains the powder, is termed the *chamber*.

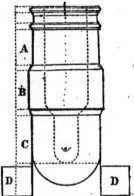

To facilitate the use of the mortar, it is placed in a solid carriage of timber, called the BED, whose different parts are strongly bolted together. By means of this it is firmly secured in its situation, so that the explosion of powder may not alter its direction. In the middle of the upper side of this carriage, are two semi-circular notches, to receive the trunnions, and keep them fast in the mortar-bed. The cap-squares are confined to the timber-work by strong pins of iron, called the eye-bolts, into whose upper ends are driven the keys, chained beneath them. On the fore part of the bed a piece of timber is placed transversely, upon which rests the belly of the mortar, or that part which contains the chamber. This piece is called the *bed-bolster*, and is used to elevate and support the mortar whilst firing.

These beds are placed upon very strong frames of timber, which are fixed in the bomb-ketch. They are securely attached to the frames, by mean of a strong bolt of iron, called the pintle, passing perpendicularly through both, and afterwards through one of the beams of the vessel. Thus the pintle, which passes through the hole in the centre, serves as an axis to the bed; so that the mortar may be turned about horizontally, as occasion requires.

Figure A in the margin is a perspective view of the bomb or shell; and figure B a section of it, whereby the thickness is exhibited. The parts *a* and *b* of the shell are its handles, by which it is lifted up or removed; and *c* is the fuse-hole, or aperture, through which the powder is poured in to charge it. The

most proper quantity of powder to charge a bomb is about two thirds of the weight which would fill the cavity.

The FUSE of the bomb is represented by *c d*, in fig. B. It is generally a conical tube of dry wood, as already mentioned, filled with a composition of sulphur, saltpetre, and mealed powder. The bomb being charged, this fuse is inserted in the cavity through the fuse-hole; and, when fired, communicates the fire to the powder in the shell. See FUSE.

The fuses for bombs are charged with great care, that nothing may prevent them from communicating the fire to the powder in the centre of the bomb. They are driven into the shell, so that only about one inch and a half comes out beyond the fuse-hole, and then the shell is said to be fixed.

These fuses are also generally charged long before there is occasion to use them; and, that the composition with which they are filled may not fall out or be damaged, by growing damp, the two ends are covered with a composition of tallow, mixed either with pitch or bees-wax. When the fuse is to be put into the shell, the little end is opened or cut off; but the great end is never opened till the mortar is to be fired.

When the proper quantity of powder, necessary to charge the mortar, is put into the chamber, it is covered with a wad, well beat down with the rammer. After this the fixed shell is placed upon the wad, as near the middle of the mortar as possible, with the fuse-hole uppermost, and another wad pressed down close upon it, so as to keep the shell firm in its position. The officer then points the mortar, or gives it the inclination necessary to carry the bomb to the place designed. When the mortar is thus fixed, the fuse is opened; the priming iron is also thrust into the touch-hole of the mortar to clear it, after which it is primed with the finest powder. This done, two men, taking each one of the matches, the first lights the fuse, and the other fires the mortar. The bomb, thrown out by the explosion of the powder, is carried to the place intended; and the fuse, which ought to be exhausted at the instant of the shell's falling, inflames the powder contained therein, and bursts the shell into splinters; which, flying off circularly, occasion incredible mischief wherever they reach. See BOMB-VESSEL.

MOULDINGS of a GUN or MORTAR. The prominent parts, as

squares or rounds, which serve for ornament; such as the breech-mouldings, rings, &c.

To MOUNT a GUN. To place a piece of ordnance on its carriage, for its management in firing.

MUSKET, or MUSQUET. The most serviceable fire-arm used by an army. It carries a ball of 29 to two pounds, and its length is 3 feet 6 inches from the muzzle to the pan.

MUSKETOON. A short and thick species of musket, the bore of which is the 38th part of its length. It carries five ounces of iron or $7\frac{1}{2}$ of lead, with a proportionate quantity of powder. The name is also applied to a fire-arm resembling a horse-pistol, of a very wide bore, and sometimes bell mouthed.

MUZZLE of a GUN. The extreme end around the mouth. Hence MUZZLE-RING is that ring which strengthens the mouth or muzzle,

To NAIL or SPIKE a GUN. To drive an iron spike into the vent or touch-hole, by which the gun is, for a time, rendered unserviceable. There are various contrivances for forcing a nail out; but they have never been found of general use. The best method, when this is impracticable, is to drill a new hole. Another method by which cannon may be rendered useless is by driving in a ball of sufficient caliber to stop the bore tightly.

ORDNANCE. A general name for all sorts of great guns used in war, as CANNON, &c. Of these, in time of service, each man is supposed to work 5 cwt. of metal. From this datum may therefore be computed the number of men required to attend each piece. See GUN, CANNON, &c.

PIECES of ORDNANCE. All sorts of great guns and mortars. BATTERING-PIECES are those which serve at sieges to make breaches, such as the 24-pounder. FIELD-PIECES are 12-pounders, &c.

PILES of SHOT and SHELLS. Shot and shells are generally piled up in the king's magazines, in three different forms: the base being either triangular, square, or a rectangle; and thence the piles are called triangular, square, and oblong.

The rules for finding the number in any pile are as follow:

TRIANGULAR PILE. Multiply the base by the base + 1, this product by the base + 2, and divide by 6.

SQUARE PILE. Multiply the bottom row by the bottom row + 1, and this product by twice the bottom row + 1, and divide by 6.

RECTANGULAR PILE. Multiply the breadth of the base by itself + 1, and this product by three times the difference between the length and the breadth of the base, added to twice the breadth + 1, and divide by 6.

INCOMPLETE PILE. These, being only frustrums, wanting a similar small pile on the top; compute first the whole pile as complete, and then the small pile wanting at top: next subtract the one from the other, and the remainder will be the content.

PLATOON. A number of men assembled for the exercise of small arms. See SMALL-ARMS.

POINT-BLANK. A term taken from the French *point blanc* or *but en blanc*, otherwise called in English the line of metal elevation. It is generally between one and two degrees. The POINT-BLANK RANGE is the distance the shot goes before it strikes the level ground, when discharged in the horizontal or point-blank direction; or sometimes this means the distance that the ball goes horizontally in a straight-lined direction.

POINTING. The laying a piece of ordnance in any proposed direction, either horizontal, or elevated, or depressed. This is usually effected by means of the gunner's level or quadrant, which, being applied to the piece, shows by a plummet the degree of elevation or depression. See QUADRANT.

PORT-FIRE. A composition driven into a case of paper, to serve instead of a match to fire guns.

Port-fires and lights are compositions that kindle readily and burn clearly. They are contained in paper tubes, rammed down, and should not go out even under water. One that is from 10 to 12 inches long, and from 3 to 5 twelfths of an inch thick, will burn from 12 to 15 minutes. The common length is 16½ inches.

A substitute for port-fires has been made of two ounces of nitre dissolved in a gallon of water, and sheets of soft brown paper dipped therein. These, when dry, were rolled up for use to about the size of common port-fires.

Port-fires may be made of any length, but seldom exceed 21 inches. The interior diameter or mould should be 10 sixteenths of an inch, and the diameter of the whole about half an inch. The paper cases must be rolled wet with paste, and one end folded down. *The composition of wet port-fire* is, saltpetre, 6; sulphur, 2; and mealed powder, 1; when it is well mixed and sieved it is to be moistened with a little linseed oil. *The composition of dry port-fire* is, saltpetre, 4; sulphur, 1; mealed powder, 2; and antimony, 1.

POUNDER. A great gun or piece of ordnance, denominated according to the weight of the ball which it carries, as a 9, 12, or 18, *pounder*, &c.

POWDER. See GUN-POWDER.

POWDER-BARRELS. See BARRELS.

POWDER-MARKS. See MARKS.

PROOF, of ARTILLERY and SMALL-ARMS. A trial whether they will stand the quantity of powder allotted for that purpose. See GUN-POWDER.

The board of ordnance allows bullets of lead of 11 in the pound for the proof of muskets, and of 29 in two pounds for service; 17 in the pound for the proof of carbines, and 20 for service; 28 in the pound for the proof of pistols, and 34 for service.

When guns of a new metal, or of lighter construction, are proved, they are, besides the common proof, fired 200 or 300 times as quick as they can be, loaded with the common charge given in actual service. Cannon are proved to ascertain their being well cast, their having no cavities or defects in the metal. In making this proof the piece is laid upon the ground, supported only by a piece of wood in the middle, of about five or six inches thick, to raise the muzzle a little; and then the piece is fired against a solid butt of earth. See CANNON.

Every species of ordnance undergoes different kinds of proof before it is received into his Majesty's service, viz. 1st. They are gauged as to their several dimensions, internal and external, as to the justness of the position of the bore, the chamber, the vent, the trunnions, &c.

2d. They are fired with a regulated charge of powder and shot, and afterwards *searched* to discover irregularities or holes produced by the firing.

3d. By means of engines an endeavour is made to force water through them; and,

4th. They are examined internally, by means of light reflected from a mirror.

Iron Guns.—The guns are first examined as to their proper dimensions, in which, in no case, more than three tenths of an inch variation is allowed; and in the diameter of the bore only one thirtieth from 42 to 18 pounders, and one fortieth from 12 to 4 pounders; but, in the position of the bore, half an inch out of the axis of a piece from a 42 to an 18 pounder, and one third of an inch from a 12 to a 4 pounder, is allowed. They are then fired twice with the charge in the following table, with one shot and two high junk wads; and examined with a searcher after each round. In this examination they must not have any hole or cavity in the bore of two tenths of an inch in depth, behind the first reinforce ring, or one quarter of an inch in depth before this ring. .

Species.	Proof charge.	Species.	Proof charge.	Species.	Proof charge.
	lbs. oz.		lbs. oz.		lbs. oz.
42-Pdrs...	25 0	12-Pdrs.	12 0	3-Pdrs....	3 0
32	21 8	9	9 0	2	2 0
24	18 0	6	6 0	1½	1 8
18	15 0	4	4 0	1	1 0

Iron guns are scaled with one twelfth of the weight of the shot.

Brass Guns.—From 1-pounders to 12-pounders the diameter of the bore must not vary more than one fortieth of an inch, and in no dimensions more than two-tenths. The following are the established charges for their proof: The heavy and medium guns with a charge equal to the weight of the shot, except the medium 12-pounder, which is proved with only 9lbs. The light guns with half the weight of the shot.—The brass ordnance have not, however, been proved of late with such charges, but with the following:

3-Pounders, light, three times, with 1lb. each round.

6-Pounders, light, three times, with 2lbs. each.

12-Pounders, light, twice, with 4lbs. each.

12-Pounders, medium, twice, with 5lbs. each.

Any hole .15 of an inch deep upwards or sideways in the bore, or .1 in the bottom, between the breech and first reinforce; or .2 of an inch upwards or sideways, or .15 in the bottom of the bore, before the first reinforce ring, will be sufficient to condemn them.

Brass Mortars and Howitzers.—The exterior dimensions are in no respect to deviate more than one tenth of an inch in an 8-inch howitzer, and one twentieth in the royals and coehorn mortars and howitzers.—Their bores and chambers not to deviate from their true diameters or positions more than one fortieth of an inch.

The brass mortars and howitzers are fired twice with their chambers full of powder, and an iron shell. The mortars on their own beds, at about 75° elevation; and the howitzers on their carriages, at about 12°. Iron mortars are proved on their iron beds, with a charge equal to the full chamber, and an iron shot equal in diameter to the shell.

Royals, or Coehorn mortars, having a hole .1 of an inch in depth in the chamber, or .15 in the chase, are rejected: royal howitzers the same.—Three-inch howitzers having a hole .15 of an inch in depth in the chamber, or .2 in the chase, will be rejected.

Carronades. The diameter and position of their bore and chamber must not deviate one twentieth of an inch.—They are proved with two rounds, with their chambers full of powder, and one shot and one wad. A hole of two tenths of an inch in depth in the bore, or one tenth in the chamber, condemns the piece.

Proof Charge.

68-Pdrs.... 13 lbs.	32-Pdrs.... 8 lbs.	18-Pdrs.... 4 lbs.
42-Pdrs.... 9 lbs.	24-Pdrs.... 6 lbs.	12-Pdrs.... 3 lbs.

All ordnance, after having undergone this proof, and the subsequent searching, are subject to the water-proof: this is done by means of a forcing pump, having a pipe or hose fixed to the mouth of the piece; after two or three efforts to force the water through any honeycombs or flaws which may be in the bore, they are left to dry; and generally the next day examined by the reflected light from a mirror. If the bore contains any small holes or flaws which have not been discovered by the former proofs, they are very readily found by this: the water will continue to weep, or run from the holes, when the solid parts of the bore are perfectly dry. Ordnance suspected of being bad are often subject to a more severe proof; that of firing thirty rounds quick, with

the service charge and two shot ; and, in doubtful cases, where
the purity of the metal is suspected, recourse has been had to
chemical trials and analysis. A quantity of clean filings taken
from a part of an iron gun free from rust, are dissolved in the
dilute sulphuric acid, and the quantity of gas disengaged during
the solution accurately ascertained. The plumbago which remains
after solution is also separated by filtration, and carefully weighed.
Now it is well known that the purer the iron, the greater the
quantity of inflammable gas obtained, and the less the proportion
of plumbago which remains after the solution : from these two
parts, therefore, a tolerable judgement may be formed of the
quality of the metal. When the plumbago exceeds $4\frac{1}{2}$ per cent.
the iron will always be found deficient in strength ; and there has
been no instance of a gun bursting where the plumbago did not
exceed 3 per cent. ; that is, where 100 grains of the metal did
not leave more than three grains of plumbago. The colour of
the plumbago is also to be attended to : when it is brown or red-
dish, it is an indication of hard metal, and when in quantities
and mixed with coals, there can be no doubt but that the iron is
too soft for cannon.

Proof of Iron Shells.—After the shells are gauged and examined
as to their dimensions and weight, they must be well scraped out,
and the iron pin at the bottom of the inside must be driven down
or broken off. They are then to be hammered all over, to knock
off the scales, and discover flaws ; and no hole, in the large shells,
is allowed, of more than three quarters of an inch deep. An
empty fuse is then driven into the fuse hole, and the shell is suspended in a tub of water, in such manner that the shell be covered
by the water, but that it does not run into the fuse ; in this situation the nose of a pair of bellows is put in at the fuse-hole, and
several strong puffs given with the bellows ; but, if no bubbles
rise in the water, the shell is concluded to be serviceable.

Ordnance condemned as unserviceable from any of the foregoing
reasons, are marked as follows : × D, or × S, or × W.—The
first signifies that they are found to be faulty in their dimensions,
by Desaguller's instrument; the second by the searcher ; and the
third by the water-proof.

QUADRANT. An instrument made of brass or wood, divided

into degrees, and each degree into ten parts, to lay guns or mortars to any degree of elevation.

The common sort is that represented on plate II. figure 7, and consists of two branches, between which is a quadrantal arch, divided into 90 degrees, and furnished with a thread and plummet.

The use of this instrument is very easy; for, if the longer branch, or bar, be placed in the mouth of the piece, and it be elevated till the plummet cut the degree necessary to hit a proposed object, the thing is done.

Sometimes, on the sides of the longer bar, are noted the division of diameters and weights of iron balls, as also the bores of pieces.

A superior sort has a spiral level fixed to a brass radius; so that, when the long end is introduced into the piece, this radius is turned about its centre till it is level: then its end shows the angle of elevation, or the inclination from the horizon; whereas the first shows that angle from the verticle. But see LEVEL.

QUADRATE. To quadrate a gun is to see it placed truly on its carriage, and that the wheels be of an equal height.

QUARTERING a SHIP's COMPANY; Remarks on.—Quartering a ship's company requires the greatest attention; and, when a ship is first put into commission, the people should be frequently exercised at their quarters, that they may be familiarised to the various occurrences which are likely to happen in action. When the men are perfect in one station at the gun, they should be appointed to another, that they may acquire a proficiency in the whole.

The men should be quartered by the watch-bill, taking equal proportions from the several watches. This plan will be found more advantageous in small ships, in which, when at sea, the people are frequently called to their quarters in the night, and, in this case, the men who belong to the watch will naturally be employed in getting their quarters ready while those below are bringing up their hammocs.

In a ship, whose crew are three watches, they should be compelled, in fine weather, to bring them up, stow them, and cover them well up, in the nettings; which, in the event of falling in with an enemy, would be of incalculable advantage.

The men at the guns should be stationed in the following manner :—the whole number divided into two equal parts, under a
first and second captain, having their respective boarders, with
their belts and cutlass ; sail-trimmers ; lantern-men, to fetch a
lantern ; fire-men with a bucket and swab ; winch-men, to pump
the ship, if required ; port-tackle-fall-men, to lower the port ;
and powder-men,. to fetch powder ; under the orders and directions of officers specifically nominated to superintend these different duties.

On beating to quarters, the first captain, with his party, is to
get the starboard guns ready ; and the second captain, with his
party, should get the larboard ones.

In fighting both sides at once, the people should be taught to
work from two guns together : thus, while one gun is in, and the
people are worming, sponging, and loading it, the other should
be run with the spare men from the gun which is in, in addition
to those belonging to the gun which is to be run out, and so continue alternately to assist each other.   When one side only is engaged, the first party of the men stationed at the gun should stand
on the fore part of the gun, and the second party on the after part.
The first captain should prick, prime, and point, the gun to the
object ; the second captain should secure the powder-horn and
stop the vent.   The boarders should sponge and load the gun ;
the fire-men should choke the tackle-falls, and handle the crows
and handspikes ; the rest of the people should work the gun.

As nothing, in action, conduces more to keep up a brisk fire
than being well supplied with powder, every necessary arrangement should be made for that purpose, by stationing a sufficient
number of men to hand it along the passages, and dividing the
supply as much as possible, that no confusion, or mistake, may
happen in distributing the cartridges.   In three-deckers it is usual
to supply the lower deck with cartridges from the grand magazine, handed up at the fore hatchway ; the middle deck, from the
fore-hanging magazine, handed along by the sail-room up the
main hatchway ; the main deck, forecastle, and quarter deck,
from the after magazine, with whips at the foot of the ladder,
coming off the middle deck.   Positive orders should be given, that
no cartridge should be given out to any person who does not deliver an empty cartridge box.

QUARTERS. Regulations of.

1st. When the drum beats to quarters observe to keep silence ; to see all the match-tubs in their proper places, and the firemen with their fire-buckets, gun-lock, tube-boxes, &c. When your men are at their guns, make them acquainted that they are all loaded. The first thing in casting them loose is to hook the relieving tackles, haul them taut, and keep a turn with the falls.

2nd. Cast off your cross and breast lashings, and haul your side-tackles well taut and belay them ; then cast off the seizing of the breechings, and let the clench go to the side-rings ; then middle your breechings in the thimble on the cascable.

3rd. Coil your tackle-falls clear, and lay them close to the side of the ship, clear of your feet ; then take your sponge, and place it from getting wet.

4th. Take out your crows and handcrow-levers, keeping the handcrow-lever abaft the gun on the starboard side, and before the gun on the larboard side ; in so doing you will find it more convenient in taking out the coins and beds, if required, to ele-vate your guns.

5th. Then cast off your muzzle-lashing, and raise the guns with bed and coin ; take out the tompions, and cast loose the aprons.

6th. Prime ; but never force the powder down the vent with the priming-iron, but rather shake it from the horn as lightly as possible, if you make no use of quill-tubes.

7th. Then man your side-tackles, and when you are working your lee guns, ease them with a turn to the ship's side ; other-wise, when let go hard against the side, you will start the shot from the first wad, so that it cannot go with the velocity as may be expected.

8th. In pointing the guns, be careful that the muzzle or the chase do not touch the side of the port ; leave always room of about two inches, looking from the venticle sight on the base-ring, to the sight on the muzzle-ring, which is a true direction ; if your gun takes the side when fired, it will fly abaft or before the port, and will cause trouble to bring it square again ; if you should meet with such misfortune, take one of your side-tackles and hook it to the breast eye-bolt of the next port; then you may bring the gun square with ease.

9th. In securing your guns, take out the coins, and lay the beds down from the axle-trees; then hook your side-tackles to the upper eye-bolts of the carriage, in which case, should you have occasion to double breech them in bad weather, the tackle-block and falls will be clear of the breeching-rings; and you may reeve your second breeching with ease, by bowsing well taught and belaying them; pass the muzzle-lashing, keeping the side-tackles fast; then get the clench of your breechings back and size it; after which pass the breast upper and cross lashings, observing that both sides of the lashing bear equal with the side-tackles, otherwise all the stress will lay on one ring at the side.

10th. In close action never put more than one wad to two shot, round and grape, or double-headed and grape, or, round and case; but if you are at a great distance, round shot only; by reason you have more than six times the weight of powder, so that you are to consider, if you charge with two round shot, it cannot do much execution; and in discharging your gun four or five times, it will become so warm as to rise from the deck; throw out the coins if not laid square with the bed, and perhaps hurt the men.

11th. In warm action lay the bed down, and the coin on the edge, it will answer more conveniently, as the gun will lay on a true level, and more ready for elevation; if required to direct a shot to the hull of a ship, force the coin more under the gun; if for a mast, or rigging, draw the coin as may be found necessary; but particular attention must be observed of the rise or fall of the ship you are on-board of: if you fire when falling, the shot will fall in the water.

12th. At the recoil of your gun stop the vent, and keep it close while the sponge is in the gun: at every four or five rounds it will be necessary to worm them, for the oftener the gun is fired the more damp is left in the chamber, and by ramming home a fresh cartridge it will stick to the cylinder, and, when fired, will remain there burning, as the damp softens the paste at the bottom of the cartridge, which occasions it to stick fast.

13th. Be always very careful never to throw any water or wet swab on the guns when warm; by so doing you will check the metal, and the next round fired may burst it. Give timely notice to the men in the magazine to reduce the powder, when in a long action.

The man who has charge of the salt-box is to stand on the side opposite to that on which you are engaging, or, if engaging on both sides, amidship. He is to be careful not to approach the match-tub, and always to keep the cover of the box shut.

14th. Never keep the lee guns on a level while loading, by reason if your relieving tackle-hooks, or falls, break, the man who is at the sponge and loading the gun, will be crushed to death between the breast of the carriage and the ship's side; when loaded, raise your guns after priming them, but if you run them out before they are primed, you may ship water and fill the bore of the guns, and also get water on the priming. These being the lee guns, it will be necessary to fire them as quickly as possible, to prevent the water doing the guns injury.

15th. Should you meet with the above-mentioned disaster, getting the bore of your gun filled with water, and the priming wet; be then brisk and bore the gun down, and fit a tube in the vent, and raise the metal with bed and coin as high as possible, so that the water may run out, and fire so soon as you can : it is better to have a gun unloaded than to remain unserviceable.

It would be adviseable to have a small iron pin, with an eye about three inches and a half long, as a turn-screw to shift the flints of every lock for the great guns, if necessary. By means of the eye, it may be spliced on the end of the lanyard which is fixed to the lock.

See that the fighting-lanterns are kept in good order, the candles always matched in them when at sea, and hooks driven for them in the most convenient places amidship. The fire-screens which are of thick fearnought should be kept dry, and often examined, to ascertain if they need repair.

It is necessary to have a double quantity of match marled up before you go to sea, and a sufficient part of that primed with a little powder boiled in vinegar. If each match be dipped one inch into it, it will take fire very readily, and be fit for immediate service.

For observations at quarters on Carronades. See CARRONADES.
QUOIN. See COIN.

RANDOM-SHOT. A shot made when the muzzle of the gun is raised above the horizon. The utmost random of any piece is about ten times as far as the bullet will go point-blank.

RANGE. The distance from a gun to that point where a shot or shell, projected or fired from it, touches the ground or water.

The following tables exhibit the ranges of carronades, cannon, and mortars, as ascertained by actual experiment.

1. RANGES WITH CARRONADES : The charge being one twelfth of the weight of the shot; and with one shell and one wad.— The line of fire from six to nine feet above the level of the water.

	Species....	68	'42	32	24	18	12
	Charge....	5lb. 8oz.	3lb. 8oz.	2lb 10oz	2 lbs.	1lb. 8oz.	1 lb.
		Yards.	Yards.	Yards.	Yards.	Yards.	Yards.
Elevation.	Point-blank	450	400	330	300	270	230
	1 Degree..	650	600	560	500	470	400
	2	890	860	830	780	730	690
	3	1000	980	900	870	800	740
	4	1100	1020	970	920	870	810
	5	1280	1170	1087	1050	1000	870

RANGES, with 8-inch SHELLS, from 68-pounder CARRONADES.

Weight of shell.	Charge.	Flight.	Elevation.	First graze.	Extreme range.
				Yards.	Yards.
lbs. oz.	3 lbs....	$1\frac{1}{2}''$	Point-blank	302	1365
43 11	8	—	5 Degrees ..	1140	
	4	$1\frac{1}{4}$	1	358	1843
	....	5	5	1137	1250
	....	—	$11\frac{1}{4}$	1767	

2. Ranges with Cannon, 32, 24, and 18, pounders.

Elevation.	Proportion of powder.	Species of shot.	Range.
			Yards.
2°	$\frac{1}{3}$	With single shot to the first graze	1200
2°	$\frac{1}{4}$	Ditto.	1000
2°	$\frac{1}{4}$	Two shot, ranged close together, to	500
4°	$\frac{1}{3}$	Single shot	1600
4°	$\frac{1}{4}$	Ditto.	1500
7°	$\frac{1}{8}$	Ditto.	2150
7°	$\frac{1}{4}$	Ditto.	2020
2°	$\frac{1}{4}$	One round shot, and one round of grape, will range with effect together, to.	600
4°	$\frac{1}{4}$	One round of grape shot alone, to	1000
2°	$\frac{1}{4}$	One double-headed or bar shot, will range to the first graze.	800

Ranges with 5½-inch Shells from an iron 24-pounder.—Length of gun, 9½ feet—Weight, 49 cwt. 26 lbs.

Elevation.	2 Pounds.			2 lbs. 8 oz.			3 Pounds.		
	Flight.	Range to First graze.	Range to Extreme.	Flight.	Range to First graze.	Range to Extreme.	Flight.	Range to First graze.	Range to Extreme.
Deg.	Sec.	Yards.	Yards.	Sec.	Yards.	Yards.	Sec.	Yards.	Yards.
1	1	213	1139	2¾	562	1456	1	277	1424
2	1¾	384	1267	1½	442	1413	1¾	526	1464
3	2¾	565	1413	2½	647	1553	2¼	740	1600
4	2¼	750	1479	3¾	896	1639	3½	880	1679
5	3¾	836	1670	4	915	1510	5	1182	1733
6	4	896	1495	5	1140	1657	6¼	1384	1787
7	6½	1180	1492	6	1205	1481	6¼	1410	1749
8	6¾	1305	1526	6½	1259	1544	7	1520	1744
9	7½	1329	1527	7	1341	1561	7¾	1722	1938
9½	6¾	1229	1453	..	....	....	8½	1748	1831

3. Ranges of 13 and 10 inch Sea-mortars.—The 13-inch, at 45 degrees, 4100 yards: the 10-inch, 3800. The former with 32 lbs., the latter with 12 lb. 8 oz., of powder.

RANGES WITH A 10-INCH SEA-MORTAR, at 21 degrees, on a horizontal plane.

Weight of mortar.	Weight of shell.	Charge.	Elevation.	Flight.	Range.
cwt. qrs. lbs.	lb. oz.	lb. oz.	Degrees.	Seconds.	Yards.
34 2 14 {	86 — 87 — }	5 8	21 {	14¾ 16	2335 2510

RANGES WITH SEA-SERVICE IRON MORTARS, at 45 degrees, upon a horizontal plane.

13-Inch.			10-Inch.		
Charge.	Flight.	Range.	Charge.	Flight.	Range.
lbs. oz.	Seconds.	Yards.	lbs. oz.	Seconds.	Yards.
2 —	13	690	1 —.	13	680
4 —	18	1400	2 —	18	1340
6 —	21	1900	3 —	21	1900
8 —	24½	2575	4 —	24½ .	2500
10 —	26¼	2975	5 —	26	2800
12 —	29	3500	6 —	27	3200
14 —	29¼	3860	7 —	29	3500
16 —	30	3900	8 —	30	3800
18 —	30½	4000	9 —	30½	3900
20 —	31	4200	9 8	30¾	4000

RECOIL, or REBOUND. The starting backward of a gun in consequence of its explosion. Guns whose vents are a little forward in the chase recoil the most. To lessen the recoil, the platforms of batteries are generally made sloping towards the embrasures. The RECOIL of SEA-SERVICE GUNS, on ship carriages, upon a horizontal platform, as ascertained by experiment, is as follows.

Charges of powder and shot.	Elevation.	32-Pdr.		24-Pdr.		18-Pdr.	
	Degrees.	Ft.	In.	Ft.	In.	Ft.	In.
⅓ of powder and 1 shot	2	11	—	11	—	10	6
⅓ of powder and 2 shot	4	19	6	18	6	13	—
⅓ of powder and 2 shot	7	11	6	12	—	12	—

RED-HOT SHOT.—Mode of charging with. The powder for firing with red-hot shot must be in strong flannel cartridges, without any holes, lest some grains should remain in the bore, when putting the cartridges home. Over the powder must be rammed a good dry wad, then a damp one, and then the hot shot; and if the gun lies at a depression, there must be a wad over the shot, which may be rammed home. If the above pre-cautions be attended to, the gun may be pointed after being loaded, without the smallest danger; as it is well known that the shot will grow cold in the gun, without burning more than a few threads of the wads next it. This is not the mode usually taught of loading with hot shot, but is that which was practised during the siege of Gibraltar. Mr. Durturbie proposes putting the shot, when heated, into a tin canister, as an effectual method of pre-venting accidents.

The grates usually made for heating shot will generally make them red-hot in three quarters of an hour. *Adye's Bombardier.*

REINFORCE. That part of a gun next to the breech, which is made stronger than the rest of the piece, in order to resist the force of the powder. There are generally two in each piece, called the first and second re-inforce; the second being smaller than the first, and divided from it by the *reinforce-ring.*

RICOCHET. This term signifies a bound or leap, such as a flat piece of stone makes when thrown obliquely along the surface of water: hence, by *Ricochet-firing* is understood the firing of guns at a low elevation, with a small quantity of powder, and so that the shot will roll on and dismount cannon, destroy troops, &c.

RIFLE. A thread, ray, or line, which is made in the barrel of a fire-arm, said to be *rifled;* or which has lines, or little canals, within its barrel, extending in a worming direction, and more or less numerous and indented, according to the fancy of the artificer. The rifled barrel possesses several advantages over the common one, which is attributed to the threads or rays by which it is indented. These threads are sometimes cut in such manner that the line which commences on the right side of the breech terminates on the left at the muzzle; by which mean the ball acquires a rotary movement, revolving once and a half round its own axis before it quits the piece, and then boring through the air with a spiral motion. The bullet for these pieces ought to be no larger than to be just pressed by the rifles, for the easier it moves in the piece, supposing it not to shift its position, the more violent and accurate will, its flight be. The whirling motion of the bullet appears by experience to terminate at the distance of 200 to 250 yards from the piece.

ROCKET. An artificial fire-work, contained in a cylindrical case of paper, filled with the composition under-mentioned; and which, being tied to a stick, mounts into the air to a considerable height, and there bursts with an explosion resembling stars. In war they are used as signals.

Those for the Navy generally weigh one pound.—Of these the composition is, saltpetre, 4 lbs ; sulphur, 1 lb.; charcoal-dust, 1lb. 8 oz.; and mealed powder, 4 oz.

The sulphur, saltpetre, and powder, to be first mealed well and mixed together, so that one shall not appear separated from the other. Meal the charcoal by itself, and mix the whole well to-. gether. A port fire cut in pieces, about half an inch long, will answer for stars.

Dimensions of a one-pound rocket.—Stick, 8 feet long ; breadth of the top, 2 inches ; $1\frac{1}{4}$ inch thick ; and tapering to $\frac{2}{10}$ at the end. The number of sheets of thick paper required, is five.

The composition for the stars is, mealed powder, 8 ounces ; saltpetre, 8 lb.; sulphur, 2 lb.; antimony, 2 lb.; isinglass dissolved, $3\frac{3}{4}$ oz.; spirits of wine, one pint; vinegar, one quart.

GENERAL TABLE OF SKY-ROCKETS.

	2-pound.	1-pound.	½-pound.	¼-pound.
	Inches.	Inches.	Inches.	Inches.
Case { Exterior diameter	2.13	1.69	1.34	1.06
Case { Interior diameter........	1.529	1.214	0.961	0.761
Case { Length before driving...	15.97	12.67	13.05	8.25
Length of gauge for the choke.	1.5	1.25	1.0	0.75
Cylinders for heading { Diameter	2.84	2.25	1.79	1.39
Cylinders for heading { Length .	4.26	3.38	2.68	2.12
Cones for heading .. { Diameter	2 84	2.25	1.79	1.39
Cones for heading .. { Height..	4.26	3.38	2.68	2.18
Mallet for driving.....Weight .	1 lb.	38 oz.	2.1	1.10
No. of strokes	31	21	18	13

Copper Ladles for filling Sky-rockets.

Length, $1\frac{1}{4}$ the exterior diameter of the case.

Diameter, equals the interior diameter of case.

Circumference, three quarters the interior caliber of the case.

Sky-rockets are driven with composition up to 4½ exterior diameters of the case from the choke ; and 1-5th of a diameter above the composition with good clay.—They are bored and reamed up to 3¼ diameters.

Dimensions of sticks for rockets.—General rules.

For rockets from half an ounce to one pound, the stick must be 60 diameters of the rocket in length : for rockets from one pound and upwards, fifty or fifty-two diameters. Their thickness at top about half a diameter, and their breadth very little more. Their square at bottom equal to half the thickness at top.

Species of rockets.	6-Pdr.	4-Pdr.	2-Pdr.	1-Pdr.	½-Pdr.	¼-Pdr.	⅛-Pdr.
	Ft. In.	Ft. In.	Ft. In.	Ft. In.	Ft. In.	Ft. In.	Ft. In.
Distance of poise from the point of the cone...	4 1½	3 9	2 9	2 1	1 10½	1 8¼	1 3

Rockets of between three and four inches in diameter have been observed to ascend as high as 1000 or 1200 yards; but the height of common rockets is between 450 and 600 yards ; and their flight usually short of five seconds.

The CONGREVE ROCKET is a species of war-rocket, invented by Colonel Congreve, of the Royal Artillery, the principle of whose projectile force is so great, as scarcely to be set in comparison with the former rocket. It is applied to various naval and military purposes, and is of different descriptions and calibers, either for explosion or conflagration, and may be armed with SHELLS, CASE-SHOT, &c.

The following statement shows the different species of this ammunition, with their extreme range and the elevation for producing it, &c.

SPECIES.	ARMED WITH	EXTREME RANGE. Yards.	ELEVATION. Degrees.
42-Pounder carcass rocket.	{ Large, 18lb. of combustible matter.. / Small, 12lb............	3500	60 not less.
42-Pounder shell rocket.	{ 5½-inch...... / 12-pounder spherical......		
32-Pounder carcass rocket.	{ Large, 18lb. combustible matter..... / Medium, 12lb. equal to a 13-inch carcass / Small, 8lb. equal to a 10-inch ditto....	2000 / 2500 / 3000	60 / 60 to 55. / 55
32-Pounder shell-rocket.	} 9-pounder spherical......	3000	50
32-Pounder rocket case-shot.	{ Case-shot which receives any increased velocity from the bursting powder. } Large, containing 200 carbine balls... / Small, 100 ditto....	2500 / 3000	55 / 50
32-Pounder explosion rocket.	} Strong iron cones, containing from 5 to 12lb. of powder, to burst by fuses......	2500 to 3000	55
12-Pounder rocket case shot.	{ Large, 72 carbine balls...... / Small, 48 ditto......	2000 / 2500	45 / 45

By this statement it is seen that the 32-pounder carcass rocket, which is the species hitherto chiefly used for bombardment, will range 3000 yards with the same quantity of combustible matter as that contained in the 10-inch spherical carcass, and 2500 yards with the same quantity as that of the 13-inch spherical carcass. It is clear, also, that the 12-pounder rocket case-shot, which is so portable that it may be used with the facility of musketry, has a range nearly double that of field artillery, carrying as many bullets as the 6-pounder spherical case.

This rocket is particularly calculated for the conveyance of case-shot to great distances; because, as it proceeds, its velocity is accelerated instead of being retarded, as happens with every other projectile; while the average velocity of the shell is greater than that of the rocket only in the ratio of 9 to 8; independent of which, the case shot conveyed by the rocket admits of any desired increase of velocity in its range by the *bursting-powder*, which cannot be obtained in any other case.

The Congreve Rockets are formed in metallic cases—the carcasses with strong iron heads, filled with a composition as hard and solid as iron itself. The penetration of the 32-pounder rocket carcass, in common ground, is 9 feet; and they have been found, in the different bombardments where they have been used, to pierce through several floors, and through the sides of houses. The sticks of these rockets are very little longer than those of the large signal rockets, and they are contrived so as to be fixed firmly, and instantaneously in action.

The velocity with which the rocket moves through the air is such that the wind has but little effect in causing it to deviate from the line of fire; and none indeed, unless the direction of the wind, when strong, be nearly at right angles to that of its flight: and its great excellence lies in the facility with which all its different species can be conveyed and applied. There is no re-action or recoil in firing the largest of these rockets; so that, by this mean, carcasses, equal to those projected from the largest mortars, may be thrown from the smallest boats: and, it is to be observed, that it is the cheapest ammunition depending on the projectile force of gunpowder.

The ROCKET LIGHT-BALL, another invention of Colonel Congreve, is a species of light-ball thrown up by means of one of his rockets, and which is detached by explosion at the summit of the ascent, and remains suspended in the air by a small parachute to which it is connected by a chain. Thus a permanent and brilliant light is obtained for about five minutes, during which time the motions of an enemy may be discovered either on-shore or at sea. It is particularly useful in chasing and for night signals.

The FLOATING ROCKET-CARCASS is another of Colonel Congreve's applications of his rocket and parachute, for the purpose of conveying combustible matter to distances far beyond the range of any other known projectile force; although it is cheap, simple, and portable. The floating carcass, like the light-ball, is thrown up attached to a rocket, from which, being separated at its greatest altitude, and suspended to a small parachute, it is driven forward by the wind; and, in a moderate breeze, affords ranges at least *double* those of the common carcass. It may, therefore, be thrown from a blockading squadron, with a fair wind, against any fleet or place without the smallest risk, or approaching within range of either guns or mortars. The rocket containing this carcass is not larger than the 32-pounder rocket carcass; and the whole expense, added to that of the rocket, does not exceed 5s. The approach of this carcass is not necessarily visible by night; as it may be contrived not to inflame until some time after it has settled.

For a more complete account of these ingenious inventions, which appear to constitute a new æra in military science, see the ' Military Dictionary' of Major James, already noticed.

ROPE. Rule to find the weight of. Multiply the square of the circumference in inches by the length in fathoms, and divide the product by 480 for the weight in hundred weights.

SAIL-TRIMMERS. See BOARDERS.

SALTPETRE or NITRE. A species of salt, found abundantly on the surface of the earth in India, South-America, Southern Africa, and some parts of Europe. It is well known with us as a component part of gunpowder.

This substance is soluble in seven times its weight of water, at the temperature of 60 degrees, and in rather less than its own weight of boiling water. When exposed to a strong heat it melts, and congeals by cooling into an opaque mass, which has been called mineral chrystal.

To refine saltpetre, put into a copper, or any other vessel, 100 weight of rough nitre, with about 14 gallons of clean water, and let it boil gently for half an hour, and as it boils take off the scum; then stir it about in the copper, and, before it settles, put it into filtering bags, which must be hung on a rack, with glazed earthen pans under them, in which sticks must be laid across for the chrystals to adhere to: it must stand in the pan for two or three days to shoot: then take out the chrystals and let them dry. The water that remains in the pans must be boiled again for an hour, and strained into the pans as before, and the saltpetre will be quite clear and transparent; if not, it wants more refining; to effect which proceed as usual, till it is well cleansed from all its earthy parts.

To pulverize saltpetre; take a copper kettle, whose bottom must be spherical, and put into it 14lb. of refined saltpetre, with two quarts or five pints of clean water; then put the kettle on a slow fire; and, when the saltpetre is dissolved, if any impurities arise, skim them off, and keep constantly stirring it with two large spattles till all the water exhales; and, when done enough it will appear like white sand, and as fine as flour; but, if it should boil too fast, take the kettle off the fire, and set it on some wet sand, by which mean the nitre will be prevented from sticking to the kettle. When pulverized it must be kept carefully in a dry place.

SALUTES.—Regulations relative to. 1. The admiral and commander-in-chief of the fleet is to be saluted with seventeen guns; he is to return fifteen to all flag-officers and thirteen to captains.

2. Admirals are to be saluted with fifteen guns, and vice and rear admirals with thirteen.

3. Every flag-officer is to return the salute of another flag-officer of the same rank with the same number of guns he is saluted with.

4. An admiral is to return two guns less to a vice or rear admiral, and four guns less to a captain. A vice-admiral is to return two guns less to a rear-admiral and four less to a captain. A rear-admiral is to return two guns less to a captain. Commodores are to salute, and to be saluted, as rear-admirals.

5. Ships meeting a squadron, in which there are more than one flag-officer, are to salute the commander only of such squadron, who is not to return the salute until all the ships saluting have

ceased firing; he is then to make one general return by firing the number of guns with which an officer of his rank is saluted.

6. When two squadrons meet, only the officers who command them are to salute.

7. A flag-officer, appointed to command in chief, shall be saluted on hoisting his flag by all the ships under his command, unless a flag-officer senior to him be present; in which case they are to salute him so soon as he shall be separated from such senior officer.

8. Flag-officers are not to be saluted by other flag-officers, nor by captains, who shall not have been separated from them six calendar months.

9. The captain of one of his Majesty's ships, is not to salute the captain of another of his Majesty's ships, in any part of the world.

10. Flag-ships are to return the salutes of foreign ships of war, in the same manner as they return the salutes of his Majesty's ships. If a captain be saluted by a foreign ship of war, he is to return it with an equal number of guns.

11. Merchant ships, whether belonging to his Majesty's subjects, or to those of any other nation, are to receive, in return to their salutes, six guns less from the admiral and commander-in-chief of the fleet, four less from all other flag-officers, and two less from captains; but, when several merchant ships salute at the same time, the officer saluted may return such a number as he' shall think proper.

12. When his Majesty or any of the royal family shall go on-board any of his Majesty's ships, the standard is to be hoisted at the main-top-gallant-mast head of that ship, and they are to be saluted with twenty-one guns on their going on-board, and on their leaving the ship, and as much oftener as, from circumstances, the commanding officer shall think proper.

13. When a nobleman, or any other person in a high public station, shall embark on-board any of his Majesty's ships, he may be saluted on his going on-board, and on his quitting the ship, with the following number of guns, viz.

A duke or ambassador with............................. 15

All other noblemen and envoys. 13

14. If any nobleman shall visit any of his Majesty's ships, he

may be saluted, on his leaving the ship, with the following number of guns, viz.

A duke with. 15
All other noblemen. 13

But, if he visit several ships of any squadron, or in the same
port; he shall be saluted by only one of them.

15. If the ship of a flag-officer anchor in any foreign port or
road, he is to inform himself what salutes have been usually given
or received by flag-officers of his rank, of other nations or by those
of his Majesty, and he is to insist on receiving the same marks of
respect.

16. If a ship, not carrying a flag, anchor in any foreign port
or road, the captain may salute the fort with such a number of
guns as may have been customary, on his receiving an assurance
from the governor, that the fort will return an equal number,
but without such assurance he is never to salute.

17. If any foreign nobleman, flag-officer, or general-officer,
shall go on-board any of his Majesty's ships, he may be saluted on
his leaving the ship with such a number of guns, as, from his
rank and quality, may be proper. And the captain of a foreign
ship of war may be saluted, on his visiting one of his Majesty's
ships, if such a compliment shall have been paid to the captain of
any of his Majesty's ships on visiting the ships of his nation.

18. His Majesty's consul or a British factory may be saluted
with eleven guns on their leaving any of his Majesty's ships which
they shall visit; but this may be done only once on the arrival
of a ship in any foreign port, and once before her departure
from it.

19. None of the before-mentioned salutes are to be fired without
the approbation of the commanding officer present.

20. The anniversary days of the birth, accession, and coronation, of the king; of the birth of the queen; of the restoration
of king Charles the Second; and of the Gunpowder Treason; shall
be solemnised by such of his Majesty's ships as are in port, with
such a number of guns as the commanding officer present shall
direct, not exceeding twenty-one in each ship.

21. All salutes are to be fired from the guns of the upper deck.

22. His Majesty's ships are not, on any account, to salute any
of his Majesty's forts or castles in the United Kingdom.

23. If a ship, which anchors in any foreign port or road, shall find there a flag-officer of the nation to which the port belongs, the captain may salute such flag-officer with as many guns as he would salute a British flag-officer of the same rank, on his being assured that his salute shall be returned, in the same manner as it would be returned to a ship of that nation.

24. Within his Majesty's seas his ships are not, on any account, to strike their topsails, nor take in their flags; nor in any way to salute any foreign ship whatever; nor are they, in any other seas, to strike their topsails, or take in their flags, to any foreign ships, unless such foreign ship shall have first struck, or shall at the same time strike, their flags and topsails to his Majesty's ships.

25. If any of his Majesty's subjects shall so far forget their duty as to attempt to pass any of his Majesty's ships without striking their topsails, the names of the ship and the master, the port to which they belong, the place from which they came, and that to which they are bound, together with affidavits of the fact, are to be sent to the secretary of the admiralty, in order to their being proceeded against in the admiralty court.

26. If any flag-officer shall die when on actual service, his flag shall be lowered half-mast, and shall continue so until he is buried; and at his funeral the commanding officer present shall direct such a number of minute-guns, not exceeding twenty-five, as he may think proper, to be fired by every ship, to begin when the corpse is put into the sea, or when it is put off from the ship to be carried on-shore.

27. If the captain of one of his Majesty's ships shall die, his pendant shall be lowered as directed in the case of the flag, and at his funeral the commanding officer present shall order such a number of minute-guns, not exceeding twenty, as he shall think proper, to be fired from the ship he commanded, beginning as in the preceding article. If the ship be alone, the officer succeeding to the command is to order this to be done.

28. If the lieutenant of one of his Majesty's ships shall die, the commanding officer present shall order three volleys of musketry to be fired at his funeral, from the ship to which he belonged.

SALUTE ON JOINING COMPANY. If a salute be required on joining company with an admiral at sea, irons should be ready heated in the fire, and the guns loaded and primed: for, it is to be observed, that irons afford the most approved method of firing a salute.

SALUTING DAYS. The number of guns fired on the holidays called SALUTING DAYS in the Navy, are as follow:

No. of guns.

Queen's Birth-day, January 18...................21

King Charles's Restoration, May 29...............17

King's Birth-day, June 4.........................21

King's Coronation, September 22.................21

King's Accession, Oct. 25.......................17

Gunpowder-Plot, Nov. 5. 17

SHELL, or BOMB. A globe or shell of cast iron, having a vent to receive a wooden fuse, &c. See BOMB and MORTAR.

TABLE of the DIMENSIONS and WEIGHT of SHELLS for Mortars and Howitzers.

Species.	Weight.			Diameter.	Powder contained in shells.	Powder for bursting.	Diameter of fuse-hole.		Thickness of metal.
							Outside.	Inside.	
	Cwt. qs. lbs. oz.			Inch.	lbs. oz.	lbs. oz.	Inch.	Inch.	Inch.
13-inch .	1 3	2		12¾	10 4	6 12	1.837	1.696	2.05
10	— 3	9		9¼	4 5	2 10	1.57	1.45	1.575
8	— 1	11¼		7¼	2 12	1 14	1.219	1.127	1.2
5½....	— —	15¼		5¼	1 —	— 12	0.894	.826	0.822
4⅖....	— —	8		4½	— 7	— 5	0.832	.769	0.653
H. Gren. {	— — 3	11		3.49	.. ..	— 1½			
{	— — 1	13		2.77					

DIMENSIONS of SHELLS for GUNS and CARRONADES made with an equal thickness of metal.

Species.			42-Pr.	32	24	18	12
			Inch.	Inch.	Inch.	Inch.	Inch.
Guns	Diameter of the shell	Exterior	6.684	6.105	5.547	5.05	4.4
		Interior	4.404	4.005	3.767	3.4	2.8
	Thickness of metal....		1.14	1.05	0.89	0.82	0.8
	Diameter of fuse-hole.	Exterior	0.894	0.894	0.893	0.832	0.832
		Interior	0.826	0.826	.826	.76	.769
	Powder for bursting...		14 oz.	11 oz.	12 oz.	9 oz.	5¼ oz.
Carronades.	Diameter of shell.	Exterior	6.64	6.05	5.48	4.935	4.295
		Interior	4.36	3.95	3.48	3.235	2.695
	Thickness of metal....		1.14	1.35	1.	.85	0.98
	Shell's weight.....lbs.			22		12	
	Contains powder ...oz.			12½		9	
	Powder for bursting oz.			10		7	

The following shells may also be fired from guns.

Hand-grenades from.................. 6-pounders.

4½-Shells........................... 12 ———————

5¼-Shells.......... .... 24 ———————

8-Inch.......................... 68-pr. carronades.

Shells may likewise be thrown from guns to short distances, in cases of necessity, though the bore be not of a diameter sufficient to admit the shell.—For this purpose the gun may be elevated to any degree that will retain the shell upon its muzzle, which may be assisted by a small line going from the lugs of the shell round the neck of the gun. To produce a greater effect, the space between the shell and the charge may be filled with wads or other substance.

To find the weight of a shell of iron.—Take nine sixty-fourths of the difference of the cubes of the external and internal diameters for the weight of the shell.

To find how much powder will fill a shell.—Divide the cube of the internal diameter of the shell in inches by 57.3, for the pounds of powder.

To find the size of a shell to contain a given weight of powder.—Multiply the pounds of powder by 57.3, and the cube root of the product will be the diameter in inches.

The Germans do not name their shells from the diameter of the bore which receives them, but from the weight of a stone ball that fits the same bore as the shell. Thus a 7lbs. howitzer admits a stone ball of that weight ; the shell for this weighs 15lbs. and answers to the English 5½-inch. The 30lbs. howitzer shell weighs 60lbs. and is rather more than 8 inches in diameter.

Note.—Shells were, till lately, made thicker at the bottom than at the fuse-hole ; but are now cast of the same thickness throughout, and are found to burst into a greater number of pieces in consequence.

SHOT. A denomination given to all sorts of balls for fire-arms ; those for cannon being of iron, and those for muskets, &c. of lead. See BALLS and BULLETS.

SKY-ROCKET. See ROCKET.

SMALL-ARMS. Muskets, carbines, pistols, &c. See the respective articles. The DIMENSIONS and PARTICULARS are as follow :

Species.	Length of Barrel.		Diameter of bore.	Balls weight for					
				Proof.			Service.		
	Ft.	In.	Inches.	oz.	dr.	gr.	oz.	dr.	gr.
Wall-piece.............	4	6	.98	2	8	8	2	5	7
Musket.	3	6	.76	1	6	11½	1	1	12
Carbine..............	3	0	.61	0	14	13	0	12	11
Pistol, common	1	2	.58	0	8	15	0	7	4¼
Ditto—carbine	1	0	.66	0	14	13	0	12	11

PARTICULARS OF CARTRIDGES FOR SMALL-ARMS.

Species.	Powder contained in each cartridge.	No. of each tied in one bundle.	No. contained in one barrel.		Weight of one barrel filled.				One sheet of paper makes.
			Whole	Half.*	Whole.		Half.		
	drams.	No.	No.	No.	cwt.	qr. lbs.	qr.	lbs.	No.
Wall-piece ...	10	6	1400	500	2	2 19	3	24	6
Musket......	6	10	2100	1000	1	3 10	3	24	12
Carbine......	4	10	2853	1500	1	3 7	3	26	16
Ditto pistol ·..	3	10	4400	1500	1	3 17	3	21	24
Common pistol	3	10		2000			3	11	24
7 Bar. guns...	1½	14		1000					

* In kegs.

SMALL-ARMS. NAVAL EXERCISE of, by Mr. Joseph Conolly, Intended to qualify the seaman to join the troops of the line in action.

The exercise, as here shewn, has been submitted to, and fully approved of by, his Royal Highness the Commander-in-chief. It comprises all that is necessary for attack and defence, in the most direct and simple manner; and ever will be the exercise of action, however military men may be instructed on the parade with a musket, in any part of the world.

EXPLANATION.

All troops of infantry fall in with the arms at the order. Standing in that position, they are sized and counted off into divisions, sub-divisions, sections, and wings; and are ready to fix bayonets, prime, and load.

The seaman, from the nature of his dress, want of pliability in his hand, and situation of his pouch, finds it necessary to make two motions in shouldering his arms (which requires but one in the line); and he is apt to drop his musket on the toes of his left hand man, and cause confusion.

The ship's pouch is fastened in front, with a belt above the hip; the bayonet-carriage is on the same belt, to the left of the pouch. The charge is considered part of the platoon, where it presents itself when the ammunition is expended.

THE MANUAL EXERCISE.

Words of command.	No. of motions.	Explanation.
Fix bayonet.	2.	1st. Slide the right thumb behind the barrel, and seize the socket of the bayonet with the left hand; the thumb downwards. 2nd. Draw and screw it on, projecting the muzzle of the piece one foot from the right shoulder, quitting the left hand, stand at the order. N.B. This may be called one motion.
Shoulder arms.	2.	1st. Slide the right thumb behind the barrel (arm at full extent). Bring the piece briskly across the body,

F F

The Manual Exercise, continued.

Words of command.	No. of motions.	Explanation.
		placing the butt in the left hand, the arm at full extent.
		2nd. Quit the right hand.
Order arms.	3.	1st. Seize the piece with the right hand, on a line with the left shoulder.
		2nd. Draw it across the body to hang in the right hand, the butt within two inches of the deck or ground.
		3rd. Place the piece at the order.

THE PLATOON EXERCISE.

From the order.

Prime and load. }	1.	Slide the right thumb behind the barrel. Throw the piece into the left hand, the little finger one inch from the feather-spring, making a half face to the right, the piece at the bevel (on a line with the left shoulder and right short rib) ; throw open the pan with the right thumb, placing the fingers before the touch-hole, the fore-finger uppermost.
Handle cart-ridge. }	1.	Take out the cartridge, bring it up briskly to the mouth, bite off the blank point; elbow down.
Prime.	1.	Fill the pan better than half full, from the cartridge, shut the pan with the three disengaged fingers, and place them round the small of the piece.
Load.	2.	1st. Cast the piece to the left side, the butt on the ground, within one inch of the left little toe (the lock outward) quitting the right hand, bring the cartridge before the muzzle at the off side.
		2nd. Shake in the powder, put in the paper and ball, and seize the rammer between the fore-finger and thumb of the right hand.

Platoon Exercise, continued.

Words of command.	No. of motions.	Explanation.
Draw rammer.	2.	1st. Draw it up at the full extent of the right arm. 2nd. Seize it back-handed, or thumb downwards, close to the muzzle of the piece, and draw it out of the loops: enter it one inch in the barrel.
Ram down charge. }	3.	1st. Force the rammer down to the grip of the fore-finger and thumb. 2nd. Seize the rammer in like manner within two inches of the top, ramming the cartridge to the bottom. 3rd. Two half motions to ram home compact.
Return rammer. }	2.	1st. Throw the rammer up, and catch it half way back-handed. 2nd. Draw it out and return it in the loops, preserving a grip with the fore-finger and thumb to steady the piece for the following motion.
Ready.	1.	Spring the piece up to a recover, and cock with the right thumb and seize the small of the piece. The piece is suspended in the left hand, with the little-finger one inch from the feather-spring. The right hand only steadies the piece. N.B. In cocking, the centre rank make one pace with the right foot, ten inches; the heel on a line with the hollow of the left foot.
Present.	1.	Level breast high, drawing back the right foot; lean forward.
Fire.	1.	Enter the fore-finger into the guard, and pull the trigger smartly at the word; when fired, bring the piece to the prime and loading position. N.B. The centre rank, when fired, bring the left heel to the right; and, in

Platoon Exercise, continued.

Words of command.	No. of motions.	Explanation.
		every succeeding fire, pace the same distance with the left.
Charge.	1.	Move forward in line; the pieces of the front rank brought down within two inches of a level, preserving a firm grip at the small with the right hand. Dress by the centre; the centre rank remains at the bevel or port.
		N.B. The centre rank bring the right heel to the left when the firing ceases, and regain the lost pace to the left.
Shut pan.		As described.

EXTRA MOTIONS.

Order arms.	2.	1st. Quit the grip at the small, bringing up the muzzle with the grip of the left hand. Seize the piece with the right hand, the thumb close to the little-finger of the left.
		2nd. Let the piece slip through the right hand to the order, quitting the left at the same time.
Unfix.	2.	1st. Project the piece about ten inches, meeting it two inches below the socket of the bayonet with the left hand.
		2nd. Strike it up at the neck with the right hand, between the fore-finger and thumb, unscrew and return it. Stand at the order.
Shoulder arms.		See shoulder arms in manual exercise.
Secure arms.	3.	1st. Seize the small across the body with the right hand.
		2nd. Seize the piece with the left hand, the thumb pointing up the tail-pipe and pressing on the rammer.
		3rd. Draw the piece out a little below, and throw the lock well up under the left

Extra Motions, continued.

Words of command.	Explanation.
	arm, quitting the right hand in the same time.
Shoulder arms.	The reverse of the above.
Order arms.	See order arms in manual exercise.
Trail arms.	See second position of the above.
Dismiss.	

LETTER OF APPROBATION.

Sir, *Horse Guards, 2d April,* 1805.

I have to acknowledge the receipt of your letter of the 21st ultimo, inclosing some proposed instructions for a naval exercise, which I have not failed to lay before the commander-in-chief, and am authorised by his royal highness to state, that the mode of performing the manual and platoon exercise as therein described, appears to his royal highness well calculated for the intended purpose.

I remain, sir, your obedient servant,

(Signed) *W. Wynyard, D. A. G.*

Mr. J. Conolly, master-at-arms
on-board his Majesty's ship
Salvador del Mundo.

To SPIKE a GUN. To fasten a coin with spikes to the deck, close to the breech of a gun-carriage, so that the gun may keep firmly and closely to the ship's side, and not break loose when the ship rolls. It likewise means to choke up the vent of a piece of ordnance, so as to render it useless. See *To* NAIL.

SQUARE NUMBER. The product of a number multiplied into itself. See INVOLUTION, p. 9.

For the convenience of the reader, and to save him the trouble of calculation, we have hereto annexed a *Table of Squares and Cubes;* by which, on mere inspection, the square and cube of every number or root from 1 to 200, and likewise the roots corresponding to the squares and cubes, may be readily found.

TABLE OF SQUARES AND CUBES, WITH THE SQUARE ROOTS AND CUBE ROOTS.

Number.	Square.	Cube.	Square root.	Cube root.
1	1	1	1.0000000	1.000000
2	4	8	1.4142136	1.259921
3	9	27	1.7320508	1.442250
4	16	64	2.0000000	1.587401
5	25	125	2.2360680	1.709976
6	36	216	2.4494897	1.817121
7	49	343	2.6457513	1.912933
8	64	512	2.8284271	2.000000
9	81	729	3.0000000	2.080084
10	100	1000	3.1622777	2.154435
11	121	1331	3.3166248	2.223980
12	144	1728	3.4641016	2.289428
13	169	2197	3.6055513	2.351335
14	196	2744	3.7416574	2.410142
15	225	3375	3.8729833	2.466212
16	256	4096	4.0000000	2.519842
17	289	4913	4.1231056	2.571282
18	324	5832	4.2426407	2.620741
19	361	6859	4.3588989	2.668402
20	400	8000	4.4721360	2.714418
21	441	9261	4.5825757	2.758923
22	484	10648	4.6904158	2.802039
23	529	12167	4.7958315	2.843867
24	576	13824	4.8989795	2.884499
25	625	15625	5.0000000	2.924018

Number.	Square.	Cube.	Square root.	Cube root.
26	676	17576	5.0990195	2.962496
27	729	19683	5.1961524	3.000000
28	784	21952	5.2915026	3.036589
29	841	24389	5.3851648	3.072317
30	900	27000	5.4772256	3.107232
31	961	29791	5.5677644	3.141381
32	1024	32768	5.6568542	3.174802
33	1089	35937	5.7445626	3.207534
34	1156	39304	5.8309519	3.239612
35	1225	42875	5.9160798	3.271066
36	1296	46656	6.0000000	3.301927
37	1369	50653	6.0827625	3.332222
38	1444	54872	6.1644140	3.361975
39	1521	59319	6.2449980	3.391211
40	1600	64000	6.3245553	3.419952
41	1681	68921	6.4031242	3.448217
42	1764	74088	6.4807407	3.476027
43	1849	79507	6.5574385	3.503398
44	1936	85184	6.6332496	3.530348
45	2025	91125	6.7082039	3.556893
46	2116	97336	6.7823300	3.583048
47	2209	103823	6.8556546	3.608826
48	2304	110592	6.9282032	3.634241
49	2401	117649	7.0000000	3.659306
50	2500	125000	7.0710678	3.684031

Number.	Square.	Cube.	Square root.	Cube root.
51	2601	132651	7.1414284	3.708430
52	2704	140608	7.2111026	3.732511
53	2809	148877	7.2801099	3.756286
54	2916	157464	7.3484692	3.779763
55	3025	166375	7.4161985	3.802953
56	3136	175616	7.4833148	3.825862
57	3249	185193	7.5498344	3.848501
58	3364	195112	7.6157731	3.870877
59	3481	205379	7.6811457	3.892996
60	3600	216000	7.7459647	3.914867
61	3721	226981	7.8102497	3.936497
62	3844	238328	7.8740079	3.957892
63	3969	250047	7.9372539	3.979057
64	4096	262144	8.0000000	4.000000
65	4225	274625	8.0622577	4.020726
66	4356	287496	8.1240384	4.041240
67	4489	300763	8.1853528	4.061548
68	4624	314432	8.2462113	4.081656
69	4761	328509	8.3066239	4.101566
70	4900	343000	8.3666003	4.121285
71	5041	357911	8.4261498	4.140818
72	5184	373248	8.4852814	4.160168
73	5329	389017	8.5440037	4.179339
74	5476	405224	8.6023253	4.198336
75	5625	421875	8.6602540	4.217163

TABLE OF SQUARES AND CUBES, WITH THE SQUARE ROOTS AND CUBE ROOTS.

Number.	Square.	Cube.	Square root.	Cube root.
76	5776	438976	8.7177979	4.235824
77	5929	456533	8.7749644	4.254321
78	6084	474552	8.8317609	4.272659
79	6241	493039	8.8881944	4.290841
80	6400	512000	8.9442719	4.308870
81	6561	531441	9.0000000	4.326749
82	6724	551368	9.0553851	4.344481
83	6889	571787	9.1104336	4.362071
84	7056	592704	9.1651514	4.379519
85	7225	614125	9.2195445	4.396830
86	7396	636056	9.2736185	4.414005
87	7569	658503	9.3273791	4.431047
88	7744	681472	9.3808315	4.447960
89	7921	704969	9.4339811	4.464745
90	8100	729000	9.4868330	4.481405
91	8281	753571	9.5393920	4.497942
92	8464	778688	9.5916630	4.514357
93	8649	804357	9.6436508	4.530655
94	8836	830584	9.6953597	4.546836
95	9025	857375	9.7467943	4.562903
96	9216	884736	9.7979590	4.578857
97	9409	912673	9.8488578	4.594701
98	9604	941192	9.8994949	4.610436
99	9801	970299	9.9498744	4.626065
100	10000	1000000	10.0000000	4.641569
101	10201	1030301	10.0498756	4.657010
102	10404	1061208	10.0995049	4.672330
103	10609	1092727	10.1488916	4.687548
104	10816	1124864	10.1980390	4.702669
105	11025	1157625	10.2469508	4.717694
106	11236	1191016	10.2956301	4.732624
107	11449	1225043	10.3440804	4.747459
108	11664	1259712	10.3923048	4.762203
109	11881	1295029	10.4403065	4.776856
110	12100	1331000	10.4880885	4.791420
111	12321	1367631	10.5356538	4.805896
112	12544	1404928	10.5830052	4.820284
113	12769	1442897	10.6301458	4.834588
114	12996	1481544	10.6770783	4.848808
115	13225	1520875	10.7238053	4.862944
116	13456	1560896	10.7703296	4.876999
117	13689	1601613	10.8166538	4.890973
118	13924	1643032	10.8627805	4.904868
119	14161	1685159	10.9087121	4.918685
120	14400	1728000	10.9544512	4.932424
121	14641	1771561	11.0000000	4.946088
122	14884	1815848	11.0453610	4.959675
123	15129	1860867	11.0905365	4.973190
124	15376	1906624	11.1355287	4.986631
125	15625	1953125	11.1803399	5.0000000
126	15876	2000376	11.2249722	5.013298
127	16129	2048383	11.2694277	5.026526
128	16384	2097152	11.3137085	5.039684
129	16641	2146689	11.3578167	5.052774
130	16900	2197000	11.4017543	5.065797
131	17161	2248091	11.4455231	5.078753
132	17424	2299968	11.4891253	5.091643
133	17689	2352637	11.5325626	5.104469
134	17956	2406104	11.5758369	5.117230
135	18225	2460375	11.6189500	5.129928
136	18496	2515456	11.6619038	5.142563
137	18769	2571353	11.7046999	5.155137
138	19044	2628072	11.7473444	5.167649
139	19321	2685619	11.7898261	5.180101
140	19600	2744000	11.8321596	5.192494
141	19881	2803221	11.8743421	5.204828
142	20164	2863288	11.9163753	5.217103
143	20449	2924207	11.9582607	5.229321
144	20736	2985984	12.0000000	5.241482
145	21025	3048625	12.0415946	5.253588
146	21316	3112136	12.0830460	5.265637
147	21609	3176523	12.1243557	5.277632
148	21904	3241792	12.1655251	5.289572
149	22201	3307949	12.2065556	5.301459
150	22500	3375000	12.2474487	5.313293

TABLE OF SQUARES AND CUBES, &c.

Number	Square	Cube	Square root	Cube root
151	22801	3442951	12.2882057	5.325074
152	23104	3511808	12.3288280	5.336803
153	23409	3581577	12.3693169	5.348481
154	23716	3652264	12.4096736	5.360108
155	24025	3723875	12.4498996	5.371685
156	24336	3796416	12.4899960	5.383313
157	24649	3869893	12.5299641	5.394690
158	24964	3944312	12.5698051	5.406120
159	25281	4019679	12.6095202	5.417501
160	25600	4096000	12.6491106	5.428835
161	25921	4173281	12.6885775	5.440122
162	26244	4251528	12.7279221	5.451362
163	26569	4330747	12.7671453	5.462556
164	26896	4410944	12.8062485	5.473703
165	27225	4492125	12.8452326	5.484806
166	27556	4574296	12.8840987	5.495865
167	27889	4657463	12.9228480	5.506879
168	28224	4741632	12.9614814	5.517848
169	28561	4826809	13.0000000	5.528775
170	28900	4913000	13.0384048	5.539658
171	29241	5000211	13.0766968	5.550499
172	29584	5088448	13.1148770	5.561298
173	29929	5177717	13.1529464	5.572054
174	30276	5268024	13.1909060	5.582770
175	30625	5359375	13.2287566	5.593445
176	30976	5451776	13.2664992	5.604079
177	31329	5545233	13.3041347	5.614673
178	31684	5639752	13.3416641	5.625226
179	32041	5735339	13.3790882	5.635741
180	32400	5832000	13.4164079	5.646216
181	32761	5929741	13.4536240	5.656652
182	33124	6028568	13.4907376	5.667051
183	33489	6128487	13.5277493	5.677411
184	33856	6229504	13.5646600	5.687734
185	34225	6331625	13.6014705	5.698019
186	34596	6434856	13.6381817	5.708267
187	34969	6539203	13.6747943	5.718479
188	35344	6644672	13.7113092	5.728654
189	35721	6751269	13.7477271	5.738794
190	36100	6859000	13.7840488	5.748897
191	36481	6967871	13.8202750	5.758965
192	36864	7077888	13.8564065	5.768998
193	37249	7189057	13.8924440	5.778996
194	37636	7301384	13.9283883	5.788960
195	38025	7414875	13.9642400	5.798890
196	38416	7529536	14.0000000	5.808786
197	38809	7645373	14.0356688	5.818648
198	39204	7762392	14.0712473	5.828476
199	39601	7880599	14.1067360	5.838272
200	40000	8000000	14.1421356	5.848035

STORES. Disposal or arrangement of. There are many things kept below in an English ship of war, which foreign officers, upon their visits, are astonished to see, as supposing them to be without. These, with arrangement and taste, might be disposed of to much advantage, both to set off their appearance, and to be in readiness at the quarters the moment they are wanted. As for example, the match-tubs, wads, salt-boxes, powder-horns, pikes, tomahawks, and tube-boxes, which are absolutely requisite to be at hand; but, particularly, in a cruising ship; and, at the same time, it furnishes the executive officer with an opportunity of displaying his abilities in disposing of them to advantage. .

The fire-buckets are generally well painted, and hung in a row round the fife-rail, and the lower part of the breast work of the poop, having their laniards flemished close down inside, which disposes of the whole that is allowed. Some ships, that do not stow hammoes in the breast work of the poop, have a breast work made of pikes, which in general appears heavy, and without taste. If there should not be any breast work, the best substitute is a half circle of tomahawks on each side, and in large ships two, which are light, and look well. The pikes, as they have no beauty in appearance, but are instruments necessary to be at hand, may be kept out of sight, (the handles either scraped very clean, or painted white, and the pike black) under the half deck. The tomahawks crossed and nailed up over each gun, with a powder-horn between them. The wads made up in cheeses, and covered with canvas, having an emblematical painting on it. The salt-boxes painted in the same manner, and fixed over the gun. The tube-boxes ranged in a dry place, painted and numbered, for the guns; they are commonly put under the half deck, against the bulk head of the cabin, under the charge of the sentinel at the cabin door. The locks are, in some ships, kept constantly on the guns, with covers cut out of solid blocks of wood, or cast lead; these covers may keep the wet from them, but cannot prevent the damp, which will, of course, render them unfit for use, and shows the impropriety of keeping them on. It appears better to place them in a dry situation, after having been fitted, with the number of the gun to which they belong affixed over them. One man at each gun should be taught to fix them on, who should be stationed to perform this particular service, when the drummer beats to quarters.

TACKLES. See GUN-TACKLES.

To TERTIATE. To examine the thickness of the metal of a piece of ordnance, in order to ascertain its strength; or, in other words, to find whether it has its due thickness at the vent, trunnions, and neck; if the trunnions and neck are in due order, and the chase straight, &c. If the piece be home-bored, take the diameter with caliber compasses, from which subtract the bore and divide by two, gives the thickness at any part required.

TOMPIONS or TAMPIONS. The wooden cylinders put into the

G G

mouth of guns, mortars, &c. to prevent the dust or wet from getting in.

TOMPIONS also signify the iron bottoms to which grape-shot are fixed; the diameter of which are as follow :

42-pounders	6$\frac{8}{10}$ inches.	9-pounders	3$\frac{2}{10}$ inches.
32	6	6	6$\frac{1}{4}$
24	5$\frac{4}{10}$	4	2$\frac{9}{10}$
18	4$\frac{8}{10}$	1$\frac{1}{2}$	2$\frac{1}{10}$
12	4$\frac{3}{10}$	$\frac{1}{2}$	1$\frac{4}{10}$

TONNAGE. The common method of finding the tonnage of a ship is by the following rule : multiply the length of the keel by the breadth of the beam, and that product by half the breadth of the beam, and divide the last product by 94, and the quotient will be the tonnage.

Ships keel 72 feet : breadth of beam, 24 feet.

$$\frac{72 \times 24 \times 12}{94} = 220.6 \text{ tonnage.}$$

The tonnage of goods and stores is taken sometimes by weight and sometimes by measurement; and that method is allowed to the vessel, which yields the most tonnage.—In tonnage by weight 20 cwt. make one ton.—In tonnage by measurement 40 cubic feet equal one ton.—All carriages, or other stores, to be measured for tonnage, are taken to pieces, and packed in the manner which will occupy the least room on-board ship.—All ordnance, whether brass or iron, is taken in tonnage, by its actual weight.—Musket cartridges in barrels or boxes; all ammunition in boxes; and other articles of great weight are taken in tonnage, according to their actual weight.

More correct, although less simple, methods of finding a ship's tonnage, may be found in the *" Elements and Practice of Naval Architecture."*

TRIMMING SHIP. The following table exhibits the total weight of shot, for trimming ship, by each man carrying two, from 10 to 100 men.

Species of shot.	Weight by 10 men.	By 20	30	40	50	60	70	80	90	100	By 100, in Tons	cwt.	qrs.	lbs.
	lbs.	lbs.	lbs.	lbs.	lbs.	lbs.	lbs.	lbs.	lbs.	lbs.				
6-Pdr. ..	120	240	360	480	600	720	840	960	1080	1200	0	10	2	24
9	180	360	540	720	900	1080	1260	1440	1620	1800	0	16	0	8
12	240	480	720	960	1200	1440	1680	1920	2160	2400	1	1	1	20
18	360	720	1080	1440	1800	2160	2520	2880	3240	3600	1	12	0	16
24	480	960	1440	1920	2400	2880	3360	3840	4320	4800	2	2	3	12
32	640	1280	1920	2560	3200	3840	4480	5120	5760	6400	2	17	0	16
Men*, wt. of.	1600	3200	4800	6400	8000	9600	11200	12800	14400	16000	7	2	3	12

* The weight of men is estimated on the assumption that 15, with their baggage, are equal to one ton.

TRUCKS. Trucks of a gun-carriage are wheels made of one piece of wood, of from 12 to 19 inches in diameter. For the dimensions, see CANNON, page 120.

TRUNNIONS. The cylindric pieces of metal on a gun by which it is supported on its carriage.

TUBES, for firing guns and mortars, are of tin; they must pass through a gauge of two tenths diameter. The composition with which they are filled is mealed powder mixed up stiffly with spirits of wine. They are made up in bundles of 100 each.

Should they get damaged by wet the composition may be cleaned out of them, and they may be fresh filled. If spirits of wine cannot be had, good rum or brandy will answer the purpose.

VALENCIENNES COMPOSITION. See Carcasses.

VELOCITY of a Ball or Shot. The rate or speed of its motion through the air, when fired from a gun, &c. This we have already sufficiently explained, in the 4th section (see pages 97, 98,); and shall therefore only add, under the present head, an explanation of the machine by which Mr. Robins made his experiments.

The machine is simply a pendulous block of wood, suspended freely by an horizontal axis, against which block are fired the balls whose velocities are to be determined.

The instrument thus fitted, if the weight of the pendulum be known. and likewise the respective distances of its centre of gravity, and of its centre of occillation, from its axis of suspension, it may thence be known what motion will be communicated to this pendulum by the percussion of a body of a known weight moving with a known degree of celerity, and striking it in a given point; that is, if the pendulum be supposed at rest before the percussion, it will be known what vibration it ought to make in consequence of such a determined blow; and, on the contrary, if the pendulum, being at rest, is struck by a body of a known weight, and the vibration which the pendulum makes after the blow, is known, the velocity of the striking body may thence be determined.

Hence then, if a bullet of a known weight strikes the pendulum, and the vibration, which the pendulum makes in consequence of the stroke, be ascertained; the velocity with which the ball moved, is thence by calculation, to be inferred.

With such machines Mr. Robins made a great number of experiments, with musket barrels of different lengths, with balls of various weights, and with different charges or quantities of powder. He has set down the results of 61· of these experiments, which nearly agree with the corresponding velocities as computed by his theory of the force of powder, and which therefore establish that theory on a sure foundation. *(Dr. Hutton)*

VENT. The small hole or aperture in a gun, commonly called the *touch-hole*, and through which the fire is communicated to the charge. The vents of all English guns are two tenths of an inch in diameter.

A variety of opinions have prevailed as to the best position of the vent; in consequence of which the king of Prussia, in 1765, ordered that a light three-pounder should be cast, with three shifting vents, one at the centre of the charge, one at the bottom, and the other at an equal distance from the bottom and centre one; so that, when one was used, the others were effectually stopped. The gun weighed 2 cwt. 1 qr. 20lb.; its length was 3 feet 3 inches, and the bottom of the bore quite flat. It was loaded each time with one fourth of the shot's weight; and it was found, that, when the lowest or bottom vent was used, the shot went farthest, and the ranges of the others diminished in proportion as they were distant from the bottom. The piece was elevated to one degree 30 minutes.

In the next year the same person caused several experiments to be tried with three small mortars of equal size and dimensions, but of different forms in their chambers; each of which held seven ounces and a half of powder. From these experiments it appeared that the concave chambers produced the greatest ranges, and that the bottom of the chamber is the best place for the vent, having in that place the greatest effect.

VINEGAR. Vinegar is frequently used in the artillery to cool pieces of ordnance. Two pints of vinegar to four of water is the usual proportion.

WAD. A substance of hay or straw, or of tow, made up tightly into a ball. It serves to put into a gun, after the powder, and is rammed home to prevent the powder's being scattered, which would have no effect if unconfined.

A Table of Wads to be expended from Junk monthly, in the Royal Navy.

GUNS.	Weight of 1.		Weight of 20.		Weight of 100.	
	lbs.	oz.	lbs.	oz.	lbs.	oz.
42-Pounders	4	8	90	0	450	0
32	3	8	70	0	350	0
24	2	12	55	0	275	0
18	2	0	40	0	200	0
12	1	8	30	0	150	0
9	1	0	20	0	100	0
6	0	12	15	0	75	0
4	0	8	12	0	60	0
3	0	6	8	0	40	0
2	0	4	5	0	25	0
1	0	2	3	1½	15	0

WAD-HOOK. A strong iron screw, resembling a cork-screw, and mounted upon a wooden handle, to draw out the wads, or any part of cartridges which may happen to remain in guns and choke up the vent.

WATCH-GUN. Regulations relative to. When a flag-officer shall be in any port or road in his Majesty's dominions, he is, at setting of the watch at night, to fire one gun, previous to which the tatoo is to be beaten on-board his ship and all the ships in company. If more than one flag-officer, or commodore with a broad pendant, be present, the senior only is to fire a gun, and the others, in succession, are to fire a volley of musketry, beginning with the second in command.—In all ships, not carrying a flag or broad pendant, the sentinels are to fire their muskets.

At the relieving of the watch in the morning, the senior flag-officer is to fire a gun, and the other flag-officers or commodore in succession a volley of musketry, and the sentinels, in all other ships, their muskets, after which the *reveillez* is to be beaten in every ship present.

If there should not be a flag-officer or commodore at any of his Majesty's ports where guard-ships are stationed, the senior captain is to fire the watch-gun; but ships at anchor in any other port, without a flag-officer or commodore, are not to fire the watch-gun, but are to set and relieve the watch by beating a drum, and the sentinels firing their muskets.

From the 25th of March to the 21st of September, the watch is to be set at nine o'clock, and from the 21st of September to the 25th of March at eight o'clock, in the evening; it is always to be relieved at day-break in the morning.

The senior officer of any number of his Majesty's ships, which may anchor in any foreign port or road, is to fire the watch-guns, except in those places in which the regulations of the port do not admit of guns being fired.

WINDAGE, The difference between the diameter of the bore of a gun and that of its shot or shell; which is, in England, one twentieth of that of the ball; but it appears that, with this windage, by its being two great, from one third to one fourth of the force is lost. The French allow only one twenty-sixth; and it must be evident that the less windage a shot has, the farther and truer it will go.

WINDAGE OF GUNS AND CARRONADES.

Species.	68	42	32	24	18	12	9	6	4	3	2	1
Guns	—	.33	.30	.27	.25	.22	.20	.17	.15	.14	.12	.09
Carronades	.15	.15	.15	.14	.12	.12						

WINDAGE OF MORTARS AND HOWITZERS.

From the 13 to $5\frac{1}{2}$-inch the windage is .15 of an inch, and that of the $4\frac{1}{4}$ is .2 of an inch.

WOODEN-BOTTOMS. Cylindrical pieces of wood, of different lengths and diameters, according to the sizes of guns. They are bottomed at one end to receive the shot, and the flannel cartridge is fastened to the other end; the whole forming one cartridge, which is put into the piece at one motion.

To WORM a Gun. To take out the charge by means of a worm. The latter is an instrument like a wad-hook, too well known to require description.

FINIS.

1811.

A NEW CATALOGUE

OF THE BEST

Charts, Pilots, Books of Navigation,

AND

Nautical Instruments;

SOLD, WHOLESALE, RETAIL, AND FOR EXPORTATION, BY

STEEL & Co.

Chart-Sellers to the Hon. Board of Admiralty,

AT THE

NAVIGATION-WAREHOUSE, 70, CORNHILL, LONDON,

NEAR THE ROYAL EXCHANGE.

CHARTS.

The Atlantic Ocean, Great Britain, and the Orkney and Shetland Isles.

	£	s	d
1° THE Atlantic, or Western Ocean, exhibiting the Coasts of Europe, Africa, and America, from the sixty-second degree of north latitude to the equator, in which all the principal points have been laid down from the most recent and decisive determinations made by the most eminent and experienced navigators, both British and foreign, upon the basis of whose surveys and observations the whole has been constructed, and may be depended on as being the most accurate chart extant; with an Annalysis of the Dangers, and Table of Variation of the Compass	0	7	6
2° The River Thames and River Medway. Coloured 5s. On canvass and rollers	0	10	6
3° The Port of London, from London to Woolwich, with the New Docks, &c. ..	0	4	0
4 The River Medway, from Sheerness to Rochester. Plain 2s. 6d. or coloured	0	3	0
5° The East Coast of England, from Folkstone to Yarmouth, by Adm. Knight, &c.	0	7	6
6° All the Entrances to the River Thames, containing Harwich, Dover, Ramsgate, new Lights at the Sunk and Galloper, &c.	0	4	0
7° A new Chart of the Downs and Margate Roads, with all the leading marks, ...	0	4	0
8° Yarmouth Roads, by John Knight, Esq. Vice-Admiral of the White	0	4	0
9° Yarmouth Roads, by Mr. Thomas Fotheringhame, of the Royal Navy	0	4	0
10 The East Coast from Yarmouth to Scarborough, including the Humber, &c.	0	7	6
11° Boston and Lynn Deeps, on a large scale	0	4	0
12 Harbour of Blakeney, on a large scale	0	4	0
13 The River Humber, from an actual survey	0	2	0
14 Scarborough to Buchanness, including Sunderland, Berwick, Aberdeen, &c...	0	7	6
15 Downie's Coast of Scotland, from the Staples to Duncansby Head	0	6	0
16 Downie's Holy-Island, Fern-Islands, and the Staples	0	3	6
17 Downie's Edinburgh-Frith from Berwick to the Limekilns	0	3	6
18 Downie's Coast of Scotland from St. Abb's Head to the Red-Head...........	0	3	0
19 Buchanness to Farout-head, with the Islands of Orkney and Shetland	0	7	6
20° The Orkney-Islands, by G. Eunson, Branch Pilot of Kirkwall; with directions	0	7	6
21 The Lewis's, from Farout-head and Cape Wrath to the Mull of Cantire.......	0	7	6
22 The Shetland Islands, on a large scale	0	4	0
23° A new, large, and correct Chart of St. George's and Bristol Channels, with the Entrances to Liverpool, the River Clyde, &c. the Harbours of Dublin, Waterford, Lamlash, &c. on an enlarged scale, compiled and drawn from the best and most accurate authorities, with considerable additions and improvements, and embellished with a great number of views, handsomely engraved and accompanied with complete directions	0	10	6

24	St. George's and the Bristol Channels from Centire to Bristol, with the Harbours	0	7
25	The N.W. and S. Coasts of Ireland, with directions on the plates............	0	7
26	The N. E. Coast of Ireland from Drogheda to the Skerries, with directions..	0	7
27	The N.W. Coast of Ireland from the Skerries to Balliconnel, with directions..	0	7
28	The West Coast of Ireland from Balliconnel to Slyne-Head; with the harbours and directions on the plates...	0	7
29	The West Coast of Ireland from Slyne-Head to Kerry-Head, with directions..	0	7
30	The S. W. Coasts of Ireland from Kerry-Head to Kilmarry, with directions..	0	7

The five preceding are from Mackenzie, on a very large scale, with the principal harbours and separate directions to each.

31*	Bear-Haven, and Bantry-Harbour, in Bantry-Bay, by Vice-Admiral Knight, with directions on the plate	0	5
32*	Cork Harbour, with views and directions, by Admiral Knight	0	5
33*	A new Chart from the Feroe, Orkney, and Shetland Isles, to the Bay of Biscay, including England, Ireland and Scotland............................	0	10

N.B.—This is a useful Chart to Mariners who go North about.

34*	A new Chart from Scotland to Barcelona, in the Mediterranean	0	10
35*	The United Kingdom, or Chart of England, Ireland, and Scotland, with the Coasts of France, Spain, Portugal, and part of the Mediterranean.........	0	14
36*	A splendid and unrivalled Chart of the British Channel; on Mercator's projection, whereon the positions of places have been laid down from new and accurate surveys (particularly from the grand trigonometrical survey made by the Board of Ordnance;) together with the precise extent, formation, and quality, of the bank of soundings, as determined by means of an excellent chronometer and numerous astronomic observations; a long-sought desideratum for determining, with certainty, the place of a ship, and facilitating her approach to the coast; including particular plans of all the principal harbours, and embellished with a numerous collection of elegant views of the principal headlands, accompanied by complete directions. By Admiral John Knight	0	14
37	A Chart of the British Channel, and directions	0	7
38*	Spithead, Portsmouth, Isle of Wight, Owers, &c.; by Vice-Admiral Knight	0	6
39*	The Bill of Portland, including the Shambles and Weymouth, by Adm. Knight	0	4
40*	Torbay, on a very large scale, surveyed by Mr. J. Dessiou	0	4
41*	Plymouth Sound, on a very large scale, from a new survey	0	4
42	Harwich Harbour, on a large scale	0	2
43	Dartmouth Harbour, on a large scale	0	4
44	Mount's Bay, with the adjacent Coast, on a large scale..................	0	2
45*	The principal Harbours in the Channel and French Coast, on one large sheet	0	5
46	The Scilly Islands, with appearances of the land, &c. on one sheet..........	0	2
47	The Islands of Guernsey, Jersey and Alderney, with part of the coast of France	0	4

The North Sea, Baltic, Gulf of Finland, Greenland, &c.

48*	The North Sea, on Mercator's projection; drawn principally from the original surveys of Admiral Knight, Murdo, Downie, and several scientific and experienced Officers in the Royal Navy. Embellished with a great number of views, and accompanied with complete directions	0	6
49*	The North Sea, reduced from the above, by Vice-Admiral Knight, with directions	0	5
50	Hammond's Chart of the North Sea, improved by J. Chandler	0	3
51*	England and Holland, from Dungeness to Lynn-Deeps, and from Cape Grisnez to the Texel; by Vice-Admiral Knight, &c.	0	7
52	The Coast of Flanders from Calais to Schowen, including all the Flemish Banks	0	7
53	The Coast of Holland from Schowen to the Texel	0	7
54*	A Survey of the Hondt, or Western Scheldt, from the Sea to Antwerp	0	14
55*	The Coasts of Batavia and Germany from the Texel to the River Hever; including the Rivers Elbe, Weser, Ems, and Eyder; with the Island of Heligoland, on a large scale	0	6
56	The South Coast of Norway, with the Entrance of the Kattegat	0	3
57	The Northern Coast of Norway, including Dronthem, &c.	0	3
58	The Sleeve, or Gulf of Jutland, with the North part of the Kattegat	0	7
59*	The Kattegat, made under the direction of P. de Lovenorn, Esq. F. R. D. S. &c.	0	5
60	The Sound from the Knoll-point to Falsterborn, with directions on the plate	0	4
61*	The Entrance to the Baltic, comprehending the Sound with the two Belts, and the Danish Islands, from the actual surveys of the Swedish Admiral Nordenanker, and improved from the Danish surveys of P. D. Lovenorn and G.		

Lous; with a particular Chart of the Great Belt, on a very large scale, from an actual survey, 1811 .... 0 7 6
62* The Baltic, or East Sea, from the Sound to the Entrances of the Gulf of Finland, including the Great and Little Belts, with directions 0 7 6
63* Particular Chart of Bornholm and the Eartholms, from an actual survey .. 0 5 0
64* The Gulf of Finland to St. Petersburgh, made by order of the Swedish and Russian Governments, with the principal Harbours, on a large scale 0 6 6
65* The Northern Coasts of Europe, from England to the White Sea 0 4 0
66 The White Sea, from the North Cape to Archangel; with directions on the plates 0 7 6
67 The whole Coast of Norway and the White Sea, with the principal Harbours, on an enlarged scale: compiled and drawn from the late surveys made by order of the respective governments of Denmark and Russia, and considerably improved from the surveys and observations of several experienced and scientific Officers of the Royal Navy, handsomely engraved on four sheets.. 0 10 0
68 England to the Coasts of Greenland, Davis's Straits, and Hudson's Bay 0 3 0
69* Potter's Charts of the Fisheries of Greenland and Davis's Straits 0 12 0

France, Bay of Biscay, Spain, Portugal and Mediterranean.

70 The Coast of France from Calais to Ushant, with Plans of several Harbours .. 0 7 6
71* Guernsey, Jersey, &c. with the Harbour of Cherbourgh, on one sheet 0 4 0
72* The Bay of Biscay, with particular plans of Brest, the River Bourdeaux, Basque Roads, &c. with views, by Vice-Admiral Knight 0 6 0
73* The North Coast of Spain, from St. Jean de Luz to Cape Finisterre, from the Spanish surveys of Tofino, and embellished with many elegant views .. 0 7 6
74* The Coasts of Spain and Portugal; compiled from the surveys made by order of the respective Governments of France and Spain, and improved from the surveys and observations of several experienced Officers of the Royal Navy 0 5 0
75* Spain and Portugal from Cape Finisterre to Gibraltar 0 7 6
76* France, Spain, and Portugal, including the Navigation from the British Channel to the Straits of Gibraltar; with the harbours, on a large scale 0 7 6
77* The Mediterranean Sea; principally constructed from the surveys made by order, and at the expense of the respective Governments of Spain, France, and Italy, and considerably improved from the surveys and observations of several experienced and scientific Officers of the Royal Navy, and embellished with several beautiful views, by Admiral Knight, with particular plans of the island of Malta and several principal harbours; handsomely engraved, and accompanied with complete directions 0 10 0
78* Spain and Barbary, with the Straits, on a large scale; by Vice-Admiral Knight 0 5 0
79* South Coast of Spain from Cadiz to Cape de Palos, and the opposite Coast, from the actual surveys of Don Vincente Tofino, &c. handsomely engraved 0 5 0
80* The East Coast of Spain from Cape de Palos to Cape de Creux, with the Islands of Majorca, Minorca, Yviza, &c. from the New Spanish surveys.... 0 5 0
81 A Set of Charts for Malta, &c. 0 15 0
82* The Adriatic Sea, or Gulf of Venice; with plans of the principal harbours, &c. 0 5 0
83 The Road of Leghorn, by Mr. John Jackson, Master in the Royal Navy 0 3 6
84* The Grecian Archipelago, on a large scale 0 5 0
85* The Black Sea, on a large scale, from the Russian surveys................ 0 6 0
86* The Harbour of Cadiz, on a large scale, from the surveys of Don V. Tofino 0 10 0
87* The Straits of Messina, from an actual survey made by order of the King of Sicily; by G. A. R. Zannoni 0 5 0
88 The River Tagus and Environs of Lisbon, from an actual survey 0 10 6

Africa and Islands adjacent.

89 Gibraltar to Cape Blanco, with a particular plan of Mogadore.............. 0 6 0
90 Cape Blanco to Cape Verd..................................... 0 2 0
91 Cape Verd to Sierra Leone 0 6 0
92 Sierra Leone to Formosa, including the Gold Coast 0 10 6
93 Formosa to Cape Negro 0 10 6
94 Cape Negro to the Cape of Good Hope, Madagascar, &c.................. 0 7 6
95 A survey of the River Congo on a large scale 0 7 6
96 ———— the River Sherbro, on a large scale 0 2 0
97* The Western Islands; from the observations made by M. Fleurieu and Don Vincente Tofino 0 4 0
98* The Madeira and Canary Islands; from the surveys made by order of the French Government, by M. le Chevalier de Borda 0 4 0
99* The Cape-Verd Islands, on a large scale, from the best authorities 0 2 0

North America, from Labrador to the Gulf of Mexico.

100* A new Chart of North America from Cape Charles, on the Coast of Labrador, and the Straits of Belle-Isle to Cape Cod; including the Gulf and River St. Lawrence, Newfoundland, the Grand Bank and Banks adjacent, Nova Scotia, New Brunswick, Bay of Fundy, Halifax, &c.; and directions 0 12 6
101* A New Chart of America, from Boston and Cape Cod to Cape Hatteras, including New York, the Delaware, Chesapeake, &c. on a large scale 0 10 6
102* Ditto from Cape Hatteras to Florida, with the harbours, on a large scale..... 0 10 6
103 The Islands of Bermudas 0 2 6
104 The Island of Newfoundland and all its Fishing Banks, with particular plans of the harbours; and directions 0 15 0
105 The Isle of Newfoundland, with separate plans of the harbours, and directions 0 7 6
106 The Coast of Labrador from Sandwich Bay to Cape Charles............... 0 4 6
107 Eastern Coast of Labrador from Belle-Isle to Cape Bluff 0 2 0
108 South Coast of Labrador from Grand Point to Checatia 0 2 0
109 The Gulf and River St. Lawrence from Newfoundland to Quebec 0 7 6
110 Nova Scotia and the Bay of Fundy; with plans of the harbours, and directions on the plates 0 7 6
111 The Straits of Belle Isle, on a large scale 0 4 0
112 The River St. Lawrence, on twelve sheets, with directions 0 12 0
113 The Gulf and River St. Lawrence, by Thomas Wright 0 10 6
114 The Bay of Fundy to New York; with particular plans of the harbours 0 7 6
115 East and West Florida, with plans of the River Mississippi, harbour of Pensacola, &c. 0 7 6

West Indies, South America, and Pacific Ocean.

116* The whole of the West Indies, including the Gulf of Mexico; from the original surveys made by the Spanish Government, and many experienced Officers of the Royal Navy, on four sheets 0 12 0
117* The Windward, or Caribbee Islands, from the Spanish surveys, on a large scale 0 5 0
118 The Gulf of Florida, Bahama Islands, Windward Passage, the Island of Jamaica, Cuba, the Bay of Honduras, and Mosquito-Shore; with directions 0 10 6
119* The Gulf-Passage or New Bahama-Channel, with the Bahama Islands, on a large scale; by Capt. James Maunderson of the Royal Navy, with directions 0 7 6
120 Bay of Honduras.. 0 2 0
121* The Windward and Mona Passages, including the Islands of Jamaica and St. Domingo, on a large scale, drawn from the latest and best authorities 0 7 6
122 The Caribbean Sea from Barbadoes to Jamaica, including the whole of Hispaniola, and plan of the Harbours 0 8 0
123* A survey of the Virgin-Islands, by George King, Land-Surveyor of those Islands, including the Island of St. Croix, on a large scale 0 7 6
124 St. Christopher, Antigua, Guadaloupe, Dominica, Martinico, St Lucia, Barbadoes, St. Vincent, Grenada, Tobago, Curaçoa, Jamaica, and Trinadad, each 0 4 0
125* The whole Coast of Guyana, the Rivers Essequibo, Demerary, Berbice, &c. 0 6 0
126* The Southern Atlantic Ocean from the Equator to Cape Horn and the Cape of Good Hope, including St. Helena, South Georgia, &c. 0 7 6
127* The whole Coast of Brazil, from Maranham to the Entrance of the River Plate, with particular plans of the Harbour of Rio Janeiro. The Bay of All Saints, and St. Salvador, Maranham, and the Island of Fernand de Noronha, on an enlarged scale; compiled and drawn from the surveys made by order of the Government of Portugal, and from the surveys and observations of several experienced and scientific Officers in the Royal Navy; accompanied with directions 0 10 6
128* The River Plate, from an actual survey made by order of the King of Spain, and improved from the observations of several experienced Officers of the Royal Navy; with particular plans of the Harbour of Monte Video and Maldonado: on a large scale, elegantly engraved 0 5 0
129* The Coast of South America from the River Plate to Cape Horn and Valparaiso, on the Coast of Chile 0 12 0
130* The Coast of Chile from Valparaiso to the Bay of Mexillones, &c. 0 7 6
131* Continuation of the Coast of Chile, to the Seventh Degree of South Latitude 0 7 6
132* Continuation of Ditto, to the Ninth Degree of North Latitude, including Panama, &c. 0 7 6
133* England to the Cape of Good Hope and Cape Horn, including the Western Isles, Madeiras, St. Helena, South Georgia, River Plate, Brazil, &c. 0 15 0
134 The Pacific Ocean, on nine sheets.................................... 2 12 6

Cape of Good Hope, Indian and China Seas, &c.

135*	The Cape of Good Hope and Mozambique Passage, with the Harbours, on a large scale, drawn from the best authorities	0	7	6
136*	A new and elegant General Chart of the Indian and China Seas, including New Holland, and all the different Passages to China, on five sheets	0	16	6
137*	An outline Chart from England to the East Indies, intended for the Use of Officers in the Hon. East India Company's service, to prick off a Ship's Track	0	10	6
138*	The Indian Ocean from the Northern Part of Madagascar to Bengal	0	10	6
139*	The Persian Gulf and Harbours	0	7	6
140*	The Andaman and Nicobar Islands	0	7	6
141*	The Coast of China from Pedra Blanca to St. John's Island, &c.	0	7	6
142*	A new Chart of Bombay-Harbour, on a large scale	0	7	6
143*	The Bay of Bengal between Point Palmiras and the Coast of Arican, with the River Hoogly, on a large scale	0	7	6
144*	The China Seas, &c. from Bengal to Canton and Endeavour Straits	0	10	6
145*	The Straits of Malacca and Sincapore on a large scale	0	7	6
146*	The River Tigris from Canton to the Island of Laukeet, by Capt. Huddart	0	7	6
147*	The Straits of Sunda, Banka, Gaspar, and Billiton	0	7	6
148*	The Straits of Sunda and Java Sea, with Batavia, on a large scale	0	7	6
149*	The Straits of Macassar, with great additions and improvements	0	7	6
150*	The Eastern Straits to China, including part of New Guinea	0	7	6
151*	The Eastern Coast of New Holland, with the Harbour of Port Jackson, &c	0	5	0
152*	The whole of the West Coast of Sumatra	0	15	0
153*	The Malabar Coast, including Ceylon, on a large scale	0	15	0
154*	Bass's Straits, and directions	1	1	0
155*	The Red Sea, or Arabian Gulf; by Sir Home Popham	0	16	0
156*	Mercator's Charts of the World, 10s. 6d.—12s.—2l. 12s. 6d. and	2	15	0
157	A variation Chart of the World	0	5	0
158	Van Deiman's Land and the Southern Extremity of New Holland	0	4	0

Besides the above, a great Variety of particular Charts and Maps of every Part of the World, from the best Authorities.—Maps and Charts mounted for the Pocket, and the use of the Counting House, on Rollers, &c.

PILOTS.

159*	The Marine Atlas, or Seaman's Complete Pilot, for all the principal Places in the World, containing a most Excellent Set of Charts, on a large Scale; the whole drawn from the latest Surveys.——Note, this is the Best Publication of this kind in England, and is quite new—in 5 vols.	16	16	0
160	Steel's European Maritime Atlas	8	8	0
161	The complete British and Irish Pilot, for the Coasts of Great Britain, Ireland, &c.	3	13	6
162	The British, Irish, and Mediterranean, Pilot	4	14	6
163	A Pilot for great Britain and the Eastern Coast of Ireland and St. George's Channel	2	12	6
164	The Complete Irish Pilot, comprehending the whole coast of Ireland, with St. George's Channel	2	2	0
165	The smaller Irish Pilot, comprehending St. George's Channel and the Coasts of Ireland	1	0	0
166*	Steel's New and Complete Pilot for the British Channel, &c.	2	2	0
	☞ *This Pilot will be found very useful to Officers in the Navy, and East India Company's Service, previous to their Examination at the Navy Office, Trinity House, or East India House.*			
167	A Pilot for the British, St. George's, and Bristal, Channels, &c.	0	18	0
168	The Newcastle and North-Country Pilot, with the Islands of Orkney and Shetland	1	5	0
169	Mr. Downie's Surveys of the East Coast of Scotland, with directions	0	16	0
170	The large North Sea Pilot, comprehending the East Coasts of Great Britain, Flanders, &c.	1	11	6
171	The Newcastle and North-Country Pilot, from the River Thames to Buchanness	1	1	0
172*	The North Sea and Hambro' Pilot; comprehending the East coast of England, from the Thames to Scarborough, &c.	1	5	0
173*	The Complete North-about Navigator	1	15	0
174*	Steel's Complete Pilot for the Baltic, or East Sea, and the Gulf of Finland	2	12	

NAVIGATION BOOKS, &c.

The Elements and Practice of Naval Architecture; with all the dimensions of 27 Classes of Ships and Vessels, and 39 large draughts, on a grand scale. One volume quarto, with draughts separately. An invaluable work both for the purpose of initiation and for constant use. 10 10 0

Complete Sets of Moulds, Sweeps, Battens, Squares &c. used in the Construction of the various Drafts and Plans of Ships and Vessels, accurately finished and handsomely fitted up in mahogany boxes, with a case of instruments 20 0 0

The Shipwright's Vade Mecum; a clear and familiar introduction to Ship-building; including practical geometry, &c. with four drafts. Boards 1 7 0

  This work may be considered as a proper companion or introduction to the former; and will, likewise, be found very acceptable to those who cannot make it convenient to purchase the larger work. But either is complete, according to its object, independent of the other; and both are calculated as well for the young beginner as for the more experienced artist.

The Elements and Practice of Rigging, Seamanship, Naval Tactics, Sail, Mast, Oar, and Block, Making. Four volumes, 8vo. with plates 2 12 6
Art of making Masts, Yards, &c. with large plates, separate 0 10 0
Improved Mast-maker's Rule, as described in the above, 9s. and 0 10 6
Art of Rigging, illustrated with Engravings 0 10 6
Art of Sail-making, ditto, a new edition 0 9 0
Hutton's Mathematics, two volumes 8vo. in boards 0 18 0
Mackay's Mathematical Tables 0 7 0
Seamanship, both in theory and practice, ... 0 7 6
The System of Naval Tactics, with coloured figures 0 7 6
Hutchinson's Practical Seamanship; fourth edition, 4to 0 18 0
Observations and Instructions for the Use of the commissioned, the junior, and other, Officers of the Royal Navy 0 7 0
Perpetual Birthling and Watch-bill Book 1 1 0
Sea-Gunner's Companion 0 2 6
Cobin's Linear Perspective, adapted to Shipping, 4th edition 0 2 0
Steel's Dimensions of a Ship of each class in the Navy. Sheet 6s.; folded.. 0 6 6
Liddel's New Seaman's Vade Mecum, fifth edition, considerably enlarged, 1811 0 17 0
Delafon's Treatise on Naval Courts-Martial 0 10 6
Improved Practical Navigator; being a complete Epitome of Navigation: with new Tables, corrected from many thousand errors of former works. By N. Bowditch and T. Kirby, 1809 .... 0 12 0
Moore's Epitome of Navigation 0 12 0
Workman on the Defects of Middle Latitude and Mercator Sailing 0 2 6
Walker on the Variation of the Compass, &c. 0 6 6
Kelly on Spherics and Nautical Astronomy 0 9 0
Ephemeris, or Nautical Almanack, for 1811, 1812, 1813, and 1814, each 0 5 0
Requisite Tables, and Supplement 0 7 6
Mackay on the Longitude, 2 vols. boards ....
Hutton's Logarithms ....
The Alien, or Foreigner's Guide, in four languages ....

Margett's Longitude Tables	5	5	0
* Mendoza-Rio's Nautical Tables, new edition, boards	1	5	0
Shepherd's Tables of Refraction, and Parallax	1	11	6
Wales on Time-Keepers	0	4	6
Seaman's Daily Assistant	0	3	6
* The New Seaman's Guide and Coaster's Companion; containing directions for the North Sea, English, Bristol, and St. George's Channels, the Kattegat, Belts, Baltic, White Sea, &c. with Tables of the Sun's Declination, up to the year 1824	0	5	6
Downie's Directions for the East of Scotland	0	2	6
Downie on the Atmosphere, or Guide to Captains who go long Voyages	0	2	6
Mackay's Epitome of Navigation	0	12	0
Directions for the Lewis's, &c	0	2	0
* Directions for St. George's Channel	0	2	6
* Directions for the British Channel; corrected by the new surveys	0	2	6
* Directions for the North Sea	0	2	6
* Directions for the Sound, Baltic, and Gulf of Finland	0	1	6
* Directions for the Mediterranean	0	2	6
* Directions for North America, complete	0	2	6
* Directions for the Gulf Passage, Bahamas &c	0	2	0
* Directions for the Coast of Brazil, &c.	0	1	6
* Steel's Atlantic and West-Indian Navigator, bound	0	6	0
Directions for Africa	0	5	0
East-India Directory; or Oriental Navigator for the East-Indies	2	2	0
* Captain Elmore's East-India Directory	2	2	0
Horsburgh's Directions for the East-Indies	2	2	0
* Ship-Master's Assistant and Owner's Manual	0	15	0
* Steel's Tables of Excise Duties and Drawbacks	0	9	0
* Seaman's and Merchant-Clerk's Ready Calculator, for the solid contents of every species of packages and casks, with a cut Index	0	6	0
India Officer's and Trader's Pocket Guide	0	5	0
India Trader's Pocket Assistant	0	4	0
* Nautical Nomenclator, or Dictionary of the British Navy	0	1	0
* Steel's List of the Royal Navy, monthly,	0	1	6
* Supplement to Prize List, from April, 1805, to June, 1806	0	1	6
* Second Supplement, up to August, 1807	0	1	6
* Tayler's Instructions for Young Mariners	0	1	0
* Mackay's Description and Use of the Sliding Gunter	0	4	6
* Ditto Use of the Sliding Rule	0	3	6
* Table of the Sun's Declination for Eleven Years	0	2	0
* Zodiacal Stars, and directions	0	5	0
Robertson's Navigation, by Wales and Gwynne, two volumes	1	4	0
Lyon's Tables for working the Lunars	0	2	6
Malham's Naval Gazetteer, boards	1	1	0
* Brookes's Gazetteer, from 4s. 6d. to	0	10	6
Flags of Nations, from 3s. 6d. to	0	6	6
East and West India Journals, from 2s. 8d. to	1	6	0
Navy and Merchant Journals, and New Navy Logs, each	0	2	8
Log Books, from 2s. to	0	8	0
Cargo Books, from 1s. 8d. to	0	2	6
Midshipman's Instructor	0	3	6
Newman's Marine Pocket Dictionary	0	7	0
Marshall's Treatise on Insurance, 2 vols.	1	10	0
Biographia Navalis, by Charnock, 6 vols. boards	2	8	0
Edwards's History of the West Indies, 3 vols.	2	2	0
Russel's Art of Rope-Making	0	5	0
* Abbot on Merchant Shipping	0	12	0
* Abbott's Transport's Monitor	0	7	0
* Steel's Naval Monitor	0	1	6
* Ferguson's Astronomy, new edition, bound	0	13	6
Midshipman's Vocabulary	0	4	6
Park's Treatise on Insurance, two volumes, boards	1	16	0
Fenning's Use of the Globes, new edition	0	4	6
Guthrie's Geography, bound in calf	0	19	0
* Maxwell's Treatise on Marine Laws, two volumes, boards	1	1	0
Pinkerton's Geography	0	12	0
Hoppus's Measurer for Timber	0	3	0
Young Man's Companion	0	4	6

An Essay on the Cause of Gravity, by the same author 0 3 0
Adams on the Use of the Globes 0 10 6
Naval Anecdotes 0 10 6
Charnock's Memoirs of Lord Nelson.. 0 10 6
M'Arthur on Courts Martial, two volumes 1 1 0
Mariner's Compass rectified ....:........... 0 3 6
Stevens on the Polar Star 0 2 0
Formulas for the Lunar Observations 0 4 0
Simson's Euclid's Elements, 8vo. 0 3 0
Moore's Daily Assistant 0 6 0
Reeves's Law of Shipping, 8vo. boards.. 0 12 0
Bonnycastle's Astronomy 0 9 6
Cary's Book of Roads 0 7 6
Wilkinson's General Atlas, 4to. bound 1 14 6
Gerrard's Trigonometrical Tables 0 10 6
Donn's Variation Atlas 2 2 0
Medicina Nautica; an Essay on the Diseases of Seamen; by T. Trottor, M.D. 3 vols. 1 3 0
*A Letter to the Rt. Hon. Ld. Visct. Melville, on the present Condition of Officers in
  the Royal Navy; with Reflections on the Necessity and Means of Melioration,
  and on several points of Economy, essentially connected with an improved
  System of Management in His Majesty's Ships. By a Post Captain 0 2 6

N. B.—ALL KINDS OF STATIONARY USEFUL AT SEA.

*The Articles marked thus * are lately published.*

NAUTICAL INSTRUMENTS.

Ebony Quadrants	from	2	12	6	to	5 15 6
Ditto Sextants	from	4	14	6	to	6 16 6
Brass Ditto	from	10	10	0	to	14 14 0
The best Brass Sextants						18 18 0
Cases and Sets of Drawing Instruments	from	0	7	6	to	5 5 0
Globes for the Pocket	from	0	9	0	to	0 14 0
Ditto, 9 inches diameter	from	3	3	0	to	
Ditto, 12 inches ditto	from	3	13	6	to	6 16 6
Ditto, 18 inches ditto	from	7	7	0	to	17 17 0
Ditto, 21 inches ditto	from	10	10	0	to	18 18 0
Barometers, Marine and others	from	2	12	6	to	8 8 0
Thermometers	from	0	8	6	to	1 11 6
Hanging, Steering, and Azimuth, Compasses	from	0	7	0	to	10 10 0
Gunter's Scale	from	0	2	6	to	0 7 0
Dividers	from	0	1	6	to	0 11 6
Watch and Pocket Compasses, in brass, wood, and silver	from	0	3	0	to	2 5 0
Donn's Improved Navigation Scale, and directions	from	0	3	6	to	0 5 0
Ebony Parallel Rulers	from	0	2	6	to	0 10 6
Pocket Telescopes	from	0	10	6	to	2 5 0
Day Telescopes	from	1	1	0	to	5 13 6
Night and Day ditto	from	2	12	6	to	5 5 0
Tape Measures in leathern boxes	from	0	6	6	to	0 18 0
Patent Solid Time and Log Glasses	from	0	1	10	to	0 14 0

Likewise a Variety of Box and Ivory Rules, Artificial Horizons, and other Instruments.

N. B. *Quadrants, Sextants, &c. cleaned and repaired.*